Excellence in Advertising

The Institute of Practitioners in Advertising is the trade association and professional body for UK advertising agencies. Its mission is to serve, promote and anticipate the collective interests of advertising agencies; and in particular to define, develop and help maintain the highest standards of professional practice within the advertising business.

The IPA's Seven Stages training programme, from which these contributions are drawn, provides continuous professional development for agency people from trainee to chief executive. Each course and workshop has been developed to provide the learning and support required at a particular stage in development, to encourage excellence at every level. This book and the Seven Stages programme are examples of the IPA mission in action.

Excellence in Advertising

The IPA guide to best practice

Second edition

Edited by
Leslie Butterfield

Published in association with the Institute of Practitioners in Advertising

ELSEVIER
BUTTERWORTH
HEINEMANN

AMSTERDAM • BOSTON • HEIDELBERG • LONDON • NEWYORK • OXFORD
PARIS • SAN DIEGO • SAN FRANCISCO • SINGAPORE • SYDNEY • TOKYO

Butterworth-Heinemann is an imprint of Elsevier
Linacre House, Jordan Hill, Oxford OX2 8DP, UK
30 Corporate Drive, Suite 400, Burlington, MA 01803, USA

First edition 1997
Reprinted 1997 (twice), 1998
Second edition 1999
Reprinted 2000, 2001, 2003 (twice), 2005, 2006

British Library Cataloguing in Publication Data
Excellence in advertising: the IPA guide to best practice, 2nd ed.
  1. Advertising
  I. Butterfield, Leslie
  659.1

Library of Congress Cataloging-in-Publication Data
A catalog record for this book is available from the Library of Congress

ISBN–13: 978-0-7506-4479-6
ISBN–10: 0-7506-4479-6

For information on all Butterworth-Heinemann publications
visit our website at books.elsevier.com

Printed and bound in *Great Britain*

06 07 08 09 10   10 9 8 7

Working together to grow
libraries in developing countries

www.elsevier.com | www.bookaid.org | www.sabre.org

ELSEVIER   BOOK AID
International   Sabre Foundation

This book is dedicated to the late Charles Channon, author of the original IPA Seven Stages programme and inspiration to many of the contributors to this book

Books in the series

Below-the-line Promotion, John Wilmshurst
The CIM Handbook of Export Marketing, Chris Noonan
The CIM Handbook of Selling and Sales Strategy, David Jobber
The CIM Handbook of Strategic Marketing, Colin Egan and Michael J. Thomas
CIM Marketing Dictionary (fifth edition), Norman A. Hart
Copywriting, Moi Ali
Creating Powerful Brands (second edition), Leslie de Chernatony and Malcolm McDonald
The Creative Marketer, Simon Majaro
The Customer Service Planner, Martin Christopher
Cybermarketing, Pauline Bickerton, Matthew Bickerton and Upkar Pardesi
Cyberstrategy, Pauline Bickerton, Matthew Bickerton and Kate Simpson-Holley
The Effective Advertiser, Tom Brannan
The Fundamentals and Practice of Marketing (third edition), John Wilmshurst
The Fundamentals of Corporate Communication, Richard Dolphin
Innovation in Marketing, Peter Doyle and Susan Bridgewater
Integrated Marketing Communications, Ian Linton and Kevin Morley
International Marketing (third edition), Stanley Paliwoda and Michael Thomas
Key Account Management, Malcolm McDonald and Beth Rogers
Market-led Strategic Change (second edition), Nigel Piercy
The Marketing Book (fourth edition), Michael J. Baker
Marketing in the Not-for Profit Sector, Margaret Kinnell and Jennifer MacDougall
Marketing Logistics, Martin Christopher
The Marketing Manual, Michael J. Baker
The Marketing Planner, Malcolm McDonald
Marketing Planning for Services, Malcolm McDonald and Adrian Payne
Marketing Plans (fourth edition), Malcolm McDonald
Marketing Professional Services, Michael Roe
Marketing Research for Managers (second edition), Sunny Crouch and Matthew Housden
Marketing Strategy (second edition), Paul Fifield
Practice of Advertising (fourth edition), Norman A. Hart
Practice of Public Relations (fourth edition), Sam Black
Profitable Product Management, Richard Collier
Relationship Marketing, Martin Christopher, Adrian Payne and David Ballantyne
Relationship Marketing for Competitive Advantage, Adrian Payne, Martin Christopher, Moira Clark
  and Helen Peck
Relationship Marketing: Strategy and Implemenation, Helen Peck, Adrian Payne, Martin
  Christopher and Moira Clark
Retail Marketing Plans, Malcolm McDonald and Christopher Tideman
Royal Mail Guide to Direct Mail for Small Businesses, Brian Thomas
Sales Management, Chris Noonan
Strategic Marketing Management, Richard Wilson and Colin Gilligan
Tales From the Marketplace, Nigel Piercy
Total Relationship Marketing, Evert Gummesson
Trade Marketing Strategies, Geoffrey Randall

Forthcoming

Direct Marketing, Brian Thomas
Principles of Customer Care and Service Quality, Colin Gilligan and Laurie Young
Services Marketing, Colin Egan

Contents

List of contributors   ix
Foreword   xv
Preface   xvii
Acknowledgements   xix

1   Building successful brands   3
    Peter Doyle

2   The advertising contribution   25
    John Bartle

3   An overview of the pressures on the client   45
    Mike Sommers

4   Strategy development   63
    Simon Clemmow

5   Quantitative data and advertising strategy development   83
    Chris Forrest

6   Analysis and interpretation in qualitative research: a researcher's
    perspective   109
    Roddy Glen

7   Creative briefing   135
    Gary Duckworth

8   Creative briefing: the creative perspective   161
    Steve Henry

9   Getting the best out of people in advertising   177
    Richard Hytner

10 The strategic importance of media   193
    Andy Tilley

11 Evaluating advertising   215
    Tim Broadbent

12 Total communications strategy   231
    Tim Pile

13 Is there a role for advertising as a driver of loyalty?   247
    Andrew Crosthwaite

14 Advertising and shareholder value   265
    Leslie Butterfield

Index   297

Contributors

John Bartle (*Joint Chief Executive, Bartle Bogle Hegarty*)
John Bartle began his career in 1965 with Cadbury's (later Cadbury Schweppes) as a marketing graduate trainee and worked there for eight years, latterly as Marketing Services Manager for the company's Foods Group. He left Cadbury Schweppes in 1973 to become a co-founder of the London office of the advertising agency TBWA. Initially TBWA's Planning Director, he became Joint Managing Director, with Nigel Bogle, in 1979, a position he held until leaving to start Bartle Bogle Hegarty in 1982. He was President of the IPA (Institute of Practitioners in Advertising) from 1995 to 1997, spent a number of years on the Council of the Advertising Association and is a Visiting Professor of Marketing at the University of Strathclyde.

Tim Broadbent (*Managing Partner, Young & Rubicam*)
Tim graduated from Sussex University in 1976 with a degree in Philosophy and another in Metaphysics. He joined Beecham in the marketing department, then switched to account planning at BMP. He was a board planning director of FCB, Saatchi & Saatchi and WCRS before joining Y&R as Head of Planning in 1994. He is also one of the agency's Managing Partners. He is the only person to have won two Grands Prix in the IPA Advertising Effectiveness Awards, for John Smith's and BMW, and won Five Stars for Colgate in the 1998 Awards. He is Convenor of Judges of the 2000 Awards.

Leslie Butterfield (*Chairman, Partners BDDH*)
Leslie Butterfield graduated in 1975 with a First Class Honours degree in Business Studies and an MA in Marketing from Lancaster University. He

joined Boase Massimi Pollitt (now BMP DDB) in the same year as an Account Planner. In 1980 he joined the fledgling Abbott Mead Vickers BBDO as Planning Director. In 1987, Leslie left to set up his own agency, Butterfield Day Devito Hockney. Now called Partners BDDH, the agency has gone from strength to strength over its twelve-year history – and counts among its clients *The Guardian*, CWS, Harley-Davidson, The Co-operative Bank, Christian Aid, Emirates Airline and Mercedes-Benz. He has been Planning Director and then Chairman of the agency since its inception. In 1998, Partners BDDH became part of Snyder Communications. Leslie is a frequent contributor to industry publications and often speaks at conferences and seminars. He was Chairman of the Account Planning Group from 1987 to 1989, and Chairman of the IPA's Training and Development Committee from 1989 to 1997. In the last two years Leslie has become increasingly involved in the whole area of Brand Valuation and Shareholder Value, and last year co-authored a book for the IPA entitled *Understanding the Financial Value of Brands*.

Simon Clemmow (*Executive Planning Director, TBWA GGT Simons Palmer*)
Simon started his career in 1982 at Benton and Bowles, moving to creative hotshop GGT in 1983. In 1988 he co-founded Simons Palmer Clemmow Johnson and in 1998 became Executive Planning Director of TBWA GGT Simons Palmer following Omnicom's acquisition of both Simons Palmer and GGT and subsequent merger of them with its TBWA Worldwide network. Simon is one of the rare professionals in the advertising industry who trained as an account planner from day one. Described by *Campaign* as 'famously brainy', he has been responsible for the strategic communications solutions behind many award-winning campaigns for blue-chip organizations such as BT, the COI, News International, Nike, Sony, Unilever and Virgin.

Andrew Crosthwaite (*Consultant*)
Andrew began his career as an account handler at Ogilvy & Mather, and then worked at Publicis (where he converted to planning) and Doyle Dane Bernbach. In 1985 he joined FCO as Planning Director and joined Euro RSCG in 1993, when the agencies merged, and became Head of Planning. In 1996 he set up a brand consultancy, Euro RSCG Upstream, to offer strategic advice to clients of Euro RSCG and external companies. In 1999 he set up as an independent consultant. He is a Fellow of the IPA, where he serves on the Value of Advertising Committee and is a member of The Marketing Society Innovations Team.

Peter Doyle (*Professor of Marketing and Strategic Management, University of Warwick Business School*)
Peter Doyle has acted as consultant to many top international businesses and has run executive programmes for senior managers throughout Europe, the United States and the Far East. He has been voted 'Outstanding Teacher' on

numerous university and corporate courses. In addition, he has published five books and over 100 articles in professional journals. He has a First Class Honours degree from the University of Manchester and an MBA and a PhD from Carnegie-Mellon University, United States.

Gary Duckworth (*Chairman and Executive Planning Director, Duckworth Finn Grubb Waters*)
Gary Duckworth was a founder partner of DFGW in 1989. He is responsible for the quality of the agency's strategic output. The agency is famous for its long-running brand campaigns. DFGW's clients include Mars, Daewoo UK and Europe, Health Education Authority – drugs education, Toshiba Computers, Pedigree Foods, Anheuser-Busch – Michelob, Co-operative Retail, Boehringer Ingelheim Self Medication – Uvistat and Pharmaton, Mothercare and Bhs. The agency now handles the Daewoo brand in eleven European countries. For Toshiba Computers their work on laptops and desktops covers seventeen European countries. DFGW won the 1998 IPA Advertising Effectiveness Grand Prix for their drugs education campaign for the HEA. Gary has written and spoken extensively on advertising topics. He was Convenor of Judges for the 1996 IPA Effectiveness awards and edited *Advertising Works*, Volume 9, published in 1997. He chairs the IPA's Training and Development Committee, and is a member of the IPA Council. Prior to starting DFGW, Gary worked at BMP, Abbott Mead Vickers BBDO and EuroRSCG. He was educated at Oxford and has an MA in PPE.

Chris Forrest (*Planning Consultant*)
Chris started his career in 1982 as a qualitative researcher at QRC and then at SRG, learning the trade from Barry Ross, Roy Langmald and Roddy Glen before joining Ogilvy & Mather's Planning Department 4 years later. He was promoted to the board of Ogilvy & Mather in 1986, making him their youngest Board Director. Having been a success at a top 3 agency he wanted to try working in a smaller, hotter agency. In 1991 he joined Duckworth, Finn, Grubb, Waters where, until Easter 1997, he was Planning Director. His innovative strategy for the launch of Daewoo Cars in the UK has been widely praised and has won him success at both the APG Awards and the IPA Effectiveness Awards. Chris has lectured at IPA 2, the Campaign Planning Course and the MRS Summer School. Forrest Associates was set up as a Planning & Research Consultancy in April 1997. Chris was Vice Chairman of the Account Planning Group until December 1997. He is married to a qualitative researcher. They have three young respondents.

Roddy Glen (*Qualitative Researcher*)
Born in Glasgow in 1949, Roddy graduated from Strathclyde University in 1972 with a BA(Hons) in Marketing and Administration. He started his career in

advertising in 1973 at CDP where he worked as an Account Executive on Whitbread, Heineken and Coty. In 1976 he left to travel the world. On returning to the UK, he joined Schlackman Surveys as a qualitative and quantitative researcher. After two years, he joined BMP as a qualitative researcher and remained in charge of the Research Department there until 1982 when he left to set up as a freelance researcher. In April 1985 he and Barry Ross founded the Strategic Research Group, one of the UK's most respected qualitative marketing research companies. Roddy teaches regularly on courses run by the Market Research Society, the IPA and the Association of Qualitative Research Practitioners, of which he was Chairman from 1987 to 1989. He lives in Rutland with his wife Maggie, an author and illustrator of children's books and his son, Calum, born in 1991. He now works as a freelance qualitative researcher and consultant.

Steve Henry (*Creative Director, HHCL*)
Steve Henry was born in Hong Kong in September 1955 during a hurricane! He took a First in English Literature, Oxford University, 1978, and from 1981 to 1985 was a Copywriter at GGT where he worked on London Docklands, London Weekend Television, Holsten Pils and *Time Out*. From 1985 to 1987 he was a Group Creative Director at WCRS and worked on Carling Black Label, Midland Bank, Prudential and Tennents Extra. He set up Howell Henry Chaldecott Lury in 1987 and his favourite clients since then include Molson lager, First Direct bank, Fuji Film, Danepak Bacon, Britvic Soft Drinks (including Tango), Mercury Communications, Martini, the Automobile Association, Mazda cars, Pot Noodles, Guinness Ireland, Egg and Thomson Holidays. Steve has won many major creative awards, including a Gold pencil at D&AD, the Grand Prix at Cannes, the Grand Prix at British Television and the President's Award at Creative Circle.

Richard Hytner (*Managing Director, Publicis*)
Richard was born in Manchester and educated at Manchester Grammar School and St John's College, Cambridge where he graduated with an MA and an LLM in Law. He has spent almost all of his career in advertising with Y & R, Still Price Court Twivy D'Souza and SP Lintas which he ran for three years. He joined Publicis, the UK's No. 5 agency, as its Chief Executive in London in 1998 from The Henley Centre for Forecasting which he also led as Chief Executive. Clients with whom he has been closely involved include Cadbury, General Foods, Elida Fabergé, Van den Bergh Foods, P & O, Virgin Atlantic, Nestlé, Renault and United Biscuits. His passions include the theatre (he was President of the ADC in Cambridge as well as a regular in Footlights), reading and the movies. One other grand passion is occupying his attention currently – he has formed Shareholders United Against Murdoch to save Manchester United Football Club, of which he has been a lifelong supporter, from the clutches of

BSkyB. He is also involved with Business in the Community, working on initiatives for both education and homelessness.

Tim Pile (*Director of Sales and Marketing, Alliance & Leicester*)
Tim is Director of Sales and Marketing with responsibility for the sales force and for all marketing within the Group: distribution strategy; brand and customer relationship management; the Customer First programme; databases; product marketing and communication. Previously, Tim was Director of Marketing Services at TSB (subsequently Lloyds TSB). During the five years at TSB, Tim had responsibility for communications, customer service, database management, the Customer Focus programme, research, marketing analysis etc. Prior to TSB, Tim was Managing Director of Dewe Rogerson and Deputy Managing Director of DMB&B and whilst at these communications agencies worked on a wide range of businesses, including Mars, P&G, Laker, Brooke Bond, Scottish Widows, British Steel etc. Tim is married with four children.

Mike Sommers (*Marketing Consultant*)
Mike Sommers has worked in marketing for 27 years, although his career began as an Account Executive at JWT. From 1975 to 1983 he was at CPC (UK) Ltd, moving from Senior Product Manager to Head of Marketing. From 1985 to 1991 he was at Woolworths plc, first as Marketing Director, then Business Director Entertainment and finally Commercial Director. After two years as Marketing and Premises Director, TSB Bank plc, he joined MGM Cinemas Ltd as Managing Director. Following the sale of MGM to the Virgin Group he went into consultancy. After a spell as a partner at Pricewaterhouse Coopers he joined SRU Ltd as a director in November 1998.

Andy Tilley (*Managing Partner, Unity*)
Having spent six years at Southampton University, including three carrying out postgraduate research on the New Forest, Andy joined BMP in late 1982 as a trainee. He became a board director in 1986, and then left to join the Delaney Brothers and Winston Fletcher at DFD as their fourth board member in 1989. With the experience of running both media and account planning in the agency as Deputy Managing Director he was headhunted to set up strategic planning at Zenith Media in 1991. He was appointed Managing Director of the agency in 1995 and during his tenure he saw planning billings grow from zero to £250 m in six years. In July 1997, Andy left to set up Unity, a strategic media planning consultancy, with two former BMP colleagues, Derek Morris and Ivan Pollard, which now works with a number of blue-chip clients including BT, HP Bulmer, Capital Radio plc, Carphone Warehouse, EMAP Consumer Magazines and The Prince's Trust. Andy is a former Chairman of the Media Circle, and sits on a number of industry committees. He is married to a magazine editor, has three children and recently moved to a small village in Oxfordshire.

Foreword

The IPA Seven Stages programme provides continual professional development for advertising agency people from trainee to chief executive level. Each course and workshop is delivered by people who have achieved excellence in their field, whether they are advertising practitioners, business academics, marketeers or professional trainers. Over the years the reputation of the programme has continued to grow, not just in the UK but worldwide, despite the fact that courses are open only to IPA member agencies. This book makes some of the more tangible evidence of this excellence available to a wider audience. Leslie Butterfield has had the vision and the determination to see this task through.

The Institute of Practitioners in Advertising is dedicated to promoting the highest standards of professional practice within the advertising business. Advertising at its very best is a collaborative and cooperative process and this book, which shares wisdom from many sources and suggests best practice in many areas of advertising, is thus a highly relevant expression of what the IPA seeks to achieve.

Nick Phillips
Director General, IPA

Preface

This book was born of an idea. For most of the last ten years, in addition to my full-time job as Chairman of one of the UK's top thirty advertising agencies, I was Chairman of the IPA's Training and Development Committee – the body that designs, supervises and organizes the majority of the educational initiatives and courses for the UK's advertising agencies. The backbone of these courses is still the IPA's Seven Stages programme – designed to parallel the seven stages of development of a career in advertising, from graduate entrant to Chief Executive. This concept was originally conceived and designed by the late Charles Channon, to whom this book is dedicated.

Over those years, and still today, some of the finest talents in the UK advertising industry deliver some outstanding individual contributions on the courses on which they are speaking. What struck me, though – and was the idea behind this book – was that each of those individually excellent papers was reaching an annual audience of only a few dozen people! My aim in putting together this compilation of papers therefore is simple: to try to capture and record the very best of those contributions and make them available to a much wider audience.

The authors of the individual chapters are themselves at the very top of their disciplines and, at the time of writing at least, will be known to most readers from the industry. For the reader from outside advertising, though, their profiles are described briefly in the List of Contributors. To each I owe a particular word of thanks, since writing a chapter for a book such as this is a much tougher task than producing speaking notes for an often quite informally delivered presentation to a small audience. Their efforts I hope are rewarded by the quality of this, the finished article!

It is also worth saying a word or two about the context in which this book has been produced. The 1990s have undoubtedly been a turbulent period in the UK advertising industry's history. There have been fundamental rethinks about the structure and purpose of the industry. Yet it is still an industry that is admired around the world. Despite the strictures of the last few years, the quality of the people in the industry and of its creative product is just as strong as it was a decade ago. Usually, it is the creative output of the industry that is most admired internationally – and most fêted within. But none I think would argue with the contention that it is because of the *composite* skills of an advertising agency that such work is forthcoming.

This book is consciously not a celebration of the creative output – there are many other sources for that. Rather it seeks to highlight excellence in all the other, less visible disciplines that contribute to outstanding advertising: planning, account management, media and so on. It also puts the spotlight on those parts of the process that the casual observer of the industry might never see: research, the development of strategy, the client's perspective, etc. All these areas are opportunities for excellence – and one of the pleasures (still) of this industry is the teamwork between talented people in these areas.

The first edition of *Excellence in Advertising* was published in 1997 – and sales exceeded all expectations. In this considerably revised and enlarged second edition, half of the chapters are updated versions of the originals, but half are wholly new. These latter seek to reflect the very latest areas of interest and opportunity within the industry such as managing relationships, total communications strategies, loyalty and shareholder value.

I challenge the reader to open this book at any chapter and *not* find something that can help improve some aspect of their day-to-day career in advertising, or their understanding of the depth and richness of advertising as an industry. It is a celebration therefore of excellence in both process and practice. Some of the views are highly personal, some controversial, but all are enthusiastically expressed and written with a verve that is a characteristic of the spirit of the industry. I hope you learn from it. Above all, I hope you enjoy it.

Leslie Butterfield

Acknowledgements

First and foremost, my thanks go to Miranda Kennett, formerly Director of Training & Development at the IPA, and her colleagues, Veronica Wheatley and Kerry Walsh, for all the help they gave me in assembling the various original papers included in this book, and for helping manage the process to completion. Thanks also to my colleagues at my agency, Partners BDDH, for putting up with my occasional absence. Apart from the contributors to this book (whom I will thank separately), there are also many other speakers, tutors and, of course, delegates who make the IPA's programme the success it is. Finally, thanks to my wife, Judy, for her forbearance over my not-too-occasional weekend working, and to my secretary, Carla Webb, for assembling all the various elements for publication. Without her computer skills all, quite literally, would have been lost!

Overview: Chapter 1

Peter Doyle and Stage 5 of the IPA's Seven Stages training programme have become almost synonymous. In fact Peter ran the first course on Advertising and Business Effectiveness in 1979, and has done so in every subsequent year. Ratings of the course never stray far from excellent and many agencies have become regular and loyal users.

While the structure of the course has evolved, its core purpose is unchanged: to enhance the strategic understanding of people in advertising of current business management and marketing techniques. As such, it aims to place advertising in its proper context: one tool among many (albeit an important one) in the businessperson's armoury.

The chapter included here was never presented in its entirety on the course. It does, however, do justice to the 'spirit' of the course, in particular by examining the issue of brands and branding, and by painting an honest picture of how advertising can contribute to these. Specifically, it covers:

- The value of successful brands
- The role of quality, service and communications in creating such brands
- The case for building as against acquiring brands
- Brand-extension strategies.

In its coverage, it sets a kind of framework for all that is to follow. Great advertising does not exist in a vacuum, it is there to serve a commercial goal. Enhancing the value of a brand is its greatest prize.

Chapter 1

Building successful brands

Peter Doyle

Introduction

The role and valuation of brands has recently become a controversial issue. Not only is the importance of successful brands emphasized by marketing managers, some financial executives have developed a new enthusiasm for brands, having seen that their inclusion in the balance sheet enhances shareholder funds, reduces company gearing, and so facilitates further growth by acquisition. This chapter explores five key questions about brands: (1) What is a successful brand? (2) What is the value of a brand? (3) How are successful brands built? (4) What are the comparative advantages of buying brands versus building and developing them internally? and (5) What are the logic and economics behind brand-extension strategies?

The successful brand

Before defining a brand it is first necessary to define a *product*. The concept of a product is not straightforward. First, products and brands are mistakenly often associated only with fast-moving consumer goods. But today, the most rapidly growing and profitable products are in services – financial, retail and management. Also, besides products and services, people, places and ideas can be thought of as 'products'. Politicians, movie-stars and privatization schemes are now marketed in much the same way as Coca-Cola or Crest toothpaste.

Second, products mean different things to people *inside* the business than they do to people *outside*. Inside, to the firm's managers and accountants, a product is something produced in the factory or the office. It is about materials, components, labour costs, quality and output specifications. But outside, to the consumer, a product is something different – it is a means of meeting his or her needs or solving their problems. These needs and problems are as likely to be emotional and psychological as functional and economic. It is a product's ability to meet these needs and aspirations which creates its value. The value of a product is not what the producer puts in but what the consumer gets out. As the chief executive of Black & Decker put it, 'Our job is not to make quarter-inch drills, but to make quarter-inch holes'. Or the chairman of Revlon Cosmetics, 'In the factory we make cosmetics, but in the store we sell hope'. Similarly, IBM has always maintained it 'doesn't sell products. It sells solutions to customers' problems' (Rodgers, 1986).

A *product* then is *anything which meets the needs of customers*. When several companies are offering rival products, they will want to identify and distinguish their particular offering. This is called 'branding', so there is a Black & Decker brand, a Revlon brand and an IBM brand. But the focus here is not on brands *per se* but on successful brands. Just because people are aware of a specific brand does not mean that it is successful. People recognized brands like the Sinclair C5, the Ford Edsel, the Co-op, or Wimpy restaurants, but they did not develop preferences for them. Some years ago a Landor Survey found, for example, that British Telecom was in the UK's top ten brands for awareness, but in terms of esteem it was rated number 300. BT has been referred to as a strong *negative* brand. It was known for all the wrong reasons.

A positive or successful brand can be defined as follows. *A successful brand is a name, symbol, design, or some combination, which identifies the 'product' of a particular organization as having a sustainable differential advantage.*

'Differential advantage' means simply that customers have a reason for preferring that brand to competitors' brands. 'Sustainable' means an advantage that is not easily copied by competitors. That is, the business creates barriers to entry, for example by developing an outstanding reputation or image for quality, service or reliability. Brands like IBM, Coca-Cola, Sony and Tesco are successful brands because they have such sustainable differential advantages, which, as shown below, invariably result in superior profit and market performance. Successful brands are *always* brand leaders in their segments.

Two implications of this definition can be noted. First, brands are only assets if they have sustainable differential advantages. If they are negative or neutral brands like BT, Woolworth's, or the Austin Maestro, they should not appear on the balance sheet, however much is spent on advertising. Any profit these brands achieve is through their property or distribution investments rather than through the brand's differential advantage.

Similarly, if the differential advantage is not sustainable, it should not appear on the balance sheet. In some markets such as games or children's toys, a successful brand often has a life expectancy of only six months and thereafter has no value.

Second, like most other assets, brands depreciate without further investment. If management fails to reinvest in enhancing quality, service and brand image then the brand will decline. Hoover, Singer, Frigidaire and MG are examples of brands which were once so successful as to be almost generic names for the product, but which have since declined or disappeared due to lack of investment.

This is often underestimated. Most models suggest that brands tend to decay logarithmically (e.g. Parsons and Schultz, 1984). This means that in the short term managers can increase profits without damaging the brand's market share by cutting back brand support. However, the mistake is in thinking that brand disinvestment can be continued. Without adequate support, typically after around a year or two (Clarke, 1976), the brand enters a period of spiralling decline.

How brands work

Brands work by facilitating and making more effective the consumer's choice process. Every day an individual makes hundreds of decisions. He or she is besieged by countless products and messages competing for attention. To make life bearable and to simplify this decision-making process, the individual looks for short-cuts. The most important of these short-cuts is to rely on *habit* – buy brands that have proved satisfactory in the past. This is particularly the case for low-involvement purchases, which make up most of the things people buy. This does not mean that people are totally brand loyal of course, since most of them know that many brands will satisfy their needs. Most people ask for Coca-Cola but they are not too disappointed when they are offered Pepsi.

But this habit rule is not just based upon experience of use, it can also be based upon long-standing *perceptions*. People can have quite strong brand preferences even though they have never bought the product. This is especially true for aspirational products. My son has had a long preference for a Porsche, even though he has still to wait another three years before he is old enough for a driving licence. Such preferences or brand images are based upon cultural, social and personality factors, as well as commercial stimuli like advertising, public relations and prominence of distribution.

Even with non-routine, supposedly highly rational purchasing situations in the industrial sector, where decisions are taken by technical personnel, it is remarkable how important brand image is in the choice process. Even industrial buyers tend to rely on experience and long-held attitudes about the brand, rather than undertake a zero-based approach to the wide range of alternative options (see Levitt, 1983a). As the cynical IBM salesman is supposed to have said to a purchasing manager, 'Nobody's ever been fired for buying IBM'.

Successful brands are those which create this image or 'personality'. They do it by encouraging customers to perceive the attributes they aspire to as being strongly associated with the brand. These attributes may be real and objective (e.g. quality, value for money) or abstract and emotional (e.g. status, youthfulness). The personality of the brand is a function of its rational characteristics but it has to be augmented and communicated to consumers through advertising, design, packaging and effective distribution and display. These position the brand's personality in the consumer's mind, generate confidence, and create the purchasing environment.

The value of a successful brand

Successful brands are valuable because they can create a stream of future earnings. It is useful to dissect the mechanisms by which brands generate these income streams.

Brands, market share and profits

A successful brand is one which customers want to buy and retailers want to stock – it achieves a high market share. Brands with a high market share are much more profitable. The well-known PIMS findings (Buzzell and Gale, 1987), based on detailed studies of 2600 businesses, showed that on average, products with a market share of 40 per cent generate three times the return on investment of those with a market share of only 10 per cent (Figure 1.1). Weak brands mean weak profits. A UK study shows that for grocery brands the relationship is even stronger. The number one brand generates over six times the return on sales of the number two brand, while the number three and four brands are totally unprofitable (Table 1.1). The pattern is similar in the United States, where a recent survey of American consumer goods showed that the number one brand earned 20 per cent return, the number two around 5 per cent and the rest lost money (*The Economist*, 1988).

The value of niche brands

The above findings do not mean that the brand has to be large in absolute terms. It is normally much more profitable to be number one in a small niche market than to be number three in a huge market. It is market share which is

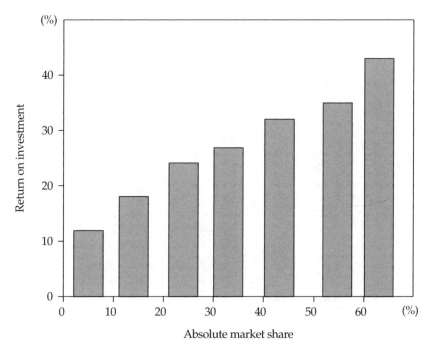

Figure 1.1 The relationship between market share and profitability. *Source*: Buzzell and Gale, 1987

the key to performance, not absolute sales. In fact, Clifford and Cavanagh (1985) provide convincing evidence that a strong brand in a niche market earns a higher percentage return than a strong brand in a big market (Figure 1.2). In large markets, competitive threats and retailer pressure can hold back profits even for the top brand.

Table 1.1 Market share and average net margins for UK grocery brands

Rank	Net margin (%)
1	17.9
2	2.8
3	−0.9
4	−5.9

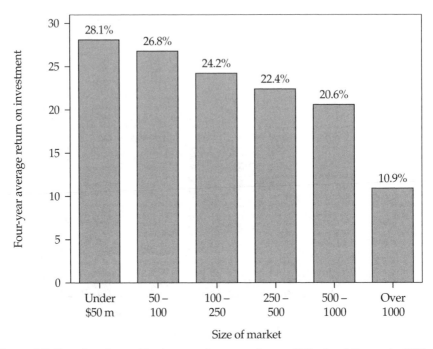

Figure 1.2 Size of market and business performance. *Source*: Clifford and Cavanagh, 1985

Brand values and prices

Because successful brands have differential advantages, they are normally able to obtain higher prices than less successful brands. Sometimes this occurs at the customer level but more frequently it is earned at the retailer level. Strong brands can resist pressure from the trade for discounts. This, in turn, generates superior earnings. Clifford and Cavanagh (1985) found that, on average, premium price products earned 20 per cent more than discount brands (Figure 1.3).

Brand loyalty and beliefs

Successful brands achieve higher customer loyalty. Unsuccessful brands or new brands have to attract customers. This hits the net margin because it is much more expensive in advertising, promotion and selling to win new customers than to hold existing satisfied ones. One study has suggested that it costs six times as much to win new customers as to retain current users (quoted in Peters, 1988).

Strong brands can also override the occasional hitches and even disasters which can destroy weaker brands. After terrorists poisoned samples of the

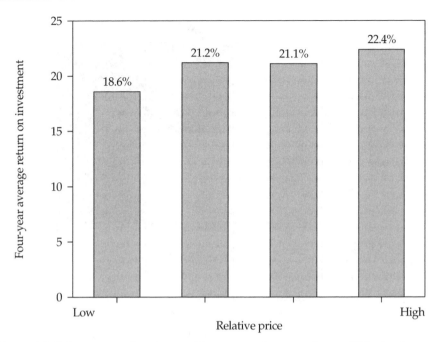

Figure 1.3 Relative price of products and business performance. *Source*: Clifford and Cavanagh, 1985

leading analgesic, Tylenol, in 1987, US retailers had to remove entirely the brand from their shelves for several months. Once the scare was over, however, customers went back to the brand they trusted, leading to a remarkably complete recovery for Tylenol. Tom Peters tells a revealing story about Federal Express, which has a superb reputation for service. He telephoned FedEx twenty-seven times over a six-month period to request service. Twenty-six times a FedEx employee answered immediately after the first ring of the telephone. On the twenty-seventh time the telephone rang repeatedly without any response. After repeated rings, he put the phone down because he assumed that *he* had made the mistake of calling the wrong number! Of course, if this had been a neutral or negative brand it would have simply reinforced one's current image of the brand.

Common products, unique brands

Today, competition can quickly emulate advances in technology or product formulation. Competitors can quickly copy a cigarette, a soft-drink formula or PC specification. But what cannot be copied is the Silk Cut, Coca-Cola or IBM brand personalities. Studies show overwhelmingly that the best feasible

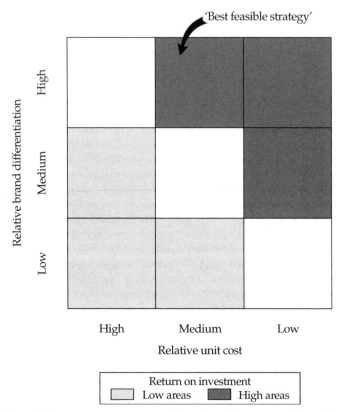

Figure 1.4 Brand differentiation, unit cost and business performance. Adapted by author from Hall, 1980

strategy is to focus on brand differentiation, rather than cost and price, as a way of building profitability and growth (Figure 1.4). While the best strategy in theory is both low cost and high differentiation, in practice it is worth paying some cost penalty to achieve strong differentiation (see Hall, 1980).

The brand growth direction matrix

The product life-cycle is a well-known phenomenon. The product peaks and eventually dies as its markets mature and new technologies replace it. But this life-cycle refers to products, not to brands. There is no reason why a brand cannot adapt to new technologies and move from mature into new growth markets. The brand growth direction matrix (Figure 1.5) indicates the main growth opportunities available. Initially brand share is the strategic focus. But most of the successful brands which have lasted the decades have

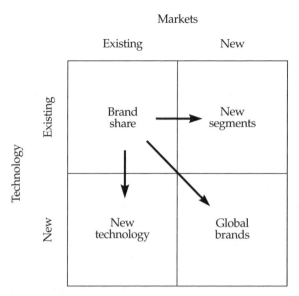

Figure 1.5 Brand growth direction matrix

shifted to incorporate *new technology*, ingredients and packaging developments to circumvent the product life-cycle. Similarly, Johnson & Johnson's
Baby Shampoo is only one of the many examples of brands which have
moved into *new market segments* to continue growth. The fourth growth
direction is towards *global branding*, which appears to offer increasing
opportunities to today's multinationals (Levitt, 1983b). Growth based upon
continuously developing successful brands appears to provide a securer
foundation than that based upon unrelated acquisitions or new untried
products where failure rates are as high as 95 per cent (Booz, Allen and
Hamilton, 1982).

Competitive depositioning

The brand leader is in an enormously strong position to fend off attacks. First,
it has financial strength – almost invariably it will have the highest market
share and the highest profit margins. This should enable it to outgun
competitors in terms of aggressive promotion and innovation. Second, the
trade is always reluctant to add new brands if the existing brand leader
satisfies the customers and themselves. Third, the brand leader can exploit its
superiority, as Coca-Cola does with its 'real thing' advertising. Without a major
strategic window (Abell, 1978), only a substantial under-investment in quality
and brand support is likely to dethrone a successful brand.

Motivates stakeholders

Companies with strong brands find recruitment easier. People want to work with companies that exhibit success. Strong brands also widen share ownership by increasing awareness and understanding of the company. Finally, successful brands elicit local authority and governmental support. Western countries, for example, compete with inducements to attract the better-known Japanese companies to build their brands with them.

The creation of successful brands

Brands are rarely created by advertising. This is often misunderstood because the advertising is generally much more visible than the factor which creates the differential advantage. For example, Singapore Airlines is a strong brand and does some attractive advertising. But the advertising is not the basis of the brand – rather, the advertising communicates and positions it. The basis of the brand is the superior customer service provided by the cabin staff. This, in turn, is largely achieved by Singapore Airlines putting in more cabin staff per plane than other airlines. Equally striking is the fact that, historically, one of Britain's strongest brands – Marks & Spencer – has done little or no advertising at all. There is often little correlation between the amount spent on advertising and the strength of the brand.

The other common mistake is to think that brand loyalty is irrational. A survey on branding by *The Economist* (1988) reflected this view: 'people all over the world form irrational attachments to different products. Humans like to take sides ... By most "tangible" measures, BMW cars and IBM computers are not significantly better than rivals, but customers will pay significantly more for them.' Levitt (1983a) provides a framework for understanding how successful brands are created and why customers are not 'irrational' to choose them (Figure 1.6).

At the core of every brand there is a *tangible* product – the commodity which meets the basic customer need. For the thirsty customer, there is water. For the production manager with a data storage problem, there is the computer. This tangible product is what economists believe rational consumers should base their choices on.

But to generate sales in a competitive environment, this tangible core has to be put in the form of a *basic* brand. It has to be packaged conveniently, the customer needs to know the features of the product and its quality. It should be designed to facilitate ease of use. But there are further ways to *augment* the brand to enhance its value by guaranteeing its performance, providing credit, delivery, and effective after-sales service. Finally, there is the *potential* brand, which consists of anything that conceivably could be done to build customer

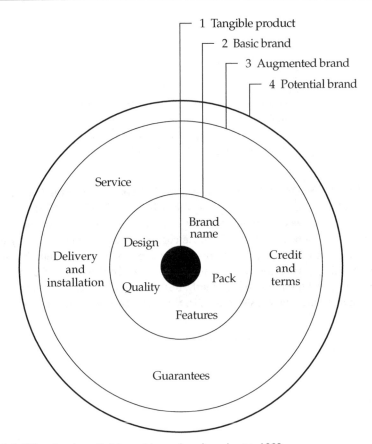

Figure 1.6 What is a brand? Adapted by author from Levitt, 1983a

preference and loyalty. Which of these dimensions appear to be most important in practice?

1 *Quality is number one.* Overwhelmingly the most important determinant of brand strength is its perceived quality. Britain's top ten brands (Table 1.2, Landor Associates, 1989), have all tended to be quality brands. The PIMS analysis showed that brands with high perceived quality earned double the return on investment and return on sales of low-quality brands (Figure 1.7). Quality generates higher margins in either or both of two ways. First, quality boosts market share, which results in lower unit costs through economies of scale. Second, by creating a differential advantage, quality permits higher relative price.
2 *Build superior service.* Service is perhaps the most sustainable differential advantage. While products are easily copied by competitors, service, because it depends on the culture of the organization and the training and attitudes of its employees, is much

Table 1.2 Britain's top ten brands

1 Marks & Spencer	6 Boots
2 Cadbury	7 Nescafé
3 Kellogg	8 BBC
4 Heinz	9 Rowntree
5 Rolls-Royce	10 Sainsbury

Source: Landor Imagepower Survey, 1989

more difficult. McDonald's, IBM, Singapore Airlines and Federal Express are all brands built on service. A study by Albrecht and Zemke (1985) showed the importance of service: in their sample survey, 67 per cent of customers changed brands because of poor service. Of those customers who did feel unhappy with the service provided by the bank, hotel or supplier, only 4 per cent bothered to complain – they just did not expect any satisfaction. Of those that did complain, 91 per cent dropped the brand permanently. But, interestingly, suppliers who dealt with complaints fast and generously held on to the vast majority of dissatisfied customers.

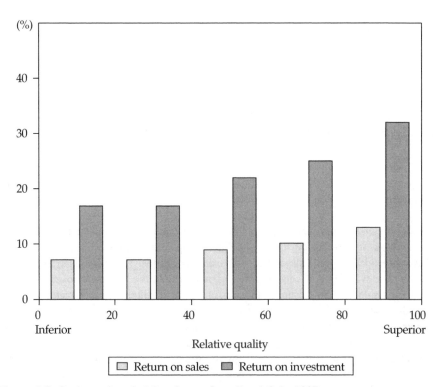

Figure 1.7 Quality and profitability. *Source*: Buzzell and Gale, 1987

In fact, there was some evidence that really effective responses to complaints actually increased brand loyalty.

3 *Get there first.* Perhaps the most common means of building an outstanding brand is being first into a market. This does not mean being technologically first, but rather being first into the mind of the consumer. IBM, Kleenex, Casio and McDonald's did not invent their respective products, but they were first to build major brands out of them and bring them into the mass market. It is much easier to build a strong brand in the customer's mind and in the market when the brand has no established competitors. This is why Clifford and Cavanagh (1985) found that pioneering brands earned on average more than one-third higher returns on investment than late entrants (Figure

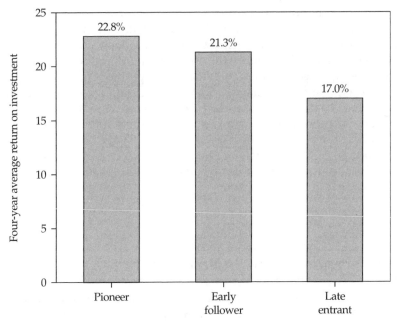

Figure 1.8 Timing of market entry and business performance. *Source*: Clifford and Cavanagh, 1985

1.8). There are five ways of 'getting there first': (1) exploiting new technology (e.g. Xerox, IBM); (2) new positioning concepts (The Body Shop, Foster's lager); (3) new distribution channels (e.g. Argos); (4) new market segments (e.g. Amstrad); and (5) exploiting gaps created by sudden environmental changes.

4 *Look for differentiation.* In building brands the principle is to invest in markets which are highly differentiated or where such differentiation can be created, as, for example, The Body Shop or Levi's jeans have done in recent years. Where markets are strongly differentiated – i.e. different segments are looking for different bundles

of attributes – then both niche brands and big power brands can potentially earn very high return on investment. Power brands like IBM, Marks & Spencer and Coca-Cola can earn high returns because they are perceived of as high-quality brands in most of the segments. Niche brands like Iron Brew can earn high profits by being preferred in one segment even though their overall rating in the broad market is not great. In markets which are undifferentiated, however – i.e. where customers do not see much difference between the brands – none typically earns exceptional returns.

To summarize, building successful brands is about quality, service, innovation and differentiation. What, then, is the role of advertising? Advertising has two functions in building successful brands. First, successful advertising accelerates the communications process. Until very recently, Marks & Spencer built a great brand without advertising. They relied primarily on their high street presence, customer experience with the brand, and word of mouth. But it took them thirty years to build the strong brand of today. Now, one cannot wait that long – competition would pre-empt the brand before it had positioned itself in the customer's mind. Advertising speeds up the process of generating awareness and interest in the brand. The second function of advertising is to position the brand's values in a manner which appeals to the target customers and increases confidence in the choice process. The creative messages of the Levi's or the Nescafé advertisements, for example, present the brand as having a set of values which match the aspirations of target customers.

Buying brands versus building brands

Today there are two routes a company can follow to obtain brands – it can build and develop them or it can acquire them, or rather acquire companies which possess them. The former is obviously a high-risk, slow and expensive route. Studies have shown clearly that a very high proportion of new brands tested and introduced into the market fail (e.g. Booz, Allen and Hamilton, 1982). It takes time and investment to build a brand and position it in the minds of consumers. In contrast, acquisitions are a deceptively quick route to obtaining a brand portfolio and it is a route which is increasingly followed today, especially by British companies. It also appears a cheap alternative, especially if the acquirer is exchanging high-valued shares in buying a company operating on a lower price–earnings ratio. Unfortunately, there is comprehensive evidence that most such acquisitions fail to generate long-term value for the acquirer's shareholders or build lasting brand portfolios (e.g. Porter, 1987). How can this dilemma be explained and resolved?

Previous studies (Doyle, 1987; Doyle *et al.*, 1986) suggest the approach companies adopt depends upon what their primary objectives are. Some companies have objectives which are primarily about marketing and market share. Others are primarily orientated to return on investment and financial objectives (Figure 1.9). Generally, companies which have objectives that are mainly marketing ones ('right-hand companies') choose to build brands. Companies whose objectives are primarily financial ('left-hand companies') are orientated towards buying brands or companies with brands.

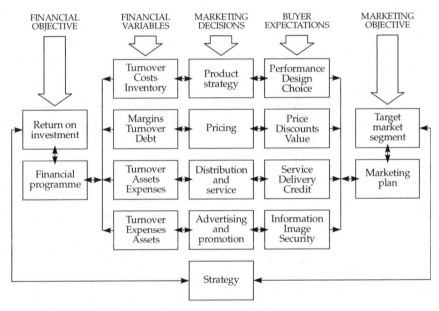

Figure 1.9 Marketing and financial objectives of the business

Japanese companies, for example, tend to be overwhelmingly right-hand orientated. The objective is market share. They believe that the most appropriate way to achieve market share is the development of strong brands which offer customers differential advantages. So they adopt a classic marketing approach – understand the expectations of customers in the target market segments and seek to match them. They seek to build brands that provide the customers with value and which beat the competition. Japanese companies rarely acquire because they believe that they have the skills to do it better. It is not surprising that many of the great global brands in the last couple of decades have been Japanese – Sony, Toyota, National Panasonic, Honda, Canon, Casio, etc.

British companies, on the other hand, have been more left-hand or financially orientated. Stock market pressures have made return on investment the primary goal and financial budgets rather than marketing plans the main planning mechanism. In these companies, products, pricing and promotional decisions are dictated mainly by financial constraints rather than marketing requirements. One result is that while there have been very few major global brands developed by British companies in the last ten years, they have led the world in acquisitions. British companies are much more aggressive in making acquisitions than companies from Japan, the United States or the rest of Europe.

The recent debate about brands in the balance sheet in Britain is essentially about acquisition strategy rather than about building customer value. Acquisition-orientated managers have observed that if brands are put in the balance sheet, then balance sheet gearing can be reduced, retained earning enhanced and so further acquisitions are facilitated. Paradoxically, companies that put brands in the balance sheet are likely to put *less* emphasis on brand building and brand development than those that do not follow this practice.

Of course, acquiring brands sometimes makes sense. The problems with acquisitions are, first, that in the long run the evidence suggests they rarely work. Second, they do not create coherent brand strategies, especially at the international level. In general, the company ends up with a rag-bag of brands with different brand names in different countries, different positioning strategies and no synergy with the existing business. Table 1.3 suggests a checklist which appraises those conditions when acquiring companies with brands makes sense.

If it is a low-growth unattractive market, building a brand costs too much. It is generally cheaper to buy competition and competitors' retail space than to beat out well-entrenched brands. This is why companies like Hanson and BTR focused their acquisition strategies on these dull mature markets. The other advantage of these types of markets is that the relative cost of acquisitions may be low. Often the stock market undervalues these apparently dull companies and there is substantial restructuring potential in selling off parts after the acquisition.

Acquisitions work when there is real potential synergy – when the acquirer can reduce joint costs or improve marketing competence by coming together. Finally, the strategic opportunities offered by the acquirer's existing brand portfolio and its corporate cash situation play a major role. If the company's current products are me-too, if it has limited skills but abundant cash spun-off from its portfolio of mature products, then acquisitions appear attractive. By contrast, it is generally better to develop and build on the company's own brands if these are operating in growth markets, if the company possesses potentially strong brands and if inside the company there are strong marketing and development skills. These five sets of factors are the key criteria in making judgements about the balance between building and purchasing brands.

Table 1.3 Building versus buying brands

	Build	*Buy*
Market attractiveness		
Market growth	High	Low
Strength of competitors	Weak	Strong
Retailer power	Weak	Strong
Relative cost of acquisitions		
Industry attractiveness	High	Low
Valuation of company	Full	Undervalued
Restructuring potential	Low	High
Brand's potential	Realized	Unrealized
Acquisition's potential synergy		
Cost reduction potential	Low	High
Marketing competence	Unchanged	Increased
Complementarity	Low	High
Relevant management expertise	Low	Transfers
Brand's strategic opportunity		
Product performance	Breakthrough	Me-too
Positioning concept	New	Mature
Market opportunity	High	Low
Corporate situation		
Growth potential	High	Low
Cash situation	Average	Abundant
Marketing/R&D capability	Strong	Weak

Brand-extension strategies

Brand-extension strategies are another controversial area in branding. Brand extension means transferring the name of a successful brand to additional products possessed by the company. The advantages of such extensions may be three: (1) it encourages customer confidence in a new product; (2) it may create scale economies in advertising and promotion; (3) it opens up distribution and retail channels. The dangers are that it confuses the brand identity and can degrade the reputation of a successful brand.

What are the principles in striking a balance? The right approach depends on the similarity of the positioning strategies of the brands. Four brand-extension options can be identified (Figure 1.10):

1 If the brands appeal to the same target market segment and have the same differential advantage, then they can safely share the same company name or range

Differential advantage

		Similar	Different
Target market segment	Similar	COMPANY OR RANGE NAME (IBM, Timotei)	COMPANY PLUS BRANDS (Kellogg's Cornflakes, Kellogg's Rice Krispies)
	Different	COMPANY PLUS GRADE ID (Mercedes Benz A-class, S-class, E-class etc.)	UNIQUE BRAND NAMES (P&G: Tide, Bold, Dreft, Ariel, …)

Figure 1.10 Brand-extension strategies

name. Here, there is consistency in the positioning strategies. Examples of this type of extension would include IBM, Dunhill and Sony – the same name applied to different products.

2 If the differential advantage is the same but the target market differs, then the company name can be extended because the benefit is similar. However, it is important to identify the 'grade'. For example, both the Mercedes-Benz 200 and 500 series offer differential advantages based upon quality, but the more expensive 500 series appeals to a much more prestigious segment of the market. The supplemental number acts to preserve the prestige positioning of the latter marque.

3 If a company has different differential advantages, then it should use separate brand names. It can find some synergy if the brands are appealing to the same target market, by using the same company name with separate brand names. For example, different brands of Kellogg's may well be selected within the same family unit.

4 But if both the target customers and the differential advantages are different then using unique brand names is logically the most appropriate strategy. So Procter & Gamble believe that it is worth losing out on the advantages of a common corporate name in order to separately position the brands in the market – to give each brand a distinct positioning appeal to a separate benefit segment. Similarly, Honda separately positioned its Acura brand because it wished uniquely to position it away from its existing models.

Summary

Successful brands are built upon the principle of seeking to build sustainable differential advantages for the customer. The levers for developing such brands are four: quality, service, innovation and differentiation. Strategies based upon acquiring brands generally fail to work because they are more usually geared to satisfying the interests of the stock market rather than the long-term interests of customers. The danger of the 'brand in the balance sheet' argument is that it leads to weaker rather than stronger branding strategies. Finally, on brand-extension strategies, there are real advantages in brands sharing a corporate logo, but care is required in not eroding a successful brand's unique positioning.

References

Abell, D.F. (1978), 'Strategic windows', *Journal of Marketing*, **42**, No. 3 (May).

Albrecht, K. and Zemke, R. (1985), *Service America*, Homewood, IL: IEE/Dow Jones/Irwin.

Booz, Allen and Hamilton (1982), *New Products Management for the 1980s*, New York.

Buzzell, R.D. and Gale, B.T. (1987), *The PIMS Principles: Linking Strategy to Performance*, London: Collier-Macmillan.

Clarke, D.G. (1976), 'Econometric measurement of the duration of advertising effect on sales', *Journal of Marketing Research*, **13**, No. 3 (Fall).

Clifford, D.K. and Cavanagh, R.E. (1985), *The Winning Performance: How America's High Growth Midsize Companies Succeed*, London: Sidgwick and Jackson.

Doyle, P. (1987), 'Marketing and the British chief executive', *Journal of Marketing Management*, **3**, No. 2 (Winter).

Doyle, P., Saunders, J. and Wong, V. (1986), 'A comparative study of Japanese marketing strategies in the British market', *Journal of International Business Studies* (Spring).

The Economist (1988), 'The year of the brand', 24 December, p. 93.

Hall, W.K. (1980), 'Survival strategies in a hostile environment', *Harvard Business Review*, **58**, No. 5 (September).

Landor Associates (1989), *The World's Leading Brands: A Survey*, London.

Levitt, T. (1983a), *The Marketing Imagination*, London: Collier-Macmillan.

Levitt, T. (1983b), 'The globalization of markets', *Harvard Business Review*, **83**, No. 3 (May).

Parsons, L.J. and Schultz, R.L. (1984), *Marketing Models and Econometric Research*, Amsterdam: North-Holland.

Peters, T. (1988), *Thriving on Chaos*, London: Macmillan.

Porter, M.E. (1987), 'From competitive advantage to corporate strategy', *Harvard Business Review*, **65**, No. 3 (May).

Rodgers, B. (1986), *The IBM Way*, New York: Harper & Row.

Overview: Chapter 2

John Bartle was President of the IPA when *Excellence in Advertising* was first published in 1997 – and few former presidents have been as committed to training and development as he. This commitment has been evidenced too by John's speaking role on the IPA's Stage 3 course: 'How to get the most out of your clients.' This course aims to enhance agency–client relationships through promoting better understanding of the context for advertising in client organizations.

John is a passionate advocate of the value of good advertising, and some of this zeal comes across in the chapter. Like many others in this book it started life as a speech (first delivered on Stage 3 in 1994), but I think the reader will sense its power even in the written word. Specifically, it covers:

- The difference between a product and a brand
- The transformation from one to the other, and the role that creativity can play in this
- The concept of head and heart in developing effective advertising
- The 'magic' that can occur when both are in play and are supported by substantial media presence.

Some of the examples used are famous across the industry, and even the non-specialist reader will get a feel for the enduring effect of great creative communication.

Chapter 2

The advertising contribution

John Bartle

Introduction

This talk – which is what this chapter originally was – made its first 'public appearance' at an IPA Stage 3 training course. One of the IPA's Seven Stages training programmes, Stage 3 has particular significance in being the first stage to provide comprehensive *client* input for people in the advertising industry.

Three to four days' exposure to a number of eminent client speakers outlining the issues, stresses and strains of what they do for a living is not only a very important eye-opener but also a particularly effective way of setting advertising into its proper business context. Potentially almost too effective!

At the end of these intensive days it could be possible to lose sight of advertising's particular contribution, its particular qualities and those things it can do particularly well.

Hence this talk, at the tail-end of the course. A reminder to all, hopefully, and a little bit of counterbalance for some, should that have been necessary.

Contribution to what?

Advertising does not 'float free'.

We all know that, don't we? It's just one marketing tool, one business tool. It operates in conjunction with a whole host of other things. We all know that but, so often, we behave as though we do not, as though advertising operates in complete isolation and is an end in itself rather than a means, and just one means at that.

A means to what? My title begs that question. A contribution to what?

Let us be in no doubt about what the answer has to be; it is the contribution to positive business performance. It is clear. It is that hard-nosed. It is not about creative accolades or agency success. Advertising stands or falls by its contribution to positive business performance.

I deliberately do not say that it is about contributing to business success – you may be trying to stop failure. That is also why I do not say that it is all about increasing sales; it may be about halting or slowing decline. Or about holding what you have got in the face of increasing competitive pressure. Or about supporting a price premium, or building one, or enhancing one.

In all these circumstances the contribution is about improving the commercial position, in a given time frame, against what would have happened without advertising at all or without the particular advertising in question.

The particular contribution

Advertising can make its contribution in a number of ways, of course, against a variety of target audiences.

It can make short-term announcements – a sale, a promotion, the latest prices. It can be used to help boost a share price or City standing. It can be used almost as PR against opinion leaders. It can be used to instil pride and confidence in a workforce. It can be used to encourage a positive trade response, to deliver shelf-space and prominent featuring as a consequence. It can simply provide information, like much government advertising does, for example.

Advertising is nothing if not versatile but, primarily, its particular contribution is in *helping to build and sustain brands* which, over long periods of time, provide the bedrock of so many consumer businesses and deliver positive business performance.

So, to understand fully the advertising contribution we need, most of all, to understand brands and, then, where and how advertising plays its part.

From product to brand

Over thirty years ago, in the very earliest days of my career, I believe now that I learned the most important lesson of all. I suspect that the last thirty years have really largely been about relearning the lesson in a whole variety of circumstances in an increasingly complex environment.

The lesson was learned when I started working, at Cadbury (before it became Cadbury Schweppes). My 'teacher' was the extensive product testing that the company carried out. Underlying that product testing programme was a belief in the vital importance of understanding basic product performance, and in assessing any product improvements, against the main competitors in the marketplace. To this end most of the tests were conducted 'blind', i.e. brand identity was completely masked.

But, sometimes, this was not the case. Then brand identity was revealed and, when undertaken in the same project with matched samples of recipients, one sample receiving the products 'blind', the other branded, the results were markedly different.

There is published evidence of this phenomenon, showing a number of different outcomes.

In the first example (Figure 2.1) a parity performance on taste when two food products are tested 'blind' becomes a clear taste preference for one (brand B) when the two brands are identified.

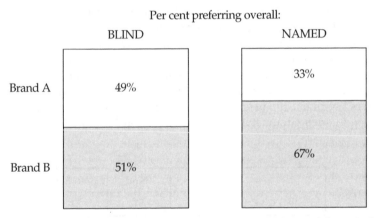

Figure 2.1 Blind versus named product test: food product (excludes don't knows). *Source:* King, 1971

In Figure 2.2, for a household product, a clear performance deficiency is removed when brand identities are revealed.

And, in the final example (Figure 2.3), where the brands are helpfully identified, there is a turn-round in taste preference without and then with disclosure.

(It is important to understand that these results are from identical questions on actual *product* performance, whether presented blind or branded, and not buying intention or brand preference questions though that, of course, is precisely what they reflect. Consumers *are* saying that the products taste different, work differently when they know what brand the product is.)

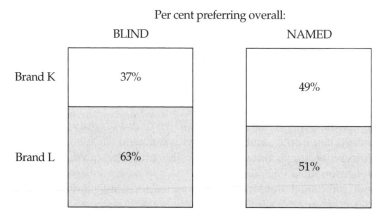

Per cent preferring overall:

Figure 2.2 Blind versus named product test: household product (excludes don't knows). *Source:* King, 1971

None of this is meant to suggest that basic product performance, as evaluated when the products are presented 'blind', is unimportant when building a strong brand. On the contrary, brand K in Figure 2.2 above, for example, might well have problems sustaining its brand values over time without some attention to its basic product. Indeed, what an opportunity it must surely have if the product can be improved. Alternatively, find those 'preferrers', segment the user base and concentrate activity accordingly. All is not gloom in such circumstances but some action is certainly indicated.

	Blind	Branded
Prefer Diet Pepsi	51	23
Prefer Diet Coke	44	65
Equal/don't know	5	12

Figure 2.3 Blind versus named product test: diet colas (%). *Source:* De Chernatony and Knox, 1990

What is very clear, however, is that pure product performance can and will be transformed when all the aspects of identity are brought to bear, when consumers bring their preconceptions and beliefs to the product experience. *Performance is transformed when all aspects of communications are added to the basic product.* Things can taste better, perform better (or worse). A product's value to the consumer can and will change.

This is what brands are – product plus communications in all its forms. (These communications include both direct ones like brand name, company name and reputation, packaging format and design and less direct ones like advertising and PR.)

A lesson learned over thirty years ago. A simple one you may think. Certainly derived from the simplest kind of research. I wish I had appreciated then just what a profound lesson it actually was. I have spent the last thirty years discovering just that!

(As an aside, one wonders whether this simplest of all research, the side-by-side blind and branded product test, is conducted anything like as frequently as it might be. As a simple barometer of relative brand strength it has so much to commend it.)

The brand difference

The difference illustrated in those product tests is nicely and simply described by Jeremy Bullmore (1991):

A product is an object or service that's available. A brand is a complex set of satisfactions delivered.

It was famously expressed by Charles Revson, Revlon's founder:

In the factory we make cosmetics but in the store we sell hope

and, again, in a more recent quote by the President of Black & Decker:

Last year one million quarter-inch drills were sold. Not because people wanted quarter-inch drills but because they wanted quarter-inch holes.

All three quotes are making some vital distinctions; between what is made and what is delivered, between production and consumption and between features (of limited consumer interest) and benefits (of, potentially, much greater interest).

A brand is not only different from a product, it is much more than a product. It is much more than its functional performance. Brands are much more complex and multi-faceted than that.

The complexity of brands

The chart which follows (Figure 2.4), derived by combining several different sources, attempts to illustrate the totality of the brand as I view it.

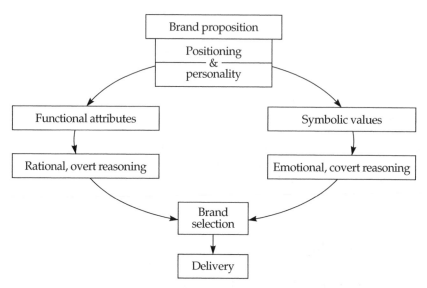

Figure 2.4 The totality of the brand. *Sources*: De Chernatony, 1992; Hankinson and Cowking, 1995

This illustrates the two broad areas, short-handed as the rational and the emotional, which combine to make up the brand. On the one side the functional attributes which feature in those 'blind' product tests, on the other all the communication aspects which surround the products. When these two are *taken together* we produce the total brand picture (and those branded product test results).

At our agency (Bartle Bogle Hegarty) we talk about the two sides of this chart as 'head' appeal and 'heart' appeal and we believe strongly that successful advertising requires *both* to be present, in a unique combination, although the particular contribution of advertising more often nowadays lies in its ability to bring 'magic' to the emotional side, a point we will return to. Nevertheless, in our view, one 'appeal' without the other is never enough.

The top part of this diagram, used by Hankinson and Cowking, is described by them as:

A brand is a product or service made distinctive by its positioning, relative to the competition, and by its personality ... Positioning defines the brand's point of reference either by price or usage. Personality consists of a unique combination of functional attributes and symbolic values with which the target audience identifies.

This reinforces the importance of functional attributes and symbolic values in combination, acknowledges that brands require both consumer perception and consumer response (which is why I have added 'delivery' without which, against expectations, no brand can be complete) and identifies the paramount importance of distinctiveness for successful brands. This, again, is an area where good advertising makes a significant contribution, to which we will return later.

Emotion about emotion

Everyone involved in brands, in marketing and advertising, will recognize that brands are constructed in the quite complex way I have just described. When dealing with brands we must never forget this.

Rationalization, and post-rationalization, tend to dominate in our measurement – rational responses to rational questions – and in our deliberations if we are not careful. But careful we have to be because it is in getting that correct rational/emotional balance, no matter how difficult, that the key to continuing brand success lies. That is why care in research methodology, analysis and interpretation are so important.

Our critics would have a field day, would they not, dismissing as nonsense all this emotional stuff. They would see the blind/branded difference as indicative of either consumer stupidity or, at best (or should it be at worst?) evidence of how easily we can manipulate.

They would be completely wrong, of course, demonstrating only their lack of understanding of consumers and of the role that brands play, and not acknowledging that, as consumers themselves, they would behave in exactly the same way.

In fact, consumers are being both human and actually rather sensible. Human in their individuality, unpredictability and, above all, their complexity. Human also in demonstrating an acceptance, indeed a desire, for 'emotion' to add interest and variety to their lives. Sensible in taking advantage of the short-cuts and, indeed, the satisfactions that brands can deliver. Eschew these, behave rationally at all times, and inaction, 'paralysis through analysis', really would occur.

Treat your customers as stupid, underestimate their ability to evaluate your brand in all its complexity or abuse your brands by failing to sustain them or to deliver against the promises made and, as we know, you will soon learn who is really in control and how fast brand strengths can disappear. This is what the marketing challenge is all about.

The extra values for brands

We have established by now, I hope, that brands are different from products and that what makes them different is that they have extra values attached.

They are products plus. If no extra values are attached then there is no brand. So, *while every brand has a product or service within it, not every product, by a long way, is really a brand.*

These extra values are in many ways 'intangible' values. They are feelings, images, associations, the statement that something makes about you. And they are not to be taken lightly or invented with no reference to consumers. Rather they are to be valued and respected since they are fundamental to our nature as social human beings. As such, we all use goods and services, in part to define ourselves, our values, our natures, our wealth, and to express these things to others.

Often we talk about 'added value' in this context. I deliberately have not, since *brands can have extra values that subtract value.*

Our product tests earlier may well illustrate this. They certainly do in relative terms and I am sure we all have examples where the extra values actually undermine the product, where the plus bit in 'products plus' is actually a minus.

In my view 'brand' is far too often used as a synonym for 'successful' when clearly this is far from always the case. There is a hierarchy of brands from the clearly unsuccessful, whose days are numbered unless remedial action is taken, all the way through to what are sometimes called the 'power brands', those which have adapted particularly well, over time, to their environment and to changing market conditions, thriving strongly as a result.

The vital ingredient – differentiation

There are many shades of grey and there is much fluidity between these two extremes, with large areas occupied by too many 'me-too' copy-cat brands. The culprits here are often research not looking beyond the tendency of consumers to respond to the familiar, and the need for security and risk aversion on the part of manufacturers or service providers. These brands may have limited success for a time, though sacrificing much if not all of any price premium in the process, but they are not likely to survive into the longer term unless action is taken to really differentiate them from the competition.

The absolute key to brand success is *motivating differentiation*. Differentiation which creates what Stephen King has described as 'a bit of a monopoly in the mind of the consumer'. Only from this can the value of the brand be fully derived and its full value reflected in the price which its consumers are prepared to pay.

As Sir George Bull (1994), former Chairman of Diageo, said:

> People pay more for brands because they offer more, satisfy more, work better, look better, feel better – in short, give better value.

Truly successful brands, as well as providing consumers with a believable 'guarantee' via their identity, also provide a mélange of values – physical, aesthetic, rational and emotional – that is seen by consumers as, in combination, *particularly* appropriate, worth paying for and, with the promise met (or exceeded), worth paying for again.

Peter Doyle (1994) summarizes this as:

> The specific characteristic of a successful brand is that in addition to having a product that meets the functional requirements of consumers it also has the added values that meet certain of their psychological needs.

(Note, again, this talk of additional values. These extra values are never, for any length of time, a compensation for functional inadequacy. They must enhance the functional or your brand is built on rapidly shifting sand.)

The importance of brands

There has been a presumption thoughout this that brands, successful ones, are 'a good thing'. And, of course, they are.

Much has been written and many words spoken about the importance of brands to consumer businesses and there are a number of examples (Nestlé's purchase of Rowntree for one) of the value that can be placed on them.

Their importance to companies was well described by Sir Michael Perry (1993) when Chairman of Unilever:

> The major assets of a consumer business, overwhelmingly, are its brands. They are of incalculable value. They represent both its heritage and its future. To succeed as a consumer products business there is no alternative but to invent, nurture and invest in brands.

Successful brands provide better security and stability, better protection, in an unpredictable world, for all involved in and with the company; shareholders, managers, the salesforce, the production line, whoever.

Brands have great value from the demand end too, of course, from the consumer perspective. Again greater reassurance and certainty are derived. Brands offer an easier and much more time-efficient purchasing life. As such, brands are needed by consumers. It is an irony that something as complex as a brand is needed to make life simpler!

But they are also *wanted* by consumers. It is not overstating to say that brands enrich their consumers' lives adding a host of possible inner- and outer-directed satisfactions, adding fun, enjoyment, self-expression, self-reward, etc.

Essentially it is the durability of successful brands that makes them so important and valuable to both companies and consumers. *If brands are nurtured, developed and evolved the life-cycle theory becomes completely redundant,* something for products but not for brands, as the longevity of so many of the great brands – Coca-Cola, Kodak, Goodyear, Gillette, Sony, Levi's – testifies. They need constant attention: complacency is the enemy and evolution a necessity but the prizes for success are huge.

Summary so far

Let me summarize where we have got to so far:

- Products and brands are different
- Brands combine non-functional values with the functional ones to provide differentiation
- Successful brands are differentiated brands
- The non-functional, intangible values are crucial to successful brand differentiation
- For successful brands these extra values represent added value
- Successful brands are of great value and importance to companies and to consumers.

... And so to advertising

Thus far, and this is called 'The Advertising Contribution', and little mention of advertising. Not really, of course. *All of what has gone before is, or could be, about advertising.* Advertising can be, and is, used in a variety of different ways but *its prime contribution is in helping to build and sustain brands for commercial benefit, often leading this process.*

Much discussion in recent times has revolved around media fragmentation and the growth in importance of non-advertising methods of communication. While these are all developments of which we must be mindful, and which we should all know a lot more about, the continuing pre-eminent position of consumer advertising is illustrated by a 1998 survey among 84 clients (see Table 2.1).

The advertising contribution

In its brand-building role the major contribution that consumer advertising can make lies in its ability to communicate the totality, that crucial combination of

Table 2.1 Relative importance of different communications techniques to business (total sample: 84 respondents)

(%)	Very	Quite	Mean
Consumer advertising	80	15	4.75
Public relations	56	35	4.42
Sales promotions	27	54	3.96
Direct marketing	43	27	3.92
Trade advertising	17	37	3.24
Sponsorship	14	39	3.28

Source: IPA Survey (1998)

the rational and emotional, the 'head appeal' and 'heart appeal' that I mentioned earlier. In particular, advertising can add emotional values in a way, in my view, that no other element of the marketing mix can. Its multi-facetedness and its potential subtlety mean that it can appeal to the senses and affect the emotions in ways that nothing else can with the same permanence, not least because we live in such a visually literate age with increasingly advertising-sophisticated consumers.

In a world of increasing complexity I would argue that the ability to add the emotional, more intangible value (the right-hand side of Figure 2.4) is becoming more rather than less important. The crucial requirement of differentiation is less and less readily delivered on a functional level. The days of the unique selling proposition (which has come to be interpreted as the rational/functional point of difference), certainly of the enduring USP, are very largely gone. Competitors are smarter and faster than ever and, in some cases, with research and development alliances, technical leads disappear by definition.

It has been reported that just one year after the introduction of the Apple PC it had eleven competitors, eight years later over 500. Sony has said that any technical lead it might have enjoyed in the past, with Walkman for example, would now be six months only. And we can all see how rapidly FMCG successes are followed by own-label competitors.

If the USP is fast disappearing then what becomes correspondingly more important is what we call the ESP (the emotional selling proposition) and this is pre-eminently the business of advertising and advertising agencies; a new, enduring source of uniqueness.

Let me say again, though, that this is not to argue that the functional is of no importance. It is important *in combination* with 'heart appeal' and all the strongest brand propositions are rooted in a product truth, even if that truth is not unique. What is added on the emotional side then creates the uniqueness. Emotional appeal alone, in my view, will result in emptiness which, however glossily presented, stays superficial and will be found wanting in time.

... In practice

These beliefs about advertising and brands inform the whole of the creative process at our agency. Indeed we 'enshrine' it in all our creative briefs, each of which asks for two descriptions; what 'the product is' and what 'the brand is' (Figure 2.5).

Figure 2.5 The creative brief

There, on every job, is a reminder that the two are different and that advertising's task is to contribute to the journey, the transformation, from one to the other. The task for the rest of the brief is to identify the role of advertising in effecting that transformation and providing support – functional and non-functional – on which to build the piece of communication under development. Thus the Häagen-Dazs 'journey' (see Figure 2.6) derived largely from consumer response to the consumption experience rather than simply from the contents of the pot, high quality though it and its ingredients are. This has lifted this brand beyond simply a very high-quality ice cream to something

Product	Super-premium, fresh cream ice cream
Brand	The ultimate sensual, intimate pleasure

Figure 2.6 Häagen-Dazs ice cream

Figure 2.7   **Figure 2.8**

altogether bigger (with, interestingly and importantly I think, no mention at all of ice cream in the brand statement).

The contribution of advertising, specifically the initial burst (examples in Figures 2.7 and 2.8), was considered and quantified in the IPA Effectiveness Awards paper (published in *Advertising Works 7*) from which Figure 2.9 is extracted.

Boddington's similarly moves, from a fine product, but one of several in a highly competitive market, to a highly distinctive entity (Figure 2.10) using press (and, later, television) executions on the Cream theme. The Cream analogies have allowed us to take a clear product characteristic and ally it with strong personality characteristics – humour, directness, unpretentiousness, urbanness and Mancunian qualities – to produce something proud to be

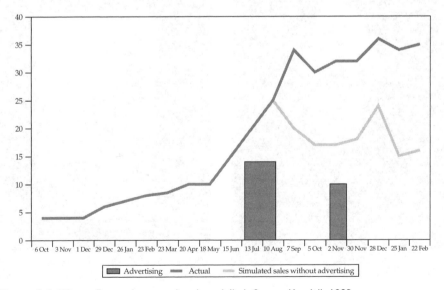

Figure 2.9 Häagen-Dazs sales, actual and modelled. *Source*: Kendall, 1993

Product	Cask conditioned ale from Manchester
Brand	The smoothest drinking bitter – with a Mancunian point of view

Figure 2.10 Boddington's beer

Mancunian and of which Manchester can be proud; truly the 'Cream of Manchester' (Figures 2.11 and 2.12).

The advertising contribution is, again, covered in *Advertising Works*, in this case Volume 8. Figure 2.13 illustrates the advertising effect for the canned variant of the brand, as an example.

Applying this same discipline to Phileas Fogg (Figure 2.14) led to the 'Medomsley Road, Consett' television campaign and, in the case of Levi's (Figure 2.15), to a memorable series of commercials for 501s, supported by press advertising.

I talk about the product/brand journey as a transformation and I would argue that advertising is the best way to effect this in a successful and *enduring* way. It can be done relatively quickly and, certainly, to a large audience, in a very public way. And, contrary to what one might be led to believe, it can be

Figure 2.11   **Figure 2.12**

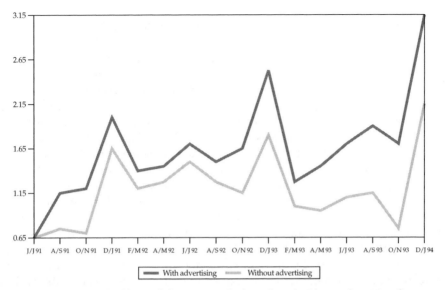

Figure 2.13 Canned Boddington's beer: rate of sale with and without advertising. *Source*: Murphy, 1995

done relatively cheaply when viewed in cost per person terms, if not in terms of absolute cost.

I do not think it is too fanciful to talk of the best of advertising, with the greatest powers of transformation, as almost performing *magic*, turning the familiar and similar into the very special and unique.

Product	A range of adult snacks from around the world
Brand	An original and authentic snack experience, eccentric through where it's made (Consett, County Durham)

Figure 2.14 Phileas Fogg snacks

Product	Five-pocket western heavyweight denim jeans
Brand	The original and definitive jeans. The embodiment of jeans values (freedom, individuality, rebellion, sex, masculinity, originality and youth)

Figure 2.15 Levi's jeans

The advertising challenge – breakthrough

This chapter and the transformation to differentiation that I have just talked about are all about the *content* of advertising. This is not the whole story, of course. Presence is the other factor in the advertising equation.

The crucial challenge for advertising, equally obviously, is to achieve breakthrough with the designated target audience. Without it we have nothing. If enough can be spent then presence, sheer advertising weight, regardless of content, can achieve that breakthrough of itself; conquest via attrition.

This cannot be denied (and it may well explain the success of some apparently average advertising). But fewer and fewer advertisers have the funds available to do this, certainly when faced with the increasing proliferation, clutter and complexity of today's media environment. Greater and greater onus, therefore, is placed upon the content of what we present.

Real creativity here (in which media creativity also has a significant role to play) must be measured by the ability to make your expenditure go further, do more, than the equivalent spent by your competitors. That is real creativity. The result is advertising which captures both the attention and the imagination, and the prize is brand and business success.

Then, the more you have to spend, the more you can look towards a real 'win–win' situation, when potent content meets the luxury of substantial presence.

In addition, of course, at its best, advertising can achieve a further dimension again, growing well beyond the confines of paid-for media altogether. A Häagen-Dazs, a Levi's, a Wonderbra or a Gold Blend would all illustrate this. When you really capture the imagination you can and do get unexpected and very considerable extra benefits, not least the benefits of fame, as identified by Jeremy Bullmore (1994):

> Just about the only thing that successful brands have in common is a kind of fame . . . Fame lends a curious value to things – and to people. Famous things can be shared, referred to, laughed about. Famous things are, literally, a talking point.

Changes

Over the years, even in the few since this talk was first given, changes have continued apace in the world of branding. In particular we have seen the ever-growing importance of service and corporate brands. Fast moving consumer goods (FMCG) no longer dominate. For services, branding becomes much more complex. Uniformity and consistency go out of the window with the intervention of people as brand embodiments. The advertising contribution, though still important, becomes one of rather more variables and much more easily undermined. For corporate brands, conversely, the branding stakes become much higher. More important but with much more to lose if it goes wrong.

Separate chapters could be written on both but, notwithstanding this, the basic principles outlined here still apply.

In conclusion

Successful brand building needs time and sustained effort as well as faith, money and consistency. And it needs to transcend the countervailing short-term pressures.

The strongest brands endure and advertising, in my view, is the best way of building endurance into brands. At its best it can produce magic.

But it cannot work miracles. Without a good product it is impossible to create a successful brand – it was Bill Bernbach, I think, who said something like 'nothing kills a bad product faster than good advertising' – but, given the product, *advertising can best provide the awareness, the breakthrough, the emotional resonance and the differentiation which will endure and without which even the best product does not leave the factory in any real volume.*

(*A footnote*:

Invited by the editor to review this chapter for the second edition, perhaps updating some of the examples, and whilst contemplating this possibility, *The Guardian* newspaper inadvertently intervened.

The City Editor, on the Finance page (and nowhere near the Media section) wrote about the premium ice-cream market, making reference to 'adverts showing nearly naked consumers in over-the-tub embraces'. Since no such advertising had appeared for a couple of years and that, when it had, the budget was modest by any standards, this seemed the best possible endorsement of precisely how substantial and enduring the advertising contribution can be; what this chapter has been all about.

It also meant I didn't feel the need to make any major changes!)

References

Bull, G. (1994), *Brands – A Load of Bull*, D&AD Festival.

Bullmore, J. (1991), *Behind the Scenes in Advertising*, NTC Publications.

Bullmore, J. (1994), *Advertising Costs Half As Much As You Think It Does. But Do You Know Which Half?*, IPA.

De Chernatony, L. (1992), *Creating Powerful Brands*, Butterworth-Heinemann, Oxford.

De Chernatony, L. and Knox, S. (1990), 'How an appreciation of consumer behaviour can help in product testing', *Journal of the Market Research Society,* **32**.

Doyle, P. (1994), *Marketing Management and Strategy,* Prentice Hall.

Hankinson, G. and Cowking, P. (1995), 'What do you really mean by a brand?', *Journal of Brand Management*, August, Henry Stewart Publications.

IPA Survey, (1998), March.

Kendall, N. (1993), 'Häagen-Dazs: dedicated to pleasure – dedicated to advertising, *Advertising Works 7*, NTC Publications.

King, S. (1971), *What is a Brand?*, JWT.

Murphy, G. (1995), 'Boddingtons: "By 'eck"', *Advertising Works 8*, NTC Publications.

Perry, Sir M. (1993), *Advertising Association Annual Luncheon*, Advertising Association.

Overview: Chapter 3

It's no accident that this chapter by Mike Sommers follows John Bartle's. Mike, too, is a passionate speaker and writer. He too has spoken on the IPA's Stage 3 course ('How to get the most out of your clients'). But his advocacy is from the position of the often misunderstood and occasionally maligned client.

This chapter (originally presented in 1992) seeks to show that whilst the ends of the marketing endeavour have remained the same for the last quarter century or so, the means of implementation have changed radically in line with changes in marketing media, increased competitive innovation, but most importantly the growth in numbers and significance of new marketing clients from the retail and services industries.

Using examples from his career with clients in very different sectors Mike Sommers shows how the day-to-day pressures on clients spring from their changing strategic focus and an increasing concern with marketing's 'account-ability'. This is followed by a discussion of how advertising agencies might adapt better to their clients by contrasting the attitudes of agencies and clients to the job in hand and finally suggesting the establishment of wholly new 'client-adapted' agency models.

Chapter 3

An overview of the pressures on the client

Mike Sommers

(*Time Wounds All Heels*)

Introduction

In order to get to know each other better, or to put it more formally, to calibrate our terms, I would like to ask you – dear reader – to consider your response to this question:

1 *Question:* You're a client. It's 9.30 a.m. on a Friday morning. You've been called out of a board meeting which convened at 7.30 to discuss the extremely poor sales position of the last several weeks. On your way to the phone your secretary uses the opportunity to tell you that the corrective promotion you had hoped to run has been declared illegal, and that the two key executives you needed to see later that morning in order to share the panic are on a buying trip to the Far East. Behind your back your colleagues – you are sure – are using your absence from the room as an opportunity to stress to the Managing Director how much the sales situation is down to your indecisive management style. You pick up the phone, it's the Creative Director of your agency who says, 'Look, I know you were pretty definite with Jeremy, but I just wanted to check if we were right down to the wire on the price issue. We really *don't* want to put a price flash on tomorrow's ad – we think it's much better if it's left to the reader's imagination. If you could come over and let the creatives explain then we've got the *Mirror* to delay its deadline on the copy – you'll

only miss the Northern Ireland edition and the position will be virtually as good as the original negotiation.'

2 *Do you:*
   (a) Suggest the board meeting is postponed due to an important development at the agency?
   (b) Ring your Account Director suggesting he run the ad as you agreed and stop the Creative Director bothering you?
   (c) Give everybody at the agency both barrels over the phone and then put a call into the Ad Agency Register?
   Here's a clue – the answer is not (a).

To many on the agency side of the fence this scenario and others like it – all featuring a harassed and somewhat dishevelled client as anti-hero – sound suspiciously like the merely urgent driving out the important from the agenda. What's critical, however, for any agency offering consultancy support of whatever sort is to understand what a client thinks of as important and why. The tactical or day-to-day pressures exemplified above are, in reality, the result of both strategic concerns and the increasing need for demonstrable account-ability which form the background to any client's approach to his work.

The best way for me to give you an insight into these pressures is to describe the situation facing each of four main client firms for which I've worked, the solutions we adopted and, in consequence, the impact on marketing spending. Along the way I'll show how advertising was sometimes critical and sometimes irrelevant to the required changes we made and finish by speculating on how agencies might better adapt their thinking and even their modus operandi to today's heterogeneous and over-pressured client community.

CPC (UK) Ltd

In 1981 I was given the task of heading up the marketing department of CPC – the division now known as Best Foods. This was at a particularly low ebb in their fortunes, with significant losses stemming from a disastrous new product foray and cost/budget reduction being the norm in consequence. The job that needed doing short term was obvious. Stop the profit haemorrhage! But the long-term problem of the business was growth. It was very much a second division player, with UK grocers becoming more and more powerful in negotiation. The company was American-owned, but the European manage-ment were German – neither nationality could understand why we couldn't make more of our brand portfolio. In fact, we had two largely US brands – Mazola and Hellmann's, and one major European brand – Knorr – which were all sub-scale in the UK when compared with their homelands. Our original

British brand, Brown & Polson, was restricted to cornflour and blancmange – which one could call mature markets if we were being polite.

German managements are very sceptical about contested acquisition – so opportunities to *buy* UK domestic scale had been turned down. The attempt to 'break out of the box' by accelerating organic growth through increased NPD investment had led to poor decision-making and mounting losses. Resisting the initial impulse to find an easier job, I sat down with the other directors to hammer out a survival strategy. A lot of what was done in terms of re-engineering the business is too technical to include here, but the most critical thing we had to do was to reassess our allocation of scarce resources (principally talent and money) and decide what would give us the biggest bang for our buck.

Portfolio appraisal

Any corporation needs some sort of priority evaluation of its product market options to overlay on its view of the strategic environment. Portfolio appraisal, as this is known, comes in many forms, the most common of which is the 'nine-box' or market attractiveness grid. At CPC the Boston Matrix was used, originally developed by the Boston Consulting Group (Figure 3.1). Without going into the theory too much, this plots products on two dimensions, the vertical axis being 'market growth' – either historical or prospective – and the horizontal is 'relative market share', which much research proved to Boston's satisfaction was an adequate measure of 'earnings potential'. Relative market share is calculated by dividing your own share by that of the largest competitor. So if you have, say, a 10 per cent market share and the next biggest competitor

Figure 3.1 The Boston Matrix

has 5 per cent the relative share would be 2.0. It stands to reason, therefore, that if you're biggest you'll have a score of more than 1.0, which is the point placed at the centre of the *x*-axis. This axis is on a log scale, since obviously it's possible to have very high relative shares – as when you have 90 per cent of a market where the next best is 2 per cent, i.e. a relative share of 45.

Products within the company's portfolio are then positioned on this two-dimensional array dependent on how fast their market is growing (versus the company average) and their relative share. Products falling in the high-share, high-growth quadrant (top left) are referred to as **Stars**. Typically they should attract investment to sustain their position. Products in the bottom left – high share, but low growth – are referred to as **Cash Cows** which should throw off funds to apply to the stars. The trickiest area is the top right – growth markets in which you have a weak share. These are referred to in the literature as **Wild Cards** or **Question Marks**. Here you must make a choice either to exploit the growing market and by investment turn your product into a star or to recognize that as market growth slows your product will fall into the bottom-right quadrant. These are low-growth low-share no-hopers referred to as **Dogs**.

If you need convincing that 'relative market share' is a useful surrogate for earnings potential, then the findings at CPC should convince you. Table 3.1 is a comparison of six major products in their portfolio at that time in descending order of their relative share with the percentage gross profit they were achieving.

The one anomaly is obviously product D which was Mazola Corn Oil. While it was the biggest brand in its market at the time (and therefore had a score greater than 1.0) it should probably have been measured against *total* own-label oils – which was more like the real purchasing situation. In that case its relative share would have fallen to 0.3 and its position in the relative share league would have matched its profitability. Apart from convincing me of the efficiency of the measurement system, this anomaly is also an object lesson in how important it is to get the market definition right when making such calculations.

Table 3.1 Comparison of six major products

Product	Relative share	Gross profit (%)
A	20.0	64
B	7.0	51
C	5.0	42
D	1.7	15
E	1.3	39
F	0.7	29

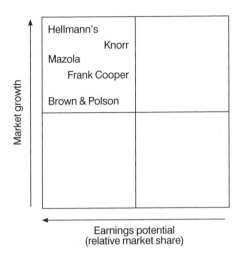

Figure 3.2 CPC: first results

The marketing teams were asked to produce plans based on their view of their product category's role in the CPC portfolio. The initial results looked something like Figure 3.2.

That taught me the simple lesson that if you leave a marketing manager alone with a calculator long enough he will come up with a marketing definition in which he is winning and deserves support. Obviously we couldn't afford the implications of this portfolio – obviously it was wrong! So we got everyone to re-do their analyses on a consistent basis. The final analysis was robust enough to highlight those areas where we needed ruthlessly to prune our range, where we seemed to be over-investing and where opportunities might lie which were capable of offering better returns.

Resource reallocation

In order to dramatize the impact portfolio appraisal can have, the final matrix for CPC is reproduced here with only two products positioned on it. It is common practice to represent the relative turnover of products in a portfolio by the size of the circle around each point (Figure 3.3).

Knorr Soup had around five times the turnover of Hellmann's, which in 1981 was marketed as a posh salad cream and was growing fast from a delicatessen heritage. According to the matrix, we should starve Knorr Soup of resources and invest in Hellmann's. And this is when the real pressure starts. Because this is *only* analysis and prejudice and inertia are much more powerful influences. Knorr Soup was regarded as the flagship product. It was felt that without support – albeit significantly outspent by Batchelors – the product's

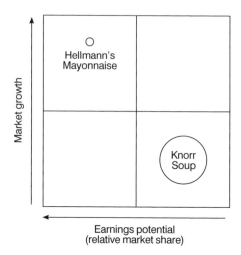

Figure 3.3 Two products competing for resources

raison d'être would be lost and we would be delisted. Without soup turnover the whole portfolio might face delisting.

In any event, after much political horse-trading, we came up with a plan which gave Hellmann's substantial investment. With soup, we developed a whole range of varieties which didn't compete directly with other brands (sweetcorn etc.) and crossed our fingers that this would keep us in distribution. The plan worked, and along with investment in Bouillon cubes and disinvestment in several failed new products it led to an immediate profit turnaround. In particular, Hellmann's volume virtually tripled over the next three years, and the advertising, which marked a radical broadening of the customer proposition, won many awards – not least, best overall campaign in the 1982 TV awards! But the critical point here for anyone involved in the advertising industry – agency or client – is that it was far more important that we correctly identified Hellmann's as an area for investment (a 'star') which was *capable* of responding to broadcast marketing. Even the best commercial in the world couldn't have helped Knorr Soup at that stage. But whilst with hindsight the decision was obvious, we were under considerable pressure at the time from our accountants and a doubting Chairman as to the advisability of such relatively massive investment in Hellmann's. The pressure on the client doesn't stop even when he makes a good decision!

Woolworths

In 1985 I became the first ever Marketing Director of Woolworths (UK). Following the takeover from the US parent in late 1982 various remedies had been tried but the chain was still a heterogeneous collection of store sizes (from 2,000 to 70,000 sq. ft.), with a badly laid out mixture of unrelated merchandise all tied together by an unreliable and expensive supply chain. We were fond of quoting the four 'Ps' and pointing out that we had the wrong products at the wrong prices in the wrong places with the wrong promotions. The 'Focus' strategy, which transformed the fortunes of the firm, was actually based on some very simple concepts – principally concentrating on Woolworths' strengths – and the analyses which backed it up were deceptively simple. Portfolio appraisal showed adult clothing and food were 'dogs' and it did seem that these were unlikely to repay an investment of management attention or promotional expenditure. These departments, representing nearly a quarter of turnover, were eliminated, freeing up space into which the expanded, more authoritative ranges of the chosen focus markets ('stars' and 'question marks') could grow. But another simple analytical tool was used in the development of the company's strategy – the so-called SWOT chart, or strategy audit. Commercial management at Woolworths sat down and generated lengthy lists of company attributes and trends in the marketplace. These were then ruthlessly pruned to leave only the most important factors, according to consensus.

When conducting this sort of analysis the participants have to be rigorous in cutting out the irrelevant. For instance, when considering the company's internal strengths and weaknesses only those factors which are *distinctive* elements, specific to the client in question, should be included.

So, while the temptation was for Woolworths to write down '800 stores' as a strength, they didn't, since Boots had over 1,000 and most other competitors (like W.H. Smith) had enough outlets to be available to the vast majority of the population.

When Woolworths went on to look at the upside and downside of the future trading environment they would face, they were similarly rigorous. 'Opportunities' and 'Threats' are the significant changes you expect to see in the company's environment going forward. When people do this sort of appraisal there's a tendency to write down the strategy you want to pursue, like 'open a chain of video stores' as an opportunity – which I suppose it is, but in this context the definition of an opportunity is something significant changing outside the company which seems potentially beneficial and which might prompt a change of resource allocation.

Strengths, Weaknesses, Opportunities and Threats were all ruthlessly cut back to a consensus of the most important three or four in each category. The beauty of being as exclusive as possible in making up the four topic lists involved in a SWOT analysis now becomes clear since all four can be summarized in Figure 3.4 which makes it easy for those involved to 'eyeball' the whole picture, and also easy to communicate to others. Now good strategy, at its simplest, is exploiting those opportunities which your strengths permit. Simply from looking at Figure 3.4 and without all the background of customer

Strengths	Weaknesses

■ Leading market positions
■ Prime high street locations
■ Brand heritage
  – price
  – traditional
  – fun
	■ Store size mix
	■ Major town exits
	■ Brand heritage
	  – incompetence
	  – old-fashioned
	  – dowdy

Opportunities	Threats
■ Demographics (+ + children) ■ Kingfisher portfolio (less competition for investment) ■ Less cyclical/steady trends	■ Rent/rate inflation ■ Labour costs ■ No real price inflation ■ Out of town erosion

Figure 3.4 SWOT analysis

research and the like that went on we can see emerging some of the reasons for Woolworths seeking to exploit young family markets, particularly in its existing product strength areas.

Far too many clients, it has to be said, pursue strategies which seek to cure weaknesses rather than build on strengths. In general terms this is fatal.

Obviously the strategy audit provided only the pointers for a more thorough appraisal of the implications of such massive change, but these techniques at least had the advantage of being easy to present and communicate to the thousands of people who were to become involved in the ensuing implementation.

Only after this 'high-level' analysis of what customers might want and how Woolworths might satisfy them was consideration given to the 'low-level' marketing and advertising implications. While the changes in media and product focus and in the tone of voice and personality of our advertising became important to the strategy's implementation, they were not our initial prime focus. Retail 'branding' tends to be the sum of a company's product-delivery attributes – 'they have what I want from them when and where I want it' – rather than an ethos which is regarded as almost separate from the product itself, as is often the case in FMCG. To make matters worse (from an ad agency's point of view) the substantial increase in marketing expenditure to support the consequent repositioning was largely funded by supplier contribution, which runs the risk of the 'tail wagging the dog' in terms of choosing what/when to advertise. But looked at from the point of view of 'accountability', the internal justification of expenditure is made a lot easier when the net cost is nothing! Any advertising agent working on a retail or service business should always bear in mind that to such clients marketing activity is often purely a matter of publicizing and incentivizing a trial of demonstrable product attributes and benefits.

The results for Woolworths were and continue to be, significant. A household name came back from the brink of extinction and now generates much more profit for its Kingfisher parent. Advertising, and marketing support in general, has been much more effective, though only rarely 'award winning'. The most important job for the client, the source of pressure on all of us, was adopting the right priorities and gaining company-wide commitment to their implementation.

TSB Bank plc

In 1991, I moved to be the Marketing Director of TSB. Peter Elwood, then Managing Director of the Retail Banking division, was looking for a retailer to help management think 'outside the box' and adapt the company's assets more closely to changing customer demand.

In many ways, like Woolworths we had the *wrong products and prices* – new competitors like Direct Line were offering better deals; in the *wrong places* – telephone banking and changes in shopping patterns were outmoding the branch network in its traditional shopping parade sites; and the *wrong promotion* – broadcast advertising with little 'cut through' beyond 'the bank that likes to say Yes'. But in financial services these were not distinctive weaknesses! Nearly everyone was just as bad.

The same analytical tools as above, SWOTs and portfolios – gave insights into a potential new focus for the TSB offer, but they didn't crack the core problem. The branch banking paradigm had passed its sell-by date and was institutionalized through a series of practices and inertia which actively militated against improved customer service. There are no standard analytical methodologies which help develop a new *vision* for a client. And there are certainly no easy ways to shift what might be termed 'legacy thinking'. It's always much easier, and *less pressured* to go with the flow.

One of the biggest contributors to the necessary change in the way the company thought about customer demand came from a wholesale reorganization of the marketing function. Out went 'supply side' ideas like management silos based on the products we made (banking, general insurance, life &

pensions and the like) and in came groupings based on the way customers saw financial services – 'Housing Finance', 'Money Management' 'Long Term Security' etc. These caused not just structural upheaval, but substantial relocation and disruption (and more pressure!). But they led to marketing being much more able to articulate demand consistently to colleagues around the company.

Priorities and budgets were focused on trying to do three things well – youth recruitment, savings and mortgages – with collateral objectives and plans put on the back burner. The immediate success of this policy did much to enhance the department's credentials.

And the biggest change – a fundamental adaptation of the distribution strategy – was realized in a test market, with, in some cases, lashed up temporary systems to simulate a future of 'transparent banking' – with 24-hour phone service, better located branches with longer opening hours, better cash machines in more convenient locations etc. This 'test' gave the firm a more concrete example of what might be done and real testbed results – which fortunately were positive.

All of this was tremendously resource-consuming and pressurized. Our advertising agencies and their work were often the last thing on our minds. But again, it was more important to ensure we were promoting the right aspects of our service than it was to refine that promotion. In many ways the experience of this turnaround was very similar to Woolworths – banking is intrinsically a retailing phenomenon. One important difference was the significance of *relationship marketing*.

Relationship marketing and accountability

It is the nature of the banking relationship that much customer information is accrued, and most companies in financial services see database marketing increasingly as a lower cost, low wastage approach to the attraction of business. The need to prove that expenditure *works*, to be *accountable*, is superficially most easily met by one-to-one campaigning: 'We spent x and 3 per cent of customers bought one which is worth more than x – result, happiness.' At TSB we were conscious that the 3 per cent positive response was only one end of a standard distribution. There was a whole bunch of people in the middle of the bell curve who 'binned' direct communication, but there was also a small percentage at the other end of the curve who could be actively antagonized by a too intrusive reliance on such techniques – and their negative response wasn't being built into the success/failure equations. Anyone involved in *broadcast* advertising in such data rich areas must be able to define the values it delivers in competition with more *narrowcast* techniques if they are to avoid seeing their budgets soaked away by the siren promises of relationship marketing. Clients under the pressure of short-term expenditure accountability need dispassionate support and help in articulating these issues.

MGM Cinemas

My last stint as a client was as Managing Director of MGM Cinemas between 1993 and 1995 when the company was sold to Virgin (some three years ahead of the original schedule and *not* to the management buyout we had hoped for!).

Despite the glamour (all those premières!) cinema is essentially another retail operation, but one in which the product on sale can vary from blockbuster in one week to turkey the next. We needed to find massive investment for new multiplex sites. The multiplex with its increased choice, ease of parking/ accessibility and adjacency to other leisure needs, especially restaurants, had by 1992 doubled cinema going in the UK from its disastrous depths in 1985. Our competitors for new sites were better funded multinational operations who were more closely associated with movie production and therefore more likely to benefit from vertical integration (e.g. Warner and UCI, a joint venture between the Universal and Paramount studios).

Marketing the movies

The solutions at MGM were probably the least associated with advertising in my career to date. Producing an ad for MGM mainly involved sticking something like Figure 3.5 in the classifieds.

Producing this (with wit and imagination of course) was hardly likely to admit the agency responsible to the innermost sanctum of MGM's marketing strategy. But we spent £4 million doing it, nevertheless!

The solutions we came up with were far more about giving us the best evaluation model in the market for new sites. A considerable investment in geodemographic analysis and modelling of cinema-going habits enabled us to improve our understanding of how much we could afford to bid, and also unearthed areas of latent demand where we could encourage developers to attempt to pull together candidate sites.

Figure 3.5 An ad for MGM

Other improvements in the cinema experience itself were on the drawing board when Virgin took over – some of which they have implemented with much more élan than we would have managed, notably their luxury screens with private bars which have significantly extended the appeal of cinema-going to a wealthier group of customers. The whole cinema industry continues to re-market itself and will need to go beyond the multiplex – which is something of a 'one trick pony' – if it's to convert infrequent visitors to the habit. Advertising will doubtless play more of a role in the future, but only disciplined and *accountable* expenditure which recognizes the real difference between stimulating awareness and usage of a retail or service product and selling *things*.

How agencies can adapt to client pressures

Since I left advertising and became a client, therefore, I've worked for a spectrum of clients where the role of advertising expenditure within the marketing task has become less and less salient. I don't think this is untypical. Even had I stayed in FMCG the maturing of consumer expenditure and the increasing power of retailers would have led to an increased need to seek improvements in efficiency and a focus on the demonstrable returns for any given expenditure; but my move into retailing and service industries parallels the increased significance of such clients within the marketing arena. All in all, the key difference in the 1990s clients from, say, their 1960s and 1970s counterparts, is that they have completely different strategic priorities. In exasperation in 1995 Andrew Seth (former Unilever marketing chief) said of ad agencies:

> Their real job is brand building which is what they used to be bloody marvellous at, and what we really paid them for, and what they deserved huge money for – which now takes second place to clever advertising, making jokes, high impact, getting awareness.

What Andrew was doing here is, however, making the same mistake as those he criticizes. He is harking back to the late 1960s when the vast majority of advertising spend was poured into fast-moving consumer goods – food, drink and tobacco.

In those days 'client' was largely synonymous with 'manufacturer'. Mega-clients built up their products' sales volumes in order to gain more economic production runs in their factories; they employed large salesforces and substantial distribution fleets to ship their products everywhere ... and then they sought to distinguish very similar product performances by 'branding' them. 'Branding' generically, means providing customers with reassurance prior to product purchase or experience. At its simplest, seeking the response 'it must be all right if it's from Heinz' or at its most complex, unconscious and almost subversive 'my family will appreciate me more if I use Heinz'.

In that golden age of FMCG 'branding' the advertising process was the highest form of marketing. It was the most important aspect of the job. What the client did that wasn't advertising was basically accountancy – running the brand budgets – and salesmanship – administering the promotional or below-the-line discounts. But are today's clients as focused on 'branding'? More importantly if they were, would they look to advertising to develop their brand?

Food manufacturing compared to food retailing

If my advertising for, say, Hellmann's mayonnaise tells you that it is 'yummy' stuff and a bottle you can put on your table without losing self-respect, then the product you obediently purchase – be it in Aberdeen or Plymouth – is identical. The base on which the branding is to build is sound and consistent. But whatever I tell you about shopping at Tesco, your response is almost wholly governed by how good or bad *relatively* your local Tesco is. And the nature of retailing means the delivery can *never* be consistent, due to the different vintage, and therefore facilities, offered by each store unit. For example, whatever the attributes of the brand MGM in *cinema* retailing, and however good customer services were at their traditional cinema in Cambridge, the opening of an eight screen multiplex a mile away led to an immediate loss of 85 per cent of its business. The new *product* was technically superior and no amount of emotional overlay could rescue the old outmoded cinema.

Advertising is not synonymous with marketing

For many of today's marketers, advertising is not synonymous with branding or even marketing as it used to seem in those far off 15 per cent commission days. If marketing means the better adaptation of the corporation's assets to customer needs then that can include radical product redesign, re-engineering of the supply chain, loyalty rewards and even radical cost reduction. In fact, if you simply lift traditional 'branding' methods from the days of FMCG dominance and apply them to the newer service industry clients then the results can backfire.

Financial services have been the prime example of this mistaken 'expertise transplant'. Midland Bank attempted to come up with a series of separately branded and segmented current accounts each with their own targeted advertising. Where are Orchard and Vector now? Or take the lengthy attempt by NatWest in recent years to invest in a branding campaign making generalized reassuring noises at a time when all banks' customers were demonstrating disaffection and all tabloid editors were actively seeking service exceptions to undermine such claims. A campaign that set out to 'provide customers with reassurances prior to product purchase' wound up looking like arrogance.

The need for new agency models

My main point is that the evolution of consumer expenditure has, for a large proportion of goods and service suppliers, outmoded the traditional advertising agency model. For many clients, agencies have either too little marketing understanding to provide them with dispassionate guidance, or, looked at the other way, too much advertising infrastructure for their needs.

Jeremy Bullmore spoke at an IPA breakfast address timed to celebrate the launch of *Advertising Works 8*. In commenting on the most successful papers he noted a common thread:

> Long before a single ad had been written, let alone run, that client company had gained insights and the confidence to change direction, modify product, restructure recruitment policy and rearrange priorities – sometimes to quite extraordinary commercial and financial advantage.

And Jeremy rightly commented that where this worked, the process of running all the way up the hierarchy to corporate strategy and back down again to the matter in hand of developing advertising was particularly suited to the traditional agency–client relationship. For three key reasons: firstly, the process had an end objective – it was focused by the need to make advertising, and this deadline forced practical conclusions on what could otherwise become an arid, never-ending analysis; secondly, he noted that the process had no common name and was a mixture of planning, research and serendipity, largely based round relatively long-term personal acquaintance; and thirdly, as he pointed out, it comes free with the ads.

This is all true but, as I've been arguing, a lot of today's clients don't find advertising central to the task of adapting their company to the customer as the examples from my career at least (I hope) have shown.

There is no doubt that the higher up the strategic hierarchy of a client's consultancy needs you go, then the more value the service has for the client. The business results of the examples Jeremy highlighted were incalculable in their positive benefit to the respective clients. Those clients, I'm sure, will therefore be less prone to argue about the percentage commission or retainer fees they are paying. In other words the more an ad agency relationship can extend up into marketing *direction* rather than allowing itself to be reduced to marketing *implementation* then the more it will be worth to its client (the more of those pressures it will alleviate) and the more it can charge them. But for an increasing number of clients the development of an ad or even a campaign does not provide the opportunity for the total business reappraisal evidenced in Jeremy's examples, even though such clients still desperately need such an insightful reappraisal of their operation.

New agency models

There's a desperate need for a new form of marketing services agency which shares some characteristics with traditional advertising agencies – particularly relatively long-term and close day-to-day client association – but which succeeds in building marketing partnerships with its clients without the need to produce important advertising. Somehow Jeremy's identified benefit 'it came free with ads' needs to be adapted to 'it came free with marketing spend'.

Various attempts are being made at 'integration' or 'unbundling' and the like but they mostly seem to me to be repackaged approaches to the production of creative advertising as opposed to recognizing, from the beginning, that advertising might not be the critical element for some clients in their continuous process of marketing reappraisal.

What is needed is a return to the 'lead agency' concept in which the agency's management, account direction and planning functions are qualified to consult with the client at the level of marketing strategy and are then equally able to propose and manage all forms of resultant marketing expenditure. Since it is unlikely that such an agency could sustain the overhead involved in being equally excellent in creative advertising, promotional work, public relations and database marketing, it seems that some or preferably all of these would be bought in – as 'à la carte' as media has already become. The 'lead agency' would maintain two key distinctions in house – the ability to think deeply and dispassionately about the management of consumer demand and the ability to coordinate all the resulting expenditures to best effect on the client's behalf. Indeed, by letting go of the traditionally in-house creative department such an agency type would *qualify* itself better as a dispassionate marketing services partner, and find it easier to avoid suspicion as an advertising chauvinist.

Until such a new 'lead agency' concept emerges which can operate as the true 'agency of record' for the sort of clients I've been referring to, they will continue to be forced to rely on their internal resources and intermittent corrective visits to expensive management consultancies. For those clients at least, the current model advertising agencies do nothing to relieve the pressures strategic adaptation has created. All too often they simply add to it.

In conclusion

I have argued that the ends clients look for from the marketing profession and its agency services have not changed over the last thirty years. But the required strategies for achieving those ends have changed considerably as continually developing consumer sophistication renders the previously esoteric common-place and brings new products and services into the spotlight – all requiring explanation and connection with latent demand.

The principal characteristic of the marketing 'market' of the 1960s and early 1970s was its homogeneity. An awful lot of products required similar marketing answers. Advertising, promotion, design and research needs were very similar and led, I think, to institutionalization and ossification in our thinking. Here was a product needing 'marketing'. We asked ourselves 'what sort of advertising does it need?' rather than 'does it need advertising?'. Indeed, marketing in many places became synonymous with advertising and promotional spend rather than the strategic adaptation of the company's offer. With the benefit of hindsight, this period of homogeneity was freakish. It is in the nature of things that different product and service categories will need very different approaches to their marketing to customers. The best sort of marketing goes back every time to first principles and tries to understand what business the company's in before adapting the offer itself to make it most readily saleable – and only then considers what means of selling to use. Today's advertising agencies face a much wider spectrum of advertiser, from those who need to be told 'Don't', through to those whose requirement is for a simple, rational explanation to be broadcast, and then on to those requiring their advertising to build branded distinction.

An agency can only be judged by how well it serves its customers, how well it shoulders the pressures on them. Too many of today's agencies are still chasing all forms of income and stretching their credibility by trying to be all things to all people. My concern is that by failing to adapt to the changing client market, agencies are losing market share most rapidly in the highest value added areas – the level at which clients describe their agency relationship as a marketing partnership. We need more initiatives to reverse that trend if we're to have happier, less pressurized clients.

Overview: Chapter 4

In taking on the task of writing the chapter on Strategy Development, Simon Clemmow faced two big challenges.

Firstly, in my view, this is the centrally most important part of the job of Account Planners in advertising agencies – so best practice here is crucial.

Secondly, in the first edition of this book this chapter was written by myself – a tough act to follow!

Fortunately, Simon has acquitted himself exceptionally on both counts. Full of contemporary examples and aided by numerous process visuals, the chapter brings to life both the complexity and the reward of this important area.

The chapter was originally presented in September 1998 on the IPA's Stage 2 Campaign Planning Course – and looks set to be a regular feature of that course in the future.

Chapter 4

Strategy development

Simon Clemmow

Introduction: how does advertising work?

After a century or so of formal study, we still do not know how advertising works! This isn't the admission of defeat it sounds; advertising is a craft, not a science, and asking how advertising works isn't like asking how a bicycle works – it's more like asking 'How does literature work?' Nevertheless, it's very important to have a good grasp of the general theories that have been advanced over the years, because they must all be part of our 'mental furniture' when we're developing an advertising strategy.

'Classic' theories of how advertising works are mainly of the single-model kind: that is, 'The way advertising works is *this* way'. These include AIDA (which states that Awareness is necessary before and leads to Interest which is necessary before and leads to Desire which is necessary before and leads to Action); USP (Unique Selling Proposition, which depends on finding a motivating point-of-difference within the product); and Brand Image (which asserts that image is more important in selling a brand than any specific product feature, and that advertising works by 'adding value' to the *gestalt*).

However, as early as the 1930s it was acknowledged that advertising could work in more than one way, and frameworks began to be constructed. The most enduring from that time is James Webb Young's 'Five Ways' (1963), which says that advertising works:

1 By familiarizing
2 By reminding

3 By spreading news
4 By overcoming inertias
5 By adding a value not in the product.

In the 1960s, the premise that the consumer is a passive, rational receiver of information began to be questioned in earnest, and Timothy Joyce (1967) suggested that advertising works via a complex relationship of interacting variables. Most importantly, Joyce's model (Figure 4.1) says that purchasing both influences attitudes ('experience and dissonance reduction') and heightens attention to advertising ('post-purchasing exposure') – undermining the validity of linear sequential models such as AIDA. It also allows for the 'natural' consumer tendency towards consistent attitudes and purchasing habit irrespective of external stimuli – James Webb Young's 'inertia' – which advertising always has to work with or against.

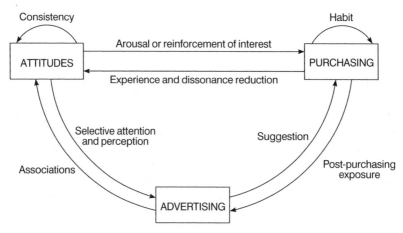

Figure 4.1 How advertising may work

The idea that it's not what advertising does to people but rather how people respond to advertising that's important was further developed in the 1970s, and Stephen King (1975) constructed a 'scale of immediacy' in terms of the desired response to a particular piece of advertising (Figure 4.2). This scale starts with the simplistic view that advertising affects action directly, then modifies it on an increasingly indirect/less immediate continuum of intervening responses, from seeking information (perhaps by filling in a coupon or telephoning a number – the 'Tell me more' response) right through to reinforcing attitudes (The 'I always knew I was right' response).

In between there are responses concerned with the receiver relating the brand to his own needs, wants, desires or motivations ('What a good idea'),

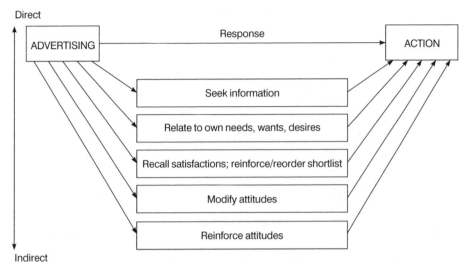

Figure 4.2 Scale of direct/indirect responses to advertising

recalling satisfactions and making shortlists ('That reminds me') and modifying attitudes (the 'Really?' response). The great strength of this model is that it recognizes that advertisements can differ in terms of either the speed or the complexity of intervening responses, or both.

Even this brief skim across the surface of some of the seminal thinking about how advertising works highlights that the planning and execution of an advertising strategy can only be a process of continuous learning and adaptation, in a competitive environment, where the norm is uncertainty and change. The proper approach is a cycle of analysis, theory, experiment, feedback, new theory, and so on. To this end, Stephen King (1977) introduced the famous 'Five Questions' which frame the planning cycle.

The planning cycle

The planning cycle consists of five fundamental questions (Figure 4.3). Question 1 is 'Where are we?' Where is our product or service now – in its marketplace, and in people's minds? Where has it come from, and where does it look as if it's going? Question 2 is 'Why are we there?' What is the combination of factors, over what period of time, that has affected our position, direction and rate of change? The answers to Questions 1 and 2 together constitute the status of the brand.

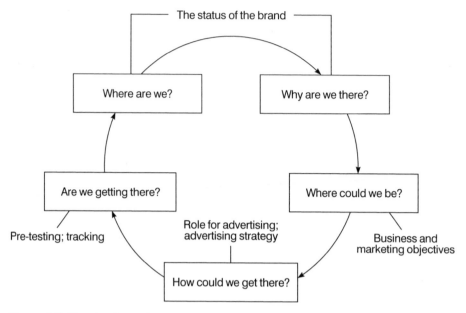

Figure 4.3 The planning cycle

Question 3 is 'Where could we be?' Again, in our marketplace, and in people's minds? How soon? This is the first of a series of creative or judgmental decisions. It is a combination of where we would like to be and where we think that, in practice, we could get to. This is where business and marketing objectives must be set and interrogated.

Note that the issue of advertising strategy doesn't arise until Question 4. Like many things in life, good strategy development depends more on perspiration than inspiration. It is clearly impossible to decide 'How could we get there?' without having first reached a decision on where to be and whether it is possible to get there (Question 3). And equally we cannot be firm about where to be without knowing why we did not get there in the past and where we are now (Questions 2 and 1).

Question 5 is 'Are we getting there?' Is it likely that our strategy would help us get there (pre-testing)? And do our measurements of progress in real life show that we're meeting our objectives (tracking)? This of course brings us back to 'Now where are we?', and a new cycle starts – we hope, from a better position than the first. This chapter is not concerned with Question 5 of the planning cycle. But it has to be concerned with Questions 1, 2 and 3 – the status of the brand, and business and marketing objectives – before it can get on to Question 4 – role for advertising and advertising strategy itself.

Strategy Startpoint: The desired response to a great ad is not 'What a great ad', but 'What a great product'

Heathrow Express gets you from Central London to Heathrow Airport in fifteen minutes, every fifteen minutes

The Virgin One account is a revolutionary new way of thinking about and organising your money to your considerable benefit

Figure 4.4 Breakthrough product propositions like these don't require much 'dressing up' to produce motivating, distinctive advertising. These strategies 'get out of the way of the product'

The status of the brand

The first thing to establish is the status of the brand, both in the marketplace and in the consumer's mind. Establishing the status of the brand in the marketplace is primarily to do with the numbers and the 'what?' Quantified information on things like market size and direction, seasonality and segmentation, purchasing profiles, penetration and frequency, brand and competitor share, distribution and pricing is generally available, objective and reliable. Even so, it's important neither to pay lip-service to the data, nor to allow it to replace judgement, interpretation and intuition. For example, consumers may not define a 'market' in the same way as a retail audit does; and 'macro' political, social and cultural trends may have more powerful implications for the future than the numbers show.

Establishing the status of the brand in the consumer's mind is more about the 'why?' of things like category buying and usage patterns, brand selection and reputation, and motivations to use and non-use. Qualitative research can be useful here, and it's the best time to do it. As Alan Hedges says (1974), the most important contribution that research can make to increasing the selling effectiveness of advertising is at the planning stage before anyone has even begun to think about particular advertising ideas. (This seems obvious, but is often ignored. Strategic conclusions are frequently reached by testing creative ideas, with the consequent erosion of time, money and goodwill all round.)

But if skimping on background research is a false economy, it's equally foolish to ignore the findings of relevant research that has recently been done, or to rush into fresh research without having properly thought through the objectives, the sample and the stimulus material. Just 'doing some research' is a waste of time and money too. Garbage in garbage out, as they say.

A completed examination into the status of the brand can take any one of several forms, from a simple checklist to a full 'brand book', and no one form is likely to be appropriate for all brands in all markets. However, we have to start somewhere, and the principles are relevant to durables and services as well as fast-moving packaged goods, so here is a framework for our guidance (Figure 4.5). We can use it as a reminder of the broad question areas that need answering and the relationship between them, and to give a systematic approach to our information search and a rationale for any research proposal arising.

Business and marketing objectives

Having established where we are and why, we need to take a view on where we could be, again in the marketplace and in the mind. What is our ambition in terms of, say, sales and share? Are we looking for increased sales, or simply

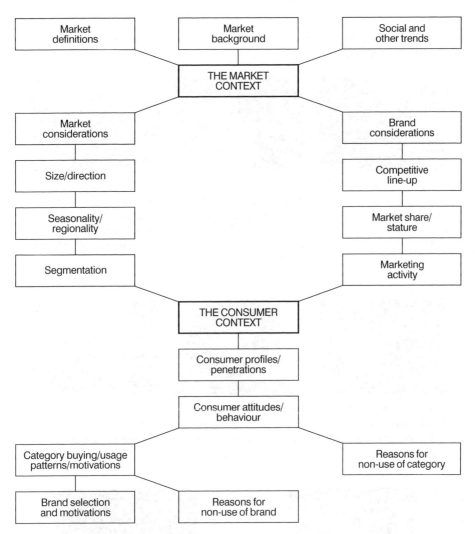

Figure 4.5 A framework to help establish the status of the brand

to halt a sales decline? Or are we looking to increase price and margin, thereby improving profitability? And does our ambition depend on gaining new users for the brand, increasing frequency amongst existing users, developing new usage methods or occasions, or what?

This ambition for the brand is based on business acumen and marketing expertize, and must be realistic given predicted 'macro' factors, competitive activity, and where we need to be in the mind. What consumer awareness and/ or attitude shift is required? Will the brand require a repositioning or a

Strategy Startpoint: 'Promise, large promise, is the soul of an advertisement' (Dr Johnson)

'For years I've lived a double life. In the day I do my job; I ride the bus, roll up my sleeves with the hoi polloi.'

'But at night I live a life of exhilaration, of missed heartbeats and adrenaline. And if the truth be known, a life of dubious virtue.'

'I won't deny I've been engaged in violence. Even indulged in it. I've maimed and killed adversaries, and not merely in self-defence.'

'I have exhibited disregard for life, limb and property, and savoured every moment.'

'You may not think it to look at me, but I have commanded armies, and conquered worlds.'

'And though in achieving these things I've set morality aside, I have no regrets.'

'For though I've led a double life, at least I can say I have lived.'

Figure 4.6 The power of Sony PlayStation to allow its users to experience a unique 'double life' is dramatized to good effect in this commercial. This strategy promises its target audience immense emotional reward.

personality change? What level of funds is available to achieve these things, and over what period of time? When are results expected? In the short term, or is a longer-term perspective viable? It is clearly unrealistic to set particular objectives if the budget is likely to be insufficient to achieve them.

It's critical to understand the difference between marketing and advertising objectives. Here are some made-up marketing objectives:

- To increase sales by generating trial amongst non-users
- To halt a decline by getting lapsed users to reconsider and infrequent users to use more
- To maintain share by reinforcing the behaviour of loyalists.

The important point is that advertising isn't necessarily required to meet any of them. A product or packaging improvement, or a distribution or pricing change, or a combination of all or some of these actions, might be more effective. We can no longer say 'The answer's advertising, now what's the question?', but must now ask 'Is the answer advertising?'.

Even if there is a role for communications, there is an increasing number of ways brands can communicate with their consumers, and advertising isn't necessarily one of them. Gone are the days when marketers could focus on network television, secure in the knowledge that their finished film would both hit the vast majority of their target audience and represent the most effective medium for doing so. Nowadays people are consuming an increasingly varied

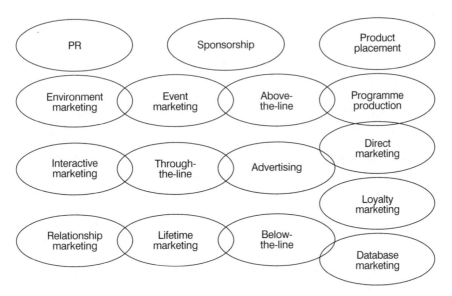

Figure 4.7 Channel proliferation means we can't presume a role for advertising

and segmented selection of media; they are using on-demand technologies to shape much more strongly what they see, and when; and new media vehicles are fast emerging, such as interactive television and the internet.

Today's channel proliferation (Figure 4.7) includes PR, sponsorship, product placement, programme production, direct marketing, environment marketing, event marketing, interactive marketing, relationship marketing, lifetime marketing, loyalty marketing, database marketing, below-the-line, through-the-line, above-the-line and – oh yes – advertising. How do we work out whether there's a genuine role for advertising amongst all this?

The role for advertising

Identifying and defining the role for advertising is fundamental to achieving excellence in advertising, because it stands as a clear 'stake in the ground' in the whole development process. If it is ill-defined – left ambiguous, inaccurate or unclear – then there are no solid foundations for developing advertising strategy or execution. Neither is there a basis for meaningful research or evaluation. In fact, it's worse than that, because there's a negative multiplier effect.

Ten per cent off on role for advertising might mean a further ten per cent off on targeting which might mean a further ten per cent off on proposition, and so on. So by the time you're looking at the finished advertising, it's got only a fifty per cent chance of meeting its objectives! When Lord Leverhulme famously said he knew that half of his advertising was wasted, but he didn't know which half, the answer was the half whose role hadn't been properly identified and defined.

So what can advertising do well, and what is it not so good at? The truth is that it is impossible to match, with any precise science, communications objectives with the 'best' channel for achieving those objectives. Even case studies which have won IPA Advertising Effectiveness Awards aren't very convincing on this point. They're generally good at demonstrating how advertising helped meet the communications and business objectives set, rigorously eliminating other variables such as marketing mix adjustment and competitive activity, thereby 'proving' the contribution that advertising made. They're not so good at justifying 'why advertising' before the event, rather than another means of communication.

However, the large body of work published under the title *Advertising Works* (Duckworth, 1981–97) does allow us to make some broad observations on the types of communication task to which advertising seems particularly suited (Figure 4.8). First, there is the plethora of case studies in which advertising is used in the almost 'classic' sense of delivering a consistent, 'added value' message on behalf of a brand, lifting an everyday product out of the ordinary.

1. Adding value to lift everyday products out of the ordinary:

Walkers (1996)   Murphy's (1996)   Gold Blend (1996)
Philadelphia (1996)   Stella Artois (1996)   PG Tips (1990)
Peperami (1994)   Boddington's (1994)
Oxo (1992)   John Smith's (1994)

2. Building emotional brand values over and above a rational proposition:

Levi's (1992)   BMW (1994)
Nike   Barclaycard (1996)

3. Spreading new news quickly and widely:

Daewoo (1996)   Direct Line (1992)

4. Putting on public display a relatively discrete product:

Wonderbra (1994)   *The Economist* (1992)

5. Providing a corporate flag to salute and a public agenda to live up to:

British Airways (1994) Safeway (1996)

6. Achieving broadscale targeting and mass social engineering:

BT (1996)   National Lottery (1996)

(Date refers to year of winning IPA Advertising Effectiveness Award)

Figure 4.8 Roles for communication that advertising can perform best

Perhaps not surprisingly, the examples are most prevalent in the food and drink categories.

In food, Walkers Crisps, Philadelphia Cream Cheese, Peperami Snacks and Oxo Cubes show how advertising can be used to build a strong and lasting bond with a brand's public, fuelling growth and resisting competitive and own-label threat. In drink, campaigns for Murphy's Stout, Stella Artois Lager and Boddington's and John Smith's Bitter in beer, the Gold Blend soap opera in coffee and the PG Tips chimps in tea have helped these brands rise above their scores of competitors.

Second, advertising is clearly useful when the communications objectives require the building of emotional brand values as well as the delivery of a rational proposition. The clothing category is an obvious area (brands like Levi's and Nike), but brands in other categories have benefited in this way too, from properties like BMW's 'ultimate driving machine' in cars to Barclaycard's bumbling secret agent, played by Rowan Atkinson, in financial services.

Third, advertising is good at spreading 'new news' quickly and widely. Daewoo cars (cutting out the dealer) and Direct Line financial services (cutting out the broker) are examples of this. Fourth, advertising can benefit a brand enormously by putting on public display products that have relatively discrete

Strategy Startpoint: 'The easy way to get into a person's mind is to be first. If you can't be first, then you must find a way to position yourself against the product . . . who did get there first' (Ries and Trout, 1981)

'Here's to the crazy ones. The misfits. The rebels. The troublemakers. The round pegs in the square holes. The ones who see things differently.'

'They're not fond of rules. And they have no respect for the status quo.'

'You can quote them, disagree with them, glorify or vilify them. About the only thing you can't do is ignore them.'

'Because they change things. They push the human race forward.'

'And while some may see them as the crazy ones, we see genius.'

'Because the people who are crazy enough to think they can change the world . . .'

'. . . are the ones who do.'

Figure 4.9 A competitor has no hope of going head-to-head against the 'no one ever got fired for buying IBM' position in computers. Many companies ignore this basic principle and suffer the consequences. Not Apple. Apple champion the creative, lateral thinker in all of us. This strategy positions the brand differently from the competition

target audiences. The poster medium is particularly suited to this 'propaganda' role, as case studies for Wonderbra and *The Economist* demonstrate.

Fifth, advertising is particularly useful when a company's communication needs to serve as a catalyst, or agenda setter, for its entire modus operandi. British Airway's self-styling as 'the world's favourite airline' is probably the most famous example, and Safeway developed crèches, mother-and-baby parking places and baby changing-rooms on the back of its child-friendly strategy personified by its advertising property, the toddler Harry.

And finally, it seems that you can't beat good old-fashioned high-spend television and multi-media advertising campaigns when it comes to the need to talk to all of the people all of the time. BT has reaped the rewards of using advertising in this way, and the launch of the National Lottery provides another example of advertising's role in mass social engineering.

Having identified that there is a role for advertising, the next problem is defining what that role is. The difficulty here is that it depends on the context. At its most obvious, the role for advertising is simple: to communicate the proposition to the target audience in the right tone of voice! (This is true, but a cop-out. It may be the role *of* a particular piece of advertising in the context of a creative brief, but the role *for* advertising needs to take account of broader issues to make a compelling and directional case.)

At the other extreme, advertising has a role to play 'beyond the strategy'. For example, the brand might benefit simply from the status of 'being advertised', or being 'TV advertised'. Or it might benefit from the way it is advertised: being the first brand in its category to use posters, or a famous person, or a tone that doesn't talk down to its audience. These are all functions that advertising can usefully perform in the context of brand marketing, but they are pleasant side-effects rather than the main kick, and lead to confusion between advertising and marketing objectives.

Clearly the role for advertising must 'fit' with the marketing objectives. Returning to our made-up examples, if we're looking to increase sales by generating trial amongst non-users, then an appropriate role for advertising might be to generate awareness or spread 'new news' if we have any. If we're looking to halt a decline by getting lapsed users to reconsider and infrequent users to use more, it may be more appropriate to charge advertising with the task of reminding consumers of the brand's benefits or modifying attitudes towards it. And if we're looking to maintain share by reinforcing the behaviour of loyalists, then the role for advertising might be to reinforce attitudes or continue adding value (Figure 4.10).

Strategy development

Having established why we're advertising and what we're trying to achieve, strategy development is about how we expect to do that. There are three key

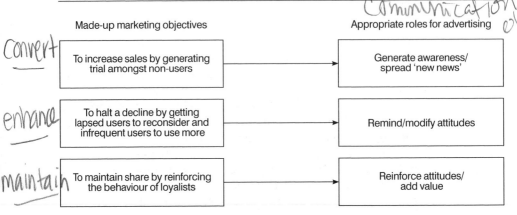

Communication objec

Convert

enhance

maintain

Figure 4.10 'Fitting' role for advertising with marketing objectives

'perspiration' tasks to strategy development before the key 'inspiration' one. The 'perspiration' tasks are product interrogation, target audience understanding and competitive analysis, and the 'inspiration' task is coming up with the proposition (which is the essence of the strategy). What we're looking for is a proposition that is true to the product *and* motivating to the consumer *and* distinctive from the competition (Figure 4.11). The better it satisfies these three criteria, the stronger the proposition will be.

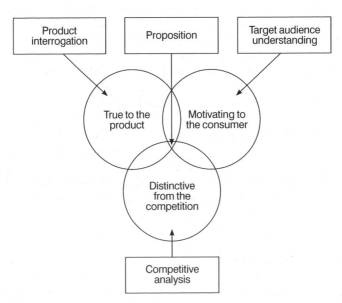

Figure 4.11 A strategy development template

Strategy Startpoint: 'Forget the logical proposition and find the personality of the brand instead' (Steve Henry, 1997)

my place now

fcuk®

i you want

fcuk®

night all long

fcuk®

 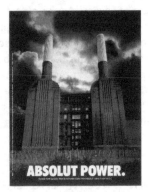

Figure 4.12 'Badge' brands like French Connection in retail fashion and Absolut vodka can often create effective advertising by recognizing that USP can stand for Unique Selling Personality as well as Unique Selling Proposition. These strategies recognize that sometimes personality sells harder than proposition

The product should be interrogated until it 'confesses to its strength'. Use it, visit the factory, read reviews, test reports, everything you can lay your hands on. Talk to the people who make it. (If you're dealing with a service brand, they may well *be* the product.) Talk to anyone who may have a point of view: experts, opinion formers, consumers. 'Formal' research may have a role here, but often equally or more revealing can be informal research – for example, watching people buying or using it can tell you a lot about the motivation behind product purchase and consumption (call it 'observational research' if you want someone to pay for your time!).

This will also help you understand the brand's target audience. Who are they? What are they like? What role does the brand play over and above the product? How does it discriminate itself from its competition? How does it fit into their world? What is their world like? This in turn will help you analyse the brand's competitive set. What is it? What is it really? Advertising landscaping, brand mapping, store visits, questions like 'If this brand didn't exist, what would you buy/use instead?' are all useful exercises.

Having done all that, a good tip is to go for a walk, both physically and mentally. There is no 'correct' process for arriving at the proposition, and no rules as to what makes a good one. Put everything you have learned to one side, and *think*. What should the advertising say that's true to the product, motivating to the consumer, distinctive from the competition, and in line with its role and objectives? Here are a few things to bear in mind that have worked well for me over the years:

- Don't try to 'be creative'. Proposition development is about arriving at a clear, unambiguous core message, not writing a strapline or slogan.
- Be single-minded. Advertising works best when it's charged with communicating one core message, not several. As the old adage reminds us, if you throw someone three tennis balls he'll probably drop them all, but if you throw him one he'll probably catch it. Advertising invariably carries 'secondary' communication in tone of voice and other executional considerations, but not in an effective proposition.
- Think of the proposition in terms of what you want the target audience to take out of the advertising rather than what you want the creatives to put in. Stimulus and response are rarely the same thing, and an effective strategy should always focus on the end rather than the means.

Conclusion: putting the theory into practice

This chapter has set out in logical sequence the steps that should be followed when developing an advertising strategy. At its heart is the planning cycle (Figure 4.3), which shows the questions that must be answered and the order they must be answered in, and at the heart of that is Question 4: 'How could we get there?', where the role for advertising must be established and the advertising strategy itself developed. The strategy development template (Figure 4.11) shows how to go about answering that part of Question 4.

But logic alone usually isn't enough. At some point during the development process, you may find it helpful to put logic to one side and ask yourself: 'What's driving the strategy?'. Figure 4.11 may look like a flat template, but it never is. During your walk around the problem, a dominant consideration will inevitably float to the surface. Perhaps the need to deliver rational product information is of overriding importance? Or the need to secure an emotional connection between consumer and brand? Perhaps the most important thing is how our brand comes across in relation to its market competition? Or maybe tone of voice is what makes us relevant and distinctive?

Use the Strategy Startpoints contained within this chapter to help you begin putting the theory into practice. There are plenty of others, and how they are used is up to the skill and judgement of whoever's responsible for developing the strategy. This book is about best practice, so this chapter has to stop here. Best practice is one thing – quality of practitioner is another.

References

Duckworth, G. (ed.) (1981–97), *Advertising Works 1–9*, NTC Publications

Hedges, A. (1974), *'Testing to Destruction'*, IPA

Henry, S. (1997), 'How to Write a Great Brief', *Admap*

Johnson, Dr Samuel, 'The Art of Advertising', *Idler*, essay No. 40, 20 January 1759.

Joyce, T. (1967), *'What Do We Know About How Advertising Works?'*, JWT.

King, S. (1975), 'Practical Progress from a Theory of Advertisements', *Admap*, October.

King, S. (1977), 'Improving Advertising Decisions', *Admap*, April.

Ries, A. and Trout, J. (1981), *Positioning: The Battle for your Mind*, McGraw-Hill.

Webb Young, J. (1963), *How to Become an Advertising Man*.

Overview: Chapter 5

Chris Forrest's enactment of the 'planner as detective' on the IPA's Stage 2 course (Campaign Planning) is as memorable for its humour as for its purpose. But the serious point it makes is a fundamentally important one: not only that quantitative data need not be daunting, sometimes it can hold the key to unlocking some of the mysteries of a market.

This chapter seeks to cover the basics of quantitative research as used in the development of advertising strategy. It outlines how to look at quantitative data and touches on the principal sources of data which advertising agencies use.

It begins by discussing the importance of having the right approach before even looking at the data. A list of useful question areas is then set out as part of the recommended approach. Finally, the data sources are discussed individually in terms of what they are most useful for and how to use them.

What the written chapter cannot replicate is Chris's consummate style in delivering the paper – nor the delight with which his acting skills have been received in each year since 1992 by some of the brightest and best young talents in the industry!

Chapter 5

Quantitative data and advertising strategy development

Chris Forrest

I've never liked maths. I passed maths O-level at 15 but then I failed additional maths O-level the following year, burnt my logarithm tables and switched to the arts stream. I thought I'd escaped.

One day in my early twenties, while working as a qualitative researcher, a busy client handed me a pile of computer tabulations and asked me to give her, within the next couple of days, a topline view of what the data was saying. My insides turned to water.

The tabs were on those scary rolls of computer print-out with the thin green lines and holes down both sides. You know, that stuff that spews unstoppably out of computer rooms in those films where the mainframe goes insane. Numbers swam before my eyes. I had to leave the building and walk around the block to control my rising panic.

So if you turned to this chapter with a sinking feeling, expecting not to like it, then you've come to the right place. If I can relax and learn to make numbers speak to me, anyone can.

The secret, which I eventually worked out the hard way, is to have an approach, a set of questions which can act as a route map through the statistics. In this sense quantitative research is very different from qualitative research. It's difficult to get badly lost in qualitative research. You can ask a group discussion which brands they buy and what they like about them and, generally, respondents will try to help you out and tell you useful things.

Numbers don't make any effort to help. They say things like '139.877' or '42 per cent' or '6' or even '0**' and then just sit there with their arms folded, waiting for you to ask another question.

Questions, questions, questions

From identifying the information need down to questionnaire design, quantitative research is all about asking questions. In fact if you're not careful you can generate such long lists of questions that it's not so much the numbers as the questions which start swimming before your eyes:

Where are the gaps in our knowledge?
Where are the unmet needs in the market?
What is the most appropriate role for advertising?
Which is more crucial, penetration or frequency?
What are the key demographics/psychographics?
What does our brand stand for?
Is the market going up or down?
When did you last see your father?
Why did the chicken...?
etc.

If quantitative research is all about asking questions then the hard part is *selecting the right questions*.

Other chapters in this book discuss advertising strategy. In this chapter my main objectives are:

1 To introduce the principle types of quantitative data you'll probably be working with.
2 (More importantly) to show how to approach quantitative data as part of your work to develop a strategy. I shall try to set out a framework for knowing which questions to ask when. If you can crack the approach then you have a context for the numbers and their relative importance. The specifics of each research technique also become less daunting. You won't have the time to become a Black Belt in every research methodology you encounter but you'll be able to work out what are the key things you need to understand about it.

Be a detective

The approach to adopt is that of a detective as opposed to a uniformed policeman. The uniformed police conduct house-to-house enquiries asking people where they were on the night of the twelfth. They are the research compilers. They follow up all leads to ensure they have interviewed everyone who might have seen anything (Figure 5.1). The detectives are the research users who are meant to cut through the mountains of paper and ask the incisive questions which ultimately solve the crime. These incisive questions are a mixture of knowing the correct procedures and relevant precedents off by heart and then adding a layer of common sense, intuition and sheer genius.

It's all too easy to lapse into compiler mode when working with quantitative market data. You can spend a lot of time trying to find out something simply because you want to tick every box, only to discover that this particular box is empty and that, with hindsight, you could have foreseen that it was going to be empty. Back in 1980 a couple of my Leeds student contemporaries who wore size nine boots were heavily questioned by police looking for the Yorkshire Ripper even though we would have been twelve years old when the killings started! The Ripper himself was interviewed and strongly suspected on a dozen separate occasions before he was finally caught. The detectives had the wrong approach. They had one set of (card index) data for men with size nine boots, a separate set of data for lorry drivers, another set for kerb crawlers and so on. They compiled more and more data without effectively cross-referencing it for useful patterns.

Even apparent patterns need to be tempered with intuition. If there's a market for hot tea and a market for iced tea it doesn't necessarily follow that there's an opportunity gap for an exciting new category called lukewarm tea.

In the first television series of *Cracker* there was an episode where the police had drawn up a psychological profile of a shopkeeper's apparently motiveless killer as young, disgruntled and unemployed. Fitz (the hero) points out that the killing took place at 6.30 a.m. and questions why anyone would get out of bed that early if they were unemployed. He suspects the killer was a tired, frustrated shift worker on the way home, points out the bus stop a hundred yards away and suggests they interview everyone who uses those bus routes in the early morning. This turns out to be the right approach and very nearly catches the baddie.

Intuition is all well and good but detectives, like musicians, cooks and artists, are most effective when they improvise from the base of a solid underlying competence in the craft skills of their respective trade. So what are the basic tools of the advertising strategists' approach to quantitative data?

Figure 5.1 (Copyright Ladybird Books Ltd)

The Big Questions

When developing advertising strategy, the Big Questions are very useful as checklists that you keep referring to, for example the classic planning cycle:

Where are we now?
Why are we here?
Where could we be?
How could we get there?
Are we getting there?

If you can answer these questions then you've got a good picture of where your brand is at. They are very useful checks but they don't really get you started on that pile of retail audit data. (Where are we now? = 74 per cent Co-op distribution in Anglia = So what?)

At a less macro level it helps to bear in mind the questions that you will ultimately need to answer in order to write an advertising strategy and thence a creative brief. An advertising strategy can be defined as a formal statement of:

Who exactly are we talking to?
What do we want them to do?
What exactly can we tell them to influence them?

To get to this point you need to have a thorough understanding of the market under the following headings:

1 Market economics and competitor analysis
2 Consumers' relationship with the product/service category
3 Consumers' relationship with the individual brands
4 Consumers' relationship with the advertising.

This should enable you to write an advertising strategy, creative brief and evaluation plan.

Thought Starters

Here are some Thought Starters for each question area.

1 Market economics and competitor analysis

This area is vital. This is the investigation that management consultants charge big money for and that clients have criticized advertising agencies for not understanding. There's no point in developing strategies solely from a demand-side perspective. We also need to understand the supply-side realities:

- How big is the market?
- Is it growing or contracting? Why?
- Is this market related to others? How?
- How many competitors are there and what share does each have?
- What positions do they take up? Why?
- Are any doing particularly well or badly? Why?
- How important to each competitor is their presence in this market? Is it a core business or more peripheral?
- How profitable a market/brand is this?

Beyond the 'realpolitik' of the economics your understanding from now on should be as much as possible from the consumer perspective. Try to look at quantitative data qualitatively, asking 'What does this mean in human terms?'.

For example, an 'out-of-stock' figure probably represents 'a lost sale' but that's not the end of the story. Think about it in behaviour terms. It means the customer either didn't buy anything on that occasion or they bought a competitive product. Which do you think they did? Which competitor does your data suggest they'd have bought? Would they have liked it, started buying it on a more regular basis since their first choice let them down?

Perhaps they were already buying the competitor. Look at Table 5.1. Brand A has the highest share of a consumer's purchases in a category. They buy lots of it. It appears to be their favourite brand. It's probably the brand leader in the market by a comfortable margin, but are its customers 'loyal' to it? The majority of their purchases are not of brand A. Surely it is more useful, less complacent, to do as Professor Andrew Ehrenburg recommends and 'think of your customers as "mostly other people's customers who occasionally buy

Table 5.1

Brand	Share of the average consumer's last ten purchases
A	4
B	2
C	2
D	1
E	1

your product"'. Bearing this sort of perspective in mind, let's return to the Thought Starters.

2 Consumers' relationship with the product

- Who is the 'consumer'? – age, sex, class, region, lifestyle
- Who are the heavy users?
- How 'important' to the consumer is the product?
- What does the consumer feel about the category?
- From where do the opinions/beliefs/knowledge derive?
- What triggers people to enter this market?
- What is the decision-making process?

3 Consumers' relationship with the individual brands

- How is the market structured in terms of brands? Why is it this way?
- What distinguishes the competing brands from each other (function, form, price, packaging, etc.)?
- What do consumers 'know' about the various brands? Why?
- What makes consumers choose between brands? What are the patterns of brand choice? Trade-offs made?
- What sort of consumers relate to our brand? Why?
- How does the consumer relate to our brand? Why?
- In what sort of repertoires does our brand sit? Why?
- What strengths and weaknesses does our brand have?
- What opportunities/threats exist for our brand? In what areas?
- What is the current brand strategy? (If there is one)
  - Price
  - Packaging
  - Promotion
  - Distribution
  - Product

4 Consumers' relationship with the advertising

- How do consumers regard the advertising in this category?
- What issues are prominent in advertising for the category or for our brand?
- What is the relative importance of advertising to this category?
- What is the advertising history of the category?
- Which brands tend to be advertised and which do not? Why?
- What is the pattern of spend? Why is it that way?
- Do any advertising conventions operate in the market? Why?
- What is our brand's history in terms of advertising (both in terms of amount of support and the content)? Why has it been that way?

- What position do we take up in the light of any conventions? Why?
- What strengths/weaknesses does our brand's advertising possess?

Now (and only now) that you know what questions the data detective must ask, you are ready to approach your data. It makes sense to start with an audit of what your information bureau, agency team and client has already got.

This will probably arrive as a pile of reports stacked in the corner of your office which grows remorselessly every day so that it appears to take on a life of its own. (Sometimes, if you listen carefully, you could swear you can hear it laughing at you.)

Waste not a second. Divide and rule it. Cut it into smaller piles. There are three points in a brand's life where measurement is particularly useful:

When it's produced
When it's bought
When it's consumed.

(For some services such as catering, the three stages happen simultaneously.) It can be useful to try to sort your data according to which of these measurement points its data are centred on (although with many research companies horizontally integrating (e.g. retail audit data and domestic panel data), this is becoming more difficult.)

When it's produced

Market study reports by companies such as Mintel and Euromonitor are very useful primers for an overview of the market, the main companies and basic consumer information. Company reports help you to see who's who and what other interests the main players have. Government data can be a treasure trove of information about the size of markets, long-term trends within them, legislative issues affecting them, predictions of further growth, etc. A client's 'ex-factory' data will tell you what has been produced. For service companies there will generally be measures of insurance policies issued, hotel 'bednights' sold, etc.

In several established markets the main players pool their sales data through an industry organization. For example, the Society of Motor Manufacturers and Traders allows members to see what they sold and what their competitors sold on a daily basis. The ex-factory data and the consumer data may not match up exactly. This could be because the ex-factory data capture is not exact but it could well be due to factors such as grey market imports where the same products are bought abroad in bulk and imported by individual traders rather than the official UK sales company. This sort of trade creates measurement problems in markets from high-fashion clothing to car tyres and, most recently, to take-home beer and wine.

When it's bought

Retail audits such as Nielsen or IRI either take retailers' electronic data or go into stores to observe what is displayed. They then crunch this information and present it in many useful ways. For example, at first sight Table 5.2 is just 140 numbers on a page. In fact it is packed with information that opens up a world of investigative possibilities. Have a good look at it before you read on. Think about what it shows and about what other thoughts it starts and lines of inquiry it might provoke.

MATs

To start with, Table 5.2 makes a useful point about MATs. Moving Annual Totals are frequently used to summarize the current state of a market. They are aggregated data for the previous twelve months, so if one data point is August 1995 to July 1996, the next will be September 1995 to August 1996, etc. In Table 5.2 MATs to September 1990 (the left-hand column) shows Own-label taking the highest share of sterling sales and brand A having the highest share of the branded sector (19.9) ahead of brand E (17.7). However, looking across the month-by-month sales figures we see the market dynamics in more detail, revealing the steady rise of Own-label and of brand E. Brand E is the current market leader. Its rise mirrors brand A's decline. Have brand E's sales come from brand A? Very possibly but we'll need to look at some consumer panel data (see later) to confirm this.

They aren't necessarily in direct competition. It may be that brand A is the old cash cow of a brand leader which has not received enough marketing and advertising support to fend off the appeal of Own-label and has become not much more than a 'manufacturer's own label', while brand E may be the new premium brand which is either growing the market or taking share from somewhere else, 'All Others' perhaps.

Value versus volume

Certainly the market is growing by value, up 17 per cent year on year as the figure at top-right shows. Is this value growth coming from volume growth, more of this stuff being bought? We need to look at volume sales to find out. It may just be that a general price rise, perhaps the cost of raw materials, has been passed on to the consumer so that although value has risen 17 per cent, volume may have declined by a greater amount. Perhaps the value rise is

Table 5.2 Product class X – Sales share, GB, Nielsen Grocery Service (£'000)

	MAT 48946 Sales Y % CHG	Sep. 1989	Oct.	Nov.	Dec.	Jan. 1990	Feb.	Mar.	Apr.	May	June	July	Aug.	Sep. (+17)
Market total	48946	3537	3833	3931	4412	3585	3689	4392	4294	4215	4224	4247	3992	4132
Brand A	19.9	22.0	20.8	19.3	18.9	19.0	19.4	20.7	20.1	19.7	20.8	21.2	20.8	17.5
Brand B	0.5	0.4	0.4	0.4	0.4	0.4	0.5	0.5	0.4	0.5	0.5	0.5	0.5	0.6
Brand C	4.6		4.4	4.3	4.3	4.7	5.2	4.9	5.1	4.8	4.6	3.9	4.4	4.5
Brand D	0.5	0.3	0.3	0.6	0.7	0.9	1.0	1.2	0.8	0.4	0.2	0.1	0.1	0.1
Brand E	17.7	18.1	18.2	17.3	17.4	17.2	18.0	17.3	17.4	16.9	16.1	10.6	18.2	22.2
Brand F	2.4	1.9	2.1	1.9	2.0	2.0	2.0	2.2	2.6	2.7	2.6	2.8	2.6	3.1
Brand G	1.6	1.1	1.0	1.0	1.3	1.3	1.5	1.6	1.6	1.7	2.3	2.2	2.2	1.0
Own-label	46.2	42.4	43.1	45.6	46.1	45.4	44.5	44.3	46.4	47.7	47.8	47.8	47.7	47.7
All others	6.8	13.8	9.7	9.0	8.9	9.1	7.9	7.3	5.0	5.6	5.1	4.9	3.5	3.3

Sep. 1990 — Latest 12 mths

Table 5.3

	Value share (%)	Volume share (%)	Value/volume index
Brand C	4.5	4.7	0.95
Brand F	3.1	2.5	1.24

attributable to consumers trading up to more premium priced, higher-quality variants. Is that what's been happening? Was brand A slow to reformulate? The value summary tables (shown) together with volume summary tables (not shown) give us enough data to work out relative price positions in the market (Table 5.3). In other words, brand F is premium priced. Its value share is 124 per cent of its volume share.

Price

Did brand A's price rise significantly in August? Could this explain the acceleration in share loss that we see? Why did any price rise occur? Is it made abroad and suffering from adverse currency fluctuations? Has it been having teething troubles switching manufacture and distribution away from its old formulation to a new improved formulation which may well take the market by storm in the next few months? I think we should be told.

Distribution

Distribution data by brand will help us get a better handle on what's been happening to the brands. If brand A has had excellent distribution throughout the year and its price has not been out of line with the market then its problems would seem to be to do with consumer preference shifting away from it. If it's been out of stock then we'd like to know why this was. Did a factory burn down or go on strike? Is it at war with one or more important retailers over the size of the retailer's margin and is the retailer delisting it to show they mean business? Look at the picture within each individual multiple.

Rate of sale

ROS is the usual way to look at relative demand for a brand. Brand A may have been selling well simply because it dominated distribution in the market. It's on sale everywhere. Brand E may not have been selling as well overall because of weaker distribution but where it was sold it may have been outselling brand A. Did the trade notice this superior ROS and, prompted by brand E's owners, give it wider and better quality distribution (e.g. more 'facings' on the shelf and/or more eye-level positions)?

ROS is the number of sales divided by the number of outlets. We usually also need to take into account the size of outlet. One Tesco hypermarket may sell more of the product category than thirty corner shops. 'Weighted (by either value or volume) distribution' takes this into account. It divides the ROS by the quality of its distribution. Technically:

$$\frac{\text{Average sales} \times \text{shop distribution}}{\text{Weighted distribution}} = \text{Weighted rate of sale}$$

Retail audit data will tell us enough to set up some working hypotheses which can be confirmed or refuted by other data sources. Don't overlook the immediate data source called 'the sales director'. It's always useful to attend those unglamorous retail audit presentations and ask the sales director(s) what they think has been happening. Now that the retail audit companies have moved to an account management system you'll also find the researcher presenting the data usually knows the market dynamics inside out and has a plausible explanation for most movements.

When it's consumed

At this point in the chapter you may be thinking that audit data tells you nearly all you need to know and that the hardbitten salesforce inhabit the real world while marketing and advertising only flutter about at a superficial level. 'Here come the Flower Arrangers' is how one of my client's sales directors likes to tease us. (Oh, how we laugh at this Wildean wit!)

But hold on a minute. We have only just started to investigate the market. We've not yet looked at our pile of data measuring the single most important agent in any market, the consumer.

Although it may appear that increased sales can be conjured out of a bit of wheeler-dealing on the distribution front, at the end of the day we need people, consumers, to actually buy the stuff otherwise all that behind-the-scenes trading effort could be pointless like in the old hippy adage: 'suppose they held a war and nobody came?'

Let's pause to remember a couple of marvellously simple common sense rules:

There are only three ways to increase profit:

1 Sell more
2 Raise prices
3 Cut costs.

There are only two ways to increase sales:

1 Get new people to use your brand
2 Get your current users to use more.

So if we are setting out to strengthen a brand in order to allow it to sell more (including extend into other areas) or to raise its prices then we need to start by understanding our brand. Brands are metaphysical entities. They live primarily in consumers' minds. We need to find out who's buying our brand and how they relate to it.

It's time to turn to your third pile of data, the one that measures the brand when it's used. Up there with retail audit data, the other data source which is most widely used in the advertising industry is TGI. BMRB's Target Group Index is a huge self-completion survey. It takes at least three hours to fill it in and all you get is a £3 Marks & Spencer voucher but 25,000 people a year have enough goodwill towards market research to dutifully complete the questionnaire giving marketers (and sociologists) a goldmine of data. The survey asks people about their purchases and usage of products across a vast range of markets combined with their media consumption patterns, leisure interests and attitudes.

It is the Bible for media planning because it shows which media a brand's users are consuming. It allows for complex cross-tabulations. If you want to, you can find out how many Mars Ice Cream heavy users read *The Economist*,

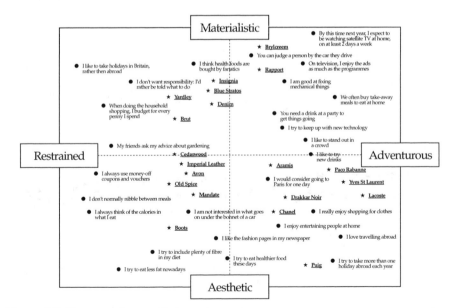

Figure 5.2 Correspondence analysis

watch *Blind Date*, bought a lawnmower in the previous 12 months and agree that 'a real man can down several pints at a sitting'.

Segmentation studies are a classic use of TGI. Statistical techniques such as correspondence analysis allow you to identify a number of clusters of people within a given target market who have similar attitudes and behaviour (Figure 5.2). This psychographic analysis can be a very useful complement to TGI's standard demographic analysis.

An example

TGI's brand buying data should reflect the retail audit's sales data. However, every so often, you come across an apparent contradiction in the numbers. Let's not kid ourselves, despite what textbooks usually tell us, life isn't always straightforward and numbers sometimes don't seem to stack up. Things are often more interesting when they go wrong. Figures 5.3 and 5.4 are one such example. What do you do when the retail audit shows one brand share pattern and TGI shows a completely different pattern? Which one of them speaks with forked tongue?

The first thing to do when you get this sort of breakdown is to go and make yourself a cup of coffee, breathe deeply and stay calm. The next thing to do is check the data's reliability. How big were the sample cells? Did the TGI data have any asterisks denoting statistically unreliable sample sizes? Next, start thinking about how the data are collected. Get hold of the original TGI questionnaire, use what you know about how people behave in this market

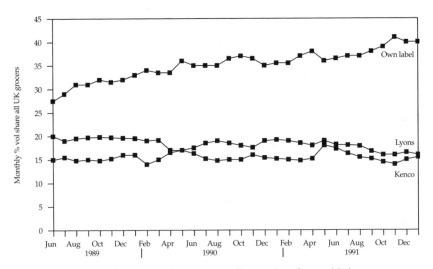

Figure 5.3 Volume brand shares in the ground coffee market. *Source*: Nielsen

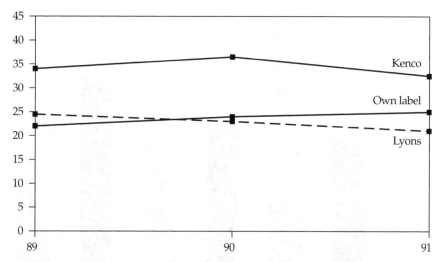

Figure 5.4 Brand penetration as a percentage of all users of ground coffee. *Source:* TGI

and try to develop an explanation for the apparent contradiction. Here's my stab at it.

If in doubt TGI is probably less reliable for this particular market. We know from qualitative research and previous quantitative studies that ground coffee is a low-involvement market where purchase intervals for light users can be as low as three-monthly. Even when people do make a purchase the labelling can be confusing. They might buy 'one in a dark brown pack that's medium roasted and suitable for cafetières'. So light users possibly aren't that certain, without a visual prompt, which one they buy. Looking at the original TGI questionnaire shows that the ground coffee questions are asked directly after the instant coffee questions. People have just been prompted with the name Kenco. Very possibly they buy it in instant form because the instant coffee market is much more brand-name oriented. Maybe they see the familiar name of Kenco coming up and tick that box again (in error).

This would explain some of the data effect, but perhaps the explanation is simpler. The penetration data wouldn't necessarily reflect brand shares because penetration doesn't necessarily correlate with weight of purchase. It might be the case that much of Kenco's penetration is accounted for by light users. Indeed an analysis of TGI by frequency of use shows that this is the case (Figure 5.5). So although more people buy Kenco, they don't buy as much of it (TGI), therefore volume share is lower (Nielsen).

From this we can also start to develop a theory that people enter this confusing market via the reassurance of brand-name products, get to like ground coffee, buy and use it more often, get confident, notice that brand names are significantly more expensive than own-label and switch to own-label.

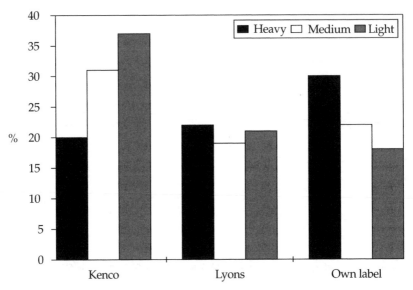

Figure 5.5 Percentage of heavy, medium and light users who claim to use each brand.
Source: TGI

Feels plausible doesn't it? So off we go to test this hypothesis through other research and we've advanced from tearing our hair out to having a new hypothesis.

Volumetrics

TGI can be used to produce estimates of the volume of product consumption, hence the importance of different demographic groups to each market by using special analysis. TGI's own example covers the vodka market, and their analysis of regional variations in vodka consumption highlights the importance of Northern Ireland to volume sales in the vodka market.

The first stage in carrying out a volumetric analysis is to translate the claimed frequency of drinking vodka into an estimate of units drunk. Table 5.4 shows the frequency scale given to TGI respondents, and the volume equivalent used in this case. To convert frequency to volume, the 'default' translation scale for the vodka market has been used, which is pre-set into Choices (BMRB's PC-based special analysis system). Users are free to alter such translation scales if required.

BMRB's example, in Table 5.5, shows that in the UK there are some 9.5 million vodka drinkers, who between them account for over 40 million measures of vodka per month.

Table 5.4

Vodka: frequency of drinking	Estimated measures per month consumed
10 or more measures per week	46.2
5–9 measures per week	29.4
3–4 measures per week	14.7
1–2 measures per week	6.3
3 or more measures per month	3.5
1–2 measures per month	1.5
Less than 1 in last month	
(at least 1 in last 6 months)	0.2

Table 5.5

Row	Cell	Total	All users: Vodka	Volume: Vodka
Total	#Resp	25853	5441	5334
	(000)	44158	9514	40341
	Vert%	100.00	100.00	100.00
	Index	100	100	100
Standard region: Northern Ireland				
	#Resp	1239	334	329
	(000)	1104	269	2630
	Vert%	2.5	2.8	6.5
	Index	100	113	261
Standard region: Yorkshire and Humberside				
	#Resp	2259	382	373
	(000)	3795	677	1450
	Vert%	8.5	7.1	3.6
	Index	100	83	42

Source: UKTGIM 93
Table base: adults 18+
WGT: POPBUKM
Copyright BMRB 1993

Broken down into region, we see that there is some variation in the concentration of vodka users throughout the UK. For example, 2.8 per cent of vodka users live in Northern Ireland (roughly in proportion to the 2.5 per cent of the entire UK population living there). However, this 2.8 per cent of vodka drinkers downs 6.5 per cent of all the vodka measures drunk in the UK – an average of virtually ten measures each, per month. By contrast, the 7.1 per cent of vodka drinkers who live in Yorkshire and Humberside consume only 3.6 per cent of the total volume.

Beyond TGI

TGI's utility lies in its sheer size. But collecting and processing all that information from 25 000 people takes time. From the first interview in one year's survey to your getting the data to look at can be an interval of up to eighteen months. In stable mature markets this isn't the end of the world but in new or dynamic markets it's a problem. Further quantitative and qualitative research is a necessary supplement to TGI.

Panels

Most FMCG panel data are collected by issuing the panel member with a barcode reading 'pen'. Panels are therefore pretty accurate records of major supermarket shopping trips. They enable similar types of analyses to TGI but with greater confidence about accuracy of data collection. Consumer panel data can be extremely valuable as a way of understanding patterns of brand switching within markets. Panels show the same individual or household's purchase choices over time. You can see if the generation 'cohort' of people who bought, for example, Budweiser five or ten years ago are still buying it or whether as their 'life stage' changed (onset of family life brings changed values) they've moved on to new brands and a new 'cohort' of Budweiser customers has taken their place. This identification of whether cohort or life stage has the greater effect on your market is often useful and is a form of analysis for which panels' longitudinal data are ideally suited. Panels aren't just for FMCG markets. There are motorists' diary panels, teenagers' panels and even panels of financial intermediaries.

Usage and attitude surveys

U&As are a useful way of delving deeper into how people relate to a brand. They are *ad hoc* quantitative surveys commissioned by you especially to look in more detail at your brand. U&As can be used to discover how many of the brand's users use it in certain ways, what repertoires it sits in and essentially any of the questions from the earlier list which still remain unanswered. I suspect that U&As aren't conducted as frequently as they were ten or twenty years ago because a combination of qualitative research and a good tracking study is often capable of meeting the same information need.

Tracking studies

Tracking studies are often the principal ongoing source of quantitative data. The first studies were originally set up by Messrs Millward and Brown as a better way of tracking advertising's effectiveness. Before tracking studies, the typical method for measuring advertising effects was a 'pre and post' survey.

Pre and posts measure consumers' attitudes to, and images of, a set of brands before you advertise and then again a few months after your campaign. These timings are your timings and may not reflect competitors' advertising cycles. Just after your post measure the main competitor might bring out a very effective new campaign but if you've already spent the research budget on your two surveys you have no way of measuring the effectiveness of competitors' activity.

Tracking studies collect continuous data. A hundred or so people are interviewed every week and the data are studied on a rolling four-weekly basis to measure factors such as:

- Brand awareness
- Advertising awareness (both spontaneous and prompted)
- Brand image
- Brand predisposition (likelihood to buy)
- Recall of advertising
- Recall of claims made by the advertising
- Recognition of unbranded ads and the degree to which they are attributed to the correct advertiser.

Tracking studies have evolved away from their initial focus on advertising to a focus on the brand. This makes them increasingly useful in the development of new advertising strategies. In this respect one of the most useful questions is the predisposition or 'brand strength' measure. In many markets predisposition can be shown to be a good predictor of future sales and if you can isolate the main influence on predisposition you're halfway to a strategy already. The Alliance and Leicester case from the IPA's *Advertising Works 7* shows a relationship between sales, propensity and awareness:

> We find that although predisposition tends not to change very quickly, it is a reasonably accurate predictor of a society's share of the market. The correlation is not exact, but we would not expect it to be. Factors such as relative price (i.e. interest rates) and, importantly, branch location will modify the extent to which potential use is converted into actual use.
>
> We also find that propensity to use correlates well with awareness; in particular, with spontaneous awareness [Figures 5.6 and 5.7]. This continues the intuitive reasoning which says that people are happiest using household names.

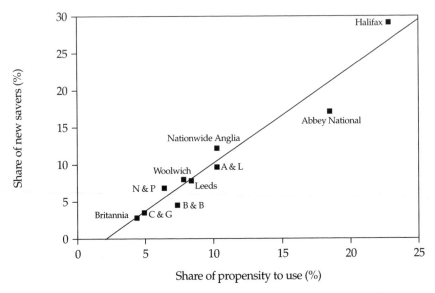

Figure 5.6 Share of propensity to use for savings and share of new savers (1990). *Source*: FRS, April 1990 (propensity)/full year (new business)

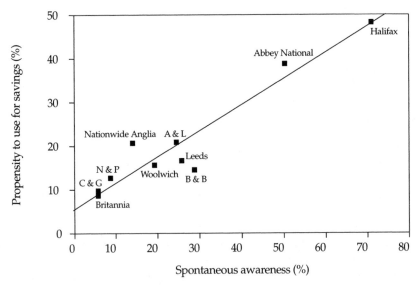

Figure 5.7 Familiarity and propensity to use (1990). *Source*: FRS, April 1990 (propensity)/full year (awareness)

Note: In the figures the share of propensity to use has been calculated by taking the percentage of adults who would 'consider using' a given society and dividing it by the total of each of the top eight societies 'considering using' rating.

Measuring predisposition with other elements (generally price) held as a constant can be an excellent measure of brand strength and very probably future sales success.

During 1995 the newly arrived Orange mobile telecoms brand was still relatively weak in sales and distribution terms and was accordingly disparaged by its rivals. (My agency was invited to pitch by two of those rivals.) I presented the data in Table 5.6 to the Chief Executives of both Mercury One2one and Vodafone and on both occasions it had the desired effect of focusing the conversation on the need to start investing in their brand rather than relying on trading muscle to keep Orange at bay:

If you decided to buy a mobile phone and all of the brands in Table 5.6 had very similar prices and offers, which of the suppliers would you be most likely to choose?

Table 5.6

	%
Orange	27
Cellnet	22
Don't know	19
Vodafone	16
Mercury One2one	13
None of these	2

Base = national sample of adults who use a mobile phone nowadays and/or expect to buy one in the next five years.
Source: *NOP 1000 Adults Omnibus*, 4 June 1995.

This question wasn't conducted via a tracking study but via an omnibus survey. Omnibuses are surveys that are conducted regularly and on which anybody can buy questions. It's a cost-effective way of asking a few questions because you share the set-up and fieldwork costs with other 'passengers'. If your market isn't changing rapidly, buying into an omnibus every quarter can be a cheaper alternative to tracking studies.

Designing questions

When writing questions for inclusion on an omnibus, or for any other use, remember to think about:

- How you want to use the answers
- How you would react to that question if someone asked you
- How to keep the respondent interested and motivated to help.

The last issue is too often overlooked, particularly in relation to image grids. We generally ask too many questions, force people to go through list after list of things they don't know or care about. Imagine being grilled by twenty minutes of questions such as:

To what extent would you agree or disagree that Shell Unleaded is 'becoming popular among people like me nowadays'?

Do you: Agree strongly? Agree slightly? Neither agree nor disagree? Disagree slightly? Disagree strongly?

And to what extent would you agree or disagree that Esso Unleaded is 'becoming popular among people like me nowadays'?

Do you: Agree strongly? Agree slightly? Neither agree nor disagree? Disagree slightly? Disagree strongly?

And to what extent would you agree or disagree that BP Unleaded is 'becoming popular among people like me nowadays'?

Do you: Agree strongly? Agree slightly? Neither agree nor disagree? Disagree slightly? Disagree strongly?
etc.
etc.

No wonder Judie Lannon once defined the answers to such questions as 'that response which the interviewee senses would most quickly release them from the instrument of torture known as an image battery'.

The respondent often doesn't have very strong views about a brand. They are not as committed or 'loyal' as we like to imagine. In markets characterized by a great deal of inertia you may find it useful to ask provocatively worded questions to get any sort of response at all. A provocatively worded question such as 'When did you stop beating your wife?' can bias towards a particular answer but you can ask an equally biased question from the opposite perspective (rotating the order of asking). If people agreed with both questions

Table 5.7

'If people had any sense, they would close their bank accounts and use a building society instead.'	
Agree strongly	12%
Agree slightly	12%
Neither agree nor disagree	16%
Disagree slightly	44%
Disagree strongly	26%
'Building societies are very limited. Most working people also need a bank account.'	
Agree strongly	36%
Agree slightly	27%
Neither agree nor disagree	8%
Disagree slightly	15%
Disagree strongly	11%

Source: NOP Omnibus, 3 April 1994

then it would demonstrate their lack of strong opinions on the issue (see Table 5.7).

Take it easy with your questions, less can be more. Always use the vernacular and always pilot your questionnaire on your neighbouring colleagues to see how it sounds.

Conclusion

It is amazingly easy to waste lots of time just swimming aimlessly in data. Don't just collect it for its own sake. When developing advertising strategy you are not the uniformed police constable who collects and files information, you are the detective who has to make a case out of it. Constantly develop and test hunches and hypotheses. Keep pursuing lines of enquiry. Keep asking yourself 'and this means that...'

One day you'll feel that your current hypothesis about:

Who exactly are we talking to?
What do we want them to do?
What exactly can we tell them to influence them?

is the 'right' one and go with it. Then you'll call it the strategy and 'sell' it to your immediate customers, your creative teams and clients.

To get to this end point, to get any sort of use out of quantitative data you need to have an approach, a set of questions which can act as a route map through the statistics. For example, I have grouped some questions under the following headings:

1 Market economics and competitor analysis
2 Consumers' relationship with the product/service category
3 Consumers' relationship with the individual brands
4 Consumers' relationship with the advertising.

This chapter has been about using quantitative data in the context of formulating advertising strategy. Advertising is about using mass communications to engage with people and either reassure them that their behaviour/attitudes are right or cause them to want to change their behaviour/attitudes. Always try to look at your quantitative data qualitatively, asking 'What does this mean in human terms?' At some point you are going to want to get inside people's minds for a greater understanding than quantitative data can provide. If you haven't already read it, you should turn next to the chapter about qualitative research (Chapter 6).

Overview: Chapter 6

This chapter on Qualitative Research is also taken from the IPA's Stage 2 Campaign Planning course and was first presented in 1983. Roddy Glen is, in my view, one of that small elite of outstanding qualitative researchers with whom it is always a pleasure to share a project, and usually an enlightenment to hear a debrief from.

It would be fair to say that, in comparison to most other 'stages' of the qualitative market research process, analysis and interpretation are not given enough prominence in terms either of general discussion and debate or in the planning and scheduling of specific projects at the time they are commissioned.

Clients don't ask about A&I much, or discuss it with researchers, preferring instead to concentrate on those more visible parts of the process for which they can be held evidently accountable. For the researchers' part, the more projects they can do in any period, the more money they make, so the less time-consuming each one is, the better.

Despite global economic uncertainty, demand for qualitative research continues to grow as we move into the new millennium.

Time pressure on projects is unlikely to decrease, and successive new generations of researchers, clients and agency planners will continue to arrive, largely unguided, at their own understanding of the qualitative process.

There will be little to encourage introspection, and more incentive to press on with the business of growing the bottom line.

In this chapter Roddy therefore has two aims:

1 To outline the processes of analysis and interpretation as they would *ideally* be conducted, thus providing a benchmark of sorts, to which new buyers and sellers may refer.
2 To demonstrate that 'interpretation' in particular is not merely the regurgitated 'voice of the consumer' on the demand side but a process which extends from the initial request for research right through to intelligent discussion of the issues which emerge.

The intelligence of Roddy's writing style reflects the depth in which he has explored this subject. The relevance of his conclusions also seems to me to have applicability beyond the field of advertising research.

Chapter 6

Analysis and interpretation in qualitative research: a researcher's perspective

Roddy Glen

Clients cannot be blamed for feeling that in buying qualitative market research (QMR) they are making a leap into faith. How do they really know what they are getting? (Indeed in some instances how do they know *who* they are getting? An important consideration in an industry where brands tend to exist, for the most part, at the level of the individual.) How can they tell if it is 'good' or 'bad'? Most importantly, how can they *ensure* that it is 'good'?

It seems all too often to be pretty haphazard, with outcomes which may be equally idiosyncratic. As a client, you may be present for the meetings prior to the fieldwork at which the objectives, methodology, sample, stimulus material and details of topics to be covered are discussed and agreed; at the interviews themselves (particularly if they are group discussions); and at the debrief presentation. But what you don't see is that part of the process in which the *meaning* of what was said in the interviews is judgementally determined through processes of analysis and interpretation. *That* tends to take place at times and in places which are the researcher's 'private territory'. In a way it parallels the creative process in advertising, where the client has an 'input' role at the start of the process, a 'receiving output' role later in the process, and very little contact with it in between.

It's not surprising, then, that the analysis and interpretation parts of the overall qualitative process are among the least talked about. Clients, being more focused on the debrief, generally ask few, if any, questions about them. Researchers for the most part volunteer nothing either, which is a little more curious as their reputations are generally maintained more through their skill at delivering insights than upon their ability actually to conduct the interviews. It's as if 'A&I' is too delicate an area of the process to withstand more than the most superficial discussion.

It remains mysterious; a sort of 'black box' into which go the data from expensive interviews and out of which comes a view of the market, the brand, the advertising, the packaging, etc. which appears at times to bear little relation to 'what respondents said'. Little wonder if there are some clients who are suspicious of it.

So how does it work? How should it work? What 'rules' are there about how it should be done?

This chapter seeks to illuminate this rather dark area of QMR, and is divided into three main sections:

1 Orientation and inputs
2 Functional issues – the mechanics of the process
3 Interpretation of consumer responses.

Orientation and inputs

Most of the better qualitative researchers enjoy not only the collecting of data (and the attention they get when conducting group discussions and when presenting the findings) but also the activities of *hypothesizing, conceptualizing* and *interpreting*. The spirit of enquiry excites them, as does the *achievement of meaning*.

They deal in *ideas*, not 'data', and they are constantly attempting to split those ideas to see what they contain. In contrast to quantitative research, they chase significance, not incidence. Of particular importance is the realization that *interpretation is integral to the progression of a qualitative research study, and not a distinct stage*. This is worth examining in greater detail.

In the past, there was a tendency to think of a qualitative study as proceeding in a sequential but discrete manner. It would start with taking the brief and then go to the stage of data collection, followed by analysis, which was then followed by interpretation, leading to the eventual debrief. At each of these stages the researcher would be required to adopt a different mental 'mode', be it passive, absorptive, active, expansive, intuitive, etc. I am sure it's possible to *attempt* qualitative research in this way, but I'm equally sure that it won't be much good. Insights will almost certainly be missed which could have been gained in the early stages of the study and which could have been of vital importance in shaping the thinking in subsequent stages.

Nowadays most practitioners believe the analysis and interpretation of qualitative data cannot be divorced from the earlier stages of a study. Sensitive interpretation begins at the briefing and design stages and the study progresses in the form of the continuous development, evolution, refinement (and often rejection) of *hypotheses*. Stephen Wells (1991) calls these 'rolling hypotheses', which seems a fair description. The good qualitative researcher, then, switches into interpretative mode as soon as the project is mentioned, and becomes fully mentally engaged with it as early as possible.

There are several stages where 'rolling hypotheses' and *active* thought are particularly important:

- The brief
- Project design elements
- What respondents 'say'
- What it all might mean
- What it means in terms of the 'Client's Thing' (the 'supply-side' structures, such as the advertising, the packaging, the product concept, the market, etc., whatever is the focus of the enquiry).

It is difficult to overestimate the importance of the first two. What happens at this stage, when the enquiry is being defined and designed, and what the researcher understands of 'the mission' is crucial. There are several different kinds of potential input, from various of the parties involved, and they each require interrogation and interpretation for the project to work optimally. Not all these inputs will fall into the researcher's lap, however, and it is important that he or she actively seeks access to all of them.

The brief

It may well be necessary to ascertain the political 'spin' on a brief and to attempt to 'decode' it. As Wendy Gordon and Roy Langmaid (1988) point out, there may be an overt brief and a 'covert brief', especially where more than one party has a direct interest in the outcome of the research. (Client marketers and agency; client NPD department and marketers are two of the most common axes here.) There are also a great many questions which may usefully be asked by the researcher at the start of a project. The answers to them, and indeed the need to ask them in the first place, all form an integral part of the process of interpretation which runs throughout the enquiry:

1 What decisions will the client/agency be using the output to assist with? (A good way, this, of sometimes getting a more succinct articulation of the brief!)
2 What other information does the client or advertising agency have which forms the context for the enquiry and therefore its findings (brand positioning, brand-share trend data, advertising tracking performance, etc.)? Odd though it seems to have to mention it, the Advertising Strategy and/or the Creative Brief are just such pieces of information where creative development research is concerned. It is surprising how many creative development projects are done with inadequate reference to these vital benchmark documents.
3 What models does the client have concerning the issue area? How do they think these might work, and what doubts do they have about their hypotheses?

This last area is one which can sometimes be contentious. Clients sometimes fear that the researcher's judgement and equanimity will be compromised if too much of the background is shared with him or her at the outset. I prefer to take the view that we're sufficiently grown-up and professional nowadays for this danger to be very remote. The disingenuously empty brief usually conceals a can of worms which the research is unlikely to remedy anyway, as well as being insulting to the researcher.

Of particular importance in creative development work is the need to understand not only *what* the proto-advertising is trying to communicate (per strategy and brief, as mentioned above) but *how* it seeks to go about this, in terms of the creative structures it employs. This is a question which unfortunately too few agencies are ready to answer at the briefing, and which has been known to send board account directors into an impromptu interpretative frenzy of their own.

Project design elements

These include:

- The sample
- Any stimulus material
- The topic guide
- The role for, and choice of, any projective techniques.

The extent to which the researcher gets to determine these varies tremendously, depending on:

- The type of project (NPD, creative development, etc.)
- The brand history
- Its research history particularly (need for continuity, etc.)
- The relationship between the researcher and the buyer
- The internal culture of the commissioning client or agency.

Interpretation at this stage often takes an anticipatory as opposed to a rationalizatory form, in that much of the thinking that goes into designing a piece of qualitative research is concerned with deciding:

1 The best quotas (what kind of respondents will help us test our hypotheses best?)
2 Interview order (how can we arrange it to get the most out of each issue area while not having those covered earlier spoil it too much for those covered later?)
3 Stimulus material (what form should it take to be most easily and unambiguously understood by respondents?)
4 Projective techniques (which would be useful, appropriate for the type of respondent and not too time consuming?)

Whether we like it or not, all of this involves hypotheses about how people relate to the market sector, the brands, the packaging, the advertising, as well, of course, as about what they may not understand, what they may learn in the course of the interview, and how they may behave during it.

In summary, interpretation, in most instances a close relative of common sense, should be regarded as a continuous process, running throughout the entire qualitative study. The more questions you ask yourself at the outset, the more hypotheses you evolve, the more you attempt to anticipate responses, the more you interrogate the product or repeatedly view the advertising before going 'into the field', the richer will be your relationship with what happens in the interviews.

I sometimes think it's better to regard the whole process as one wherein we are being asked to *think* and to clarify some issues, and *as part of this* the client is paying for our stimulation in the form of access to relevant groups in the community via structured conversation.

Functional issues – the mechanics of the process

Although the activity of interpretation should run throughout any project, it is nevertheless the case that at some points in the process there are large data inputs, and these require to be 'digested' in some coherent way. The most notable of these is the point after completion of fieldwork.

At this stage the researcher has accumulated a pile of tape recordings, a few notes made after each group, notes from any observers of the groups, possibly a transcript or two if time has permitted, and a collection of hazy memories of the interviewing experience interspersed with recollections of fatigue, motorway service areas at night, and white bread sandwiches lovingly prepared by northern night porters.

What do we actually *do* with all this? Here, two principal types of problem arise. Alan Hedges (1983) identifies them as:

1 Functional – how does one cope with this mass of data? How does one break it down and digest it? It can be a daunting prospect.
2 Interpretative – how does one decide what it means? What to take literally, and what not to believe? How to decide what it all adds up to? And how then to relate it back to the structures the client can work with?

There are three main areas of interpretation of consumer responses, which involve increasing levels of conceptual thought, with the functional activity called 'analysis' coming immediately after the first stage, which is itself an integrated input to it. The overall order of the stages of the process is as follows:

- Interpretation (Level 1) – What do respondents each feel and mean?
- Analysis – Sifting, differentiating, separating, sorting, ordering the data
- Interpretation (Level 2) – What patterns emerge, and what do *they* mean?
- Interpretation (Level 3) – What does it mean re the 'Client's Thing'?

While noting that the first level of interpretation occurs before and during the activity of analysis – indeed it takes place in the researcher's head as each interview progresses, a point I will return to – it is best to consider the two types of problem separately. This section deals with those which come under the heading 'Analysis'.

There is no magic formula for coping with data, no unique prescription for success. Everyone has to develop their own personal style of working. It is worth here considering the options available at this stage in the process. Some are much more satisfactory than others, and you should be aware of the trade-offs which pertain when deciding which method of data organization to use (see Figure 6.1).

Tapes

After the interviews, a complete aural record of them exists in the form of the tape recordings made. You can use these in any of four basic ways:

1 To listen to and make notes from, of an interpretative sort. The researcher notes the content in paraphrase form, and records observations in a margin. These observations are of a hypothetical nature, and may also be remarks about patterns arising or commonality with events on other tapes.
2 To listen to and make complete verbatim transcripts. The researcher may at the same time make notes in the margin as described above.

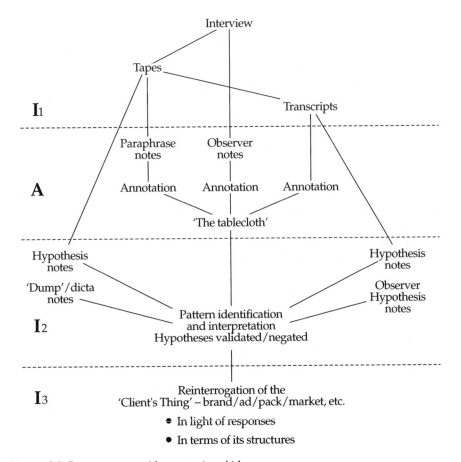

Figure 6.1 Process stages – 'the mysterious bit'

3 To send out for full verbatim transcription. The idea here is that the researcher receives back a full written transcript of the group discussion/depth interview from which they can subsequently work. Transcripts are useful as a source of illustrative quotes (for the report).
4 To listen to while following what is said on a full verbatim transcript. This is perhaps the best and most thorough method of content analysis, and allows the researcher to re-experience the interview and make remarks on the transcript and on a 'hypothesis notepad'. Better sense can be made of the transcript this way – repeated remarks can be traced to individuals and a better feeling for consensus or disagreement can be obtained.

It is important in my view that researchers listen to some of the tapes, to invigorate the nerve-endings; to rekindle the 'buzz' of the interviews. It is essential to remind oneself of the ways in which respondents expressed themselves and of the *tone* of different parts of the discussion (flat, enthusiastic, chatty, hostile, etc.), the silences, the terminology, etc. If *forced* to make a limited selection, it is probably good to choose tapes of interviews in which views were expressed which were in some way puzzling, and those where the proceedings crackled along, rich in comments which were particularly stimulating. The dangers of this should be clear, however. We are more likely to base our interpretation on more vividly recalled data, and hence bias is highly likely to creep into the process as a result of selectively reviewing them. It is *not* best practice.

One great benefit of listening back to the recordings is that in addition to hearing what was said (and not said) again, the researcher can restimulate the thoughts *they* had during the interview, but had no time to examine. This, for me, is vital. I find I often have thoughts 'in the heat of battle' which, if not major insights or end points themselves, are frequently good beginnings of productive trains of thought. By the end of an evening's fieldwork, I've forgotten half of them.

Much of this is *not* accessible through simply reading transcripts – specially those parts *where people do not say what they mean or do not mean what they say*. In the UK today, the media has changed both what people know about and the way they speak. Ordinary people know something of surrealism. Under-statement has long been an English verbal characteristic. Irony has more recently become a common expressive mode. 'Everyone's Dali now' and 'It's quite good' are both dependent on inflection for precise interpretation. Try them in front of the bathroom mirror, with different 'voice musics' and you will realize how much transcripts cannot offer.

Transcripts

I personally use these only infrequently, finding them less restimulating than tape reviewing. This is because I'm an audial person, more than a visual one. Full verbatim transcripts are favoured by many researchers as the 'source' from which they conduct the analysis and interpretation. This always assumes that there is time enough between fieldwork and debrief for transcripts to be made, and for the researcher then to conduct a comprehensive analysis of them.

When reading full verbatim transcripts, the researcher should devise some way of beginning a distillation process in respect of the content. A system whereby marks, comments, abbreviations, etc. are written in the margins of the transcripts is a good one. This 'coding' of the transcripts can then save a great deal of time at the next stage.

When reading transcripts, as when reviewing the tapes, the researcher should refer constantly to *the objectives* of the research and, second, to the *topic guide*. The objectives are the agreed framework within which the client expects the findings, conclusions and recommendations to be couched. You should never stray far from them. While always referring to these 'guides' the researcher can write on the transcript thus:

- Summarize a majority view/behaviour/attitude
- Underline comments or quotes which illustrate this and code them in the margin for ease of retrieval
- Pick out a minority viewpoint
- Ignore obviously eccentric comments
- Annotate responses by type, using your own 'system' of codes and abbreviations, e.g. for positive or negative responses, comprehension problems, good illustrative quotes, etc.

You can also annotate in a more interpretative way by summarizing sections in the margin, e.g. hero unaspirational; presenter patronizing/insincere; proposition incredible, etc. These would be interpretative comments based on the responses to a series of questions or projectives.

It is useful again to have a parallel 'hypothesis notepad' when reading and annotating transcripts. This may be used as a respository for such interpretative comments and for jotting down, in no particular order, hypotheses, 'profound' thoughts and tentative conclusions. It is good discipline to use this pad only for 'global' thoughts and observations, not allowing specific quotes or responses to be mentioned. These notes will later provide a very useful series of ideas and frameworks through which the 'findings' may be appraised, and perhaps even explained and presented.

Thus at the end of this (time-consuming) process all the transcripts may be read quickly by looking at the annotations, and the interpretative framework is beginning to build.

Once this stage has been reached, you are ready to gain a more coherent overall view of responses, patterns, attitudes, etc. One good way preferred by many researchers is then to transfer the notes made on the transcripts (or from listening to tapes) on to a very large sheet of paper. I call this the 'tablecloth'. This sheet will be ruled into rows and columns, each column representing an interview or group. Each 'row' represents an area of the discussion, either literally (in terms of *responses*) or in hypothesis form. It may be highly mechanistic – simply a charting of responses which may then be examined for patterns – or it may be more interpretative (Table 6.1). The completed grid can then be marked, perhaps using different-coloured pencils to highlight response patterns, attitudes, behavioural traits and comments which appear to support or negate various of the rolling hypotheses.

From here, conclusions may begin to form, although only on a superficial level. It is the combination of this discipline and the application of hypotheses and conceptual frameworks of various sorts from which conclusions of a more penetrating and usable sort will emerge.

Table 6.1 The 'tablecloth'

	25–34 BCI South	35–50 BCI North	25–34 C2D North	35–50 C2D South
Cells				
Topic areas				
Sector appeal				
Brands aware (spont.)				
Brands used/in repertoire				
Differences between brands				
Brand A – personality				
Brand B – personality				
etc....				

Notes taken by skilled and briefed observer

The opportunity sometimes exists for two researchers to attend the interview. It can be very useful if (and only if) both of them are fully briefed on the objectives of the study and on the proposed method of investigation of the various issue areas. One may take notes during the group as the other conducts it. These notes would ideally be as nearly as possible a full transcript – but may in fact be a mixture of verbatims and, if there is time, observations, hypotheses, conjectural thoughts, etc. This method of working is more suited to experienced researchers who will, by virtue of their experience, be more able to generate hypotheses quickly and judge the mood and tone of the interview as it proceeds. Importantly, it is *not* a substitute for the subsequent listening to tapes (or at least some of them), nor for the subsequent analysis of full verbatim transcripts. It does, however, come into its own when there is little time allowed between the completion of fieldwork and the debrief presentation. In such cases – which ought to be regarded as *in extremis* – the notes thus made would be 'distilled' down in the manner already described so that patterns, behaviours, attitudes, etc. can be clearly identified.

One of the characteristics of QMR, which some might say is a weakness, is the fact that it is usually the potentially idiosyncratic product of one mind. Most companies do not have a sufficiently robust margin that they can double-head all the fieldwork. Double-heading a project with a colleague is, however, something I think everyone in the business should experience, so stimulating is it when you come to interpretative tasks. It is an excellent way of hothousing issues and generating secondary and tertiary thoughts and ideas, much as respondents do in groups.

'Dump' notes and/or dicta-tapes

A good habit to cultivate is the *immediate* recording, either on tape or in written form, of the researcher's impressions, thoughts, feelings and hypotheses *after each interview*. These should be made after (not during) the interview, and should be brief. They should endeavour to capture something of the mood or spirit of the group so that when it comes to reading the full verbatim transcript the feeling or 'buzz' of the event is rekindled to some extent. I use a tape to 'dump' the thoughts I had while conducting the interview, so that I needn't worry about forgetting them. These notes should not be 'findings' as such, but should constitute the collection of hypotheses which will 'roll' throughout the study. You should also be sufficiently flexible to record suggestions for methodological revisions to the study as well. The benefit of making such immediate post-fieldwork notes is that they start the hypotheses 'rolling', and focus your thinking in a beneficial way.

One further very important point is worth making about the process of analysis and interpretation. As Wendy Gordon (1983) says in her paper on this subject:

> *Whilst the fieldwork is in progress or after the groups or interviews are completed you will find that a subconscious process of interpretation takes place. Thoughts will creep into your mind whilst you're driving. Whilst cooking a meal a sudden flash of insight on a particular aspect of the study will hit you like a bolt from the blue even though you were unaware that you were really thinking about it. These subconscious interpretative thoughts are like gold dust – value them and treasure them.*

This is absolutely right. Like a process of fermentation these thoughts occur spontaneously and unbidden, *and you could not have had them had you not experienced the interview or group*. Trust them. They often take the form of very important hypotheses.

In summary, the process of content analysis is one for which there are no short-cuts. It takes time and concentration. It cannot be rushed or skimped. Only when it is done thoroughly can you be confident that you have not been superficial or impressionistic. Your understanding may not be quite the same as someone else's but it *is* based on sound procedure.

You have reached the point where, as Wendy Hayward (Robson and Foster, 1989) describes it, you have held on to the data and now you must let them go. We each have our own metaphor for this part of the process, as it's difficult to describe otherwise. It is one of the areas which inexperienced qualitatives find the most alarming because it is almost counter-intuitive. Their difficulty is that they daren't stop looking at the trees for fear they will forget some part of the wood. The way to see the wood, however, is to get above it. Time to fly...

Interpretation of consumer responses

When we reach the post-fieldwork stage, where a mass of raw qualitative 'data' has accumulated, we should have some ideas already about what certain parts of it might mean. Much interpretation, however, still remains to be done, in order to create meaning out of the apparent chaos of the 'data'.

Analysing and interpreting qualitative 'data', however, is not just a matter of semantic content analysis, but of looking for *meaning* – the music as well as the words. There are three levels on which the interpretation of interview data operates in QMR:

1 Interpreting what people say to get to what they mean
2 Interpreting what the whole thing might mean
3 Interpreting what this means in terms of the 'Client's Thing'

Interpreting what people say to get to what they mean

This level of interpretation, of course, occurs both during the interviews and at the start of the whole process of post-interview analysis and interpretation, when listening to tapes or reading transcripts. In the interviews we are, as moderators, constantly having to respond to what is going on. We listen, assess, seek elaboration, probe, prompt and generally make on-the-spot judgements about *what* is being said and *how*. We don't have questionnaires, but are instead much more flexible, being both proactive and reactive. This is similar to the interpretative activity that we all carry on whenever we converse with anyone. The difference here is that our conversation has a purpose which goes beyond simply understanding what is said.

Qualitative researchers inhabit, by virtue of their primary task, a world which lies between *people* and *things*. We attempt to understand and illuminate people's *relationships* with things, usually with the purpose of assisting the proprietors or creators of those things in strengthening this relationship in motivational terms. *Meaning* is ascribed by people to things. It does not reside inherently in products, brands, advertisements, or any *thing*. So meaning is a construction, and is the only reality that matters, in market research at least.

There are difficulties involved in establishing the meanings people place on things, however, and merely analysing what people *say* is unlikely to overcome them. These problems arise because in the research situation we are dealing with:

■ People (!)
■ Respondents
■ Users/non-users of certain types of products or services.

In these multiple capacities, people are likely to be unreliable conveyors of meaning, and the good researcher will develop (with experience) a greater understanding of people in these 'roles' and the pressures they experience which contribute to this unreliability. People:

■ Are often poor at expressing themselves
■ May be inconsistent and self-contradictory
■ Often have not thought about what they believe or why they do things
■ May not want to admit to others (or even to themselves) how they feel or behave, and hence may distort or even lie
■ May be subject to group or other social pressures
■ Are in an artificial situation (i.e. they are *respondents*, being interviewed).

In groups they behave in ways which further act to conceal the true meaning of their relationship with the subject of the enquiry. Frequently they:

■ 'Follow a leader'
■ Feel obliged to be critical
■ Are defensive, lest they appear stupid (a big fear!)
■ Compete for attention
■ Seek to agree
■ Fight for informal leadership.

In short, they don't/can't always say what they mean, and don't always mean what they say.

A good researcher will develop a sensitivity to these group dynamic factors which attend and affect the group process, as well as gaining a basic knowledge of 'body language', allowing them to interpret what various postures usually mean – particularly those to do with acceptance/rejection and agreement/disbelief. With experience, too, of working across many different markets, and (yes! it's allowed) drawing on their own experience as a consumer as a start point for hypotheses, researchers can develop a sensitivity to the conventions, totems and taboos of various product fields. In this way there is a greater chance of reaching a better understanding of people in their roles as consumers, users, non-users, etc.

Mini-case

In the late 1980s the Meat and Livestock Commission ran a television campaign in support of British pork. It featured lighthearted vignettes of families being served different pork-based dishes (visual recipe suggestions). The family members were shown looking eager and enthusiastic at the arrival of the dishes, and their attraction was rendered humorously visual by showing them leaning over sideways towards it. The proposition offered to the viewer was a dual one which sought to encourage greater *reliance* on pork as an attractive dinner meat, and which underpinned this with the idea that pork is (perhaps surprisingly) *lean*, and therefore healthy. The endline was 'Lean on (British) Pork'. Research was examining some potential new scripts for the campaign.

Respondents in groups said they liked the ad, that it was 'quite good', and generally had no difficulty in replaying the communication. When asked what it was saying, it was striking how many people replayed the communication almost verbatim from the strategy document. It would also have been easy to miss the equally striking number who prefaced their response with the words 'I suppose...'.

The proposition was not in fact adopted by most respondents. This was in large part because, as expressed via the commercials, it was something most people found counter-intuitive. At the time of research, the prevailing opinion of pork was that it was a fatty meat.* Additionally their perceptions of the visual 'joke' and, more particularly, of the reason for it (a visual-semantic bridge – often dodgy in my experience) seemed to mean that it remained as a *perceived intention* rather than as anything more enrolling. Being nice people, however, they made a concession for it.

The word 'suppose', used in the way they used it, has a very special function. It means something like 'I can see what they're trying to say, and can imagine that there may be some people, more easily amused than I am, who would enjoy the way they've gone about it. It doesn't quite make it for me, however, and so I don't really feel obliged to take it that seriously. Points for trying, though.'

Advertising to which the audience condescends may ultimately be only a little better than that which patronizes the viewer.

The problems of interpreting what respondents *mean* from what they *say*, and what they *think* from what they *say and do*, are aggravated by the fact that qualitative interviews rarely deal with the more cut-and-dried areas of attitude and behaviour, and have to cope with intangible or even subconscious attitudes and motivations.

Our job, then, is to build up a picture of each individual, and of how they affect and are affected by the interview situation. We then try to understand how they each view the things they are asked to consider (market, brand, advertising, packaging, propositions, etc.) and to gauge the levels of enthusiasm, commitment, and sincerity with which these views are held. What do

---

* It is fair to say that the campaign was never expected to change people's minds overnight. It was in fact the start of what was recognized by the Meat and Livestock Commission as necessarily a long-term education process, which has, with perseverance through the subsequent years, been measurably successful.

they seem involved with? What do they block? What 'language do they use? How honest are they being? How consistent are they being? When are they being ironic or disingenuous, and when should they be taken literally?

Most researchers have had the experience of playing a piece of proto-advertising only to be told by respondents that the message was that the brand could be enjoyed or used by everybody. In a few cases (e.g. Coca-Cola's classic campaign) this may be *part* of the intended communication. In most cases, however, it is a response offered, sometimes disingenuously, because it is not instantly apparent what the real message is. Here, the researcher has to be alert to the possibility of respondents hoping that this answer will prevent any further questions about something they find too difficult or obscure.

It's fair to say that in making those assessments, common sense is the main guide, and that we are essentially using the same tools as we use in everyday conversation, only using them more intensively and more objectively. The 'antennae' which we develop in childhood to interpret others' moods and dispositions are simply deployed here in a different way which does not have ourselves as the end-beneficiary. The process can be made to sound more arcane and mystical than is in fact the case, and it's true that a balance has to be maintained between being fanciful and being over literal or naive. It is likewise important, as Alan Hedges (1983) points out, to realize that the process has no definite end-point, in terms of the attainment of *'the answer'*:

> It's important to dispel the fallacy that there's a hard, cold, clean pristine Platonic Truth underneath it all if we only had the analytic tools to scrape away the surface junk. Underneath that muddled, chaotic, inconsistent surface there may well lie a muddled, chaotic, inconsistent reality. People are ambivalent, untidy bundles of latencies, not clear-cut and deterministic machines.

Interpreting what the whole thing might mean

Once you've decided what you think people mean, what conclusions do you draw from it? What patterns emerge from across the different types of people in the sample which might confirm or negate the various hypotheses you have been examining? How do the response patterns stack up with the conventional wisdoms surrounding the issue areas? This is a higher-level interpretative problem, which involves making judgements about the application and the decision-making context of the study.

An example illustrates the two levels of problem. Suppose you show people some advertising and they claim to dislike it. You may have a problem on the first level – that of deciding if they said what they meant and meant what they said. Can you believe their comments represent their real feelings? Were they reacting to the *style* of the stimulus material rather than the content of the ad? Did the group setting invite people to assume more critical postures than they felt? Were they led by one strong hostile voice?

But there's also a problem on the higher level. Assuming you conclude that they genuinely disliked the ad, does it actually *matter* that they don't like it? Is that an appropriate 'test' for an ad in the particular sector involved? If it was doing all the right things in terms of communication and seemed likely to be impactful and memorable, isn't that the overriding consideration? In recent research into new advertising for Christian Aid this was precisely the case, with few people liking the ads, and a great many being provoked in other ways entirely. The intention was to create disturbance and discomfort, which would lead to outrage and, hopefully, action.

At this second level the objectives both of the study and of the advertising become important. What do the former ask you to do? Are you just supposed to be *describing* people's responses? Or are you supposed to be *explaining* why they say what they say, and what implications it has? Are you expected to 'evaluate' and 'provide guidance'? The more you try to judge and explain, the more you get involved in the higher-level interpretative problems. But the less you try to judge and explain, the more your client is left grappling with the interpretation of evidence he or she can't possibly understand as well as you do. Consistent responses such as 'It'd be better if they kept it as a cartoon', 'People will be offended' and 'It's aimed at (another target group)' are not uncommon, and invariably require judgements as to their ultimate relevance.

It is not simply enough to describe people's responses in most cases. To do so is to remain in the realm of reportage as opposed to that of interpreted findings, and on the level of *specifics* as opposed to achieving a more useful *general* portrayal of the nature of their relationship with the issues or material under investigation.

The researcher's task at this stage is not simply to present the client with discrete pieces of evidence of how people claimed to feel about specific aspects of, say, the proposed packaging or advertising, but to deal in *boundaries, lines of generality*, in a more conceptual way.

Interpreting what this means in terms of the 'Client's Thing'

In taking the project forward from our interpretation of the aggregated views of the consumers interviewed, we need to establish how these various interpretations or conclusions relate usefully to the client view or model or to their 'Thing' – be it a new product, packaging, advertising or the market itself. The key frequently lies in the following activity:

Reinterrogating the 'Client's Thing'
– in structural and conceptual terms
– in light of the responses.

The important word here is *conceptual*. For it is concepts, abstract notions, general ideas which embrace or illuminate many specifics, which enable us to make more sense out of the world and consequently to make decisions, the purpose of which we are clear about.

As researchers we come into contact over time with many product fields and types of advertising. As professionals it is our duty to be curious about these, and to be students of them. We will begin to evolve mental maps, models, typologies which may assist in the interpretation of qualitative 'data'. Some are little more than straightforward 'checklists' of areas for examination, others are more evolutionary in nature. For example, in an attempt to understand 'the market' within which a brand operates we would examine:

Users
Usage patterns and occasions
Purchasing
The role and importance of brands
Salient evaluative criteria for differentiating between brands
Brand positionings on these dimensions
Brand images, personalities, essences
...and so on.

Within each of these areas there may be further known subdivisions which are expressible in concept form, albeit in 'jargon', e.g.

Purchasing:
   Premeditated   Impulse
   Distress   Stock-keeping, etc.

Within each area of marketing activity there may be numerous hypotheses we wish to test, e.g.

- That consumers see the market as divided into the same categories as does the manufacturer's marketing department (a good one this, with spirits and fortified wines, countlines and moulded bars)
- That the salient criterion for differentiating between brands is taste
- That brand loyalty is high
- That the market is an added-value one, showing price positivity
- That purchasing is always premeditated
- That the advertising must always show typical usage occasions, or type of user, etc.

The litany may indeed be a long one.

There is a similarly long (although nowhere does it seem to have been written down) list of types of advertising platforms or structures, each of which is likely to give rise to key issues with which consumers will be concerned, e.g.:

Type	*Issue*
Expert testimonial ⎫	
User testimonial ⎭	Credibility
Celebrity endorsement	Identification with user, credibility
Knowing-brand-in-conspiracy	Targeting, identification
Humour	Branding, targeting, identification
Cartoons	Targeting

We can learn to identify these types of advertising, and watch to see if the 'predicted' issues arise, and put responses in better perspective accordingly.

Researchers should have, as intelligent people, a stock of concepts by which distinctions may be made, and models constructed which move towards explaining why respondents responded in the way they did. A few examples are:

- **Product-values centred advertising** (e.g. archetypal old-style washing powder advertising, whisky and bitter advertising which major on heritage), as distinct from *user-values centred advertising* (e.g. most 'knowing-brand-in-conspiracy with ad-literate audience' model advertising, advertising which targets by means of style or attitude).
- **Adopted Proposition** versus **Perceived Intention** (cf. 'Lean on Pork' mini-case above).
- **Identity** (issues around *who* I am/*who* I want to be) versus *Disposition* (issues around *how* I feel/*how* I want to feel). A lot of advertising effort is spent trying to convey the nature of a shown brand-user's experience. It is often the case that the audience never gets as far as considering this, because they get hung up on the protagonist's identity.
- **Relevance and Credibility** – the two most common *boundaries* operating in respect of propositions and brand positionings.
- **Denotive** (overtly expressed, or 'spelled out') versus *Connotive* (implied or indicated by commonly understood associations) communication – these are usually both present in advertising and packaging. How do they work with respect to each other? Are they relevant and credible?

In advertising we should attempt to separate and gauge the contributions of:

1 The *communicative content* (the strategy, albeit in synoptic form).
2 The *vehicle* (the core creative idea used to convey the intended message).
3 *Executional detail* (the specifics of the articulation that is given to the vehicle).

Using the sorts of conceptual distinctions and frameworks mentioned, such reinterrogation can be most revealing. Aspects of the brand or advertising which were hitherto not obvious may suddenly become apparent. They may not be intentional, and may never be recognized by the owners or creators of those things, but it may be that consumers and audiences pick up on them at levels they find difficult to articulate.

This is the most exciting part of qualitative research – the sudden understanding of why people appear to react in the way they do in respect of a particular product or advertisement, and then the development of a model of the 'towards a general theory' sort. Once this reinterrogation is completed it is usually not difficult to see why responses were the way they were. A model that explains this can be built, which can be used to guide the development of the brand or advertising. I'll end with a case history which illustrates some of this.

Mini-case: Halifax 'house'

When asked in qualitative interviews what advertising people can recall for banks or building societies, this commercial often gets an early mention, and almost always has a very positive reception. I don't know what weight of airtime it has received, but I do know it is now quite old. It seems to have become a 'classic', at least within the sector, if not among all UK TV ads of recent years.

The sort of things, in no particular order, that people say about it *include* (not a comprehensive list) the following:

- Easy to recall who it's for, because of the 'X'
- It makes you feel they're nice people at the Halifax
- They are the biggest, so your money will be safe there and they won't muck you about
- They care about people, perhaps a bit more than some of the others
- The advert doesn't talk down to you, or make out that you're stupid
- It's very watchable, with all the different people gradually making up the house
- It gives a very nice warm feeling, seeing it, with all the people working together to make a home
- The music says it all – it's about 'home' and has words that fit very well.

These sort of comments include some which are about perceptions of the brand (consumer perspective) and some which are about the ad itself (viewer perspective). The comments demonstrate that the ad is successful in respect of the main indices of *relevance* (i.e. 'my kind of stuff', both as an ad – *rewarding*, and as a brand – *beneficial*), *credibility* and *distinctiveness*.

They do not, however, explain by themselves *why* the commercial seems so effective, and scores so well on quantitative tracking measures. The responses are *consequences* of the way the ad has been written, and in order to understand *that* we need to look at it in terms of its *structure* and the internal relationships between its various elements.

Examining the components by themselves may take us a bit further in terms of divining the success of 'House', but, like cataloguing the responses and comments, it will not take us all the way there. The film is made up of lots of ordinary-looking people who are cleverly organized and filmed jumping up on each other's shoulders and finally forming themselves into a house. We know it's not absolutely for real, but find the apparent process fascinating, as well as the result. The music runs throughout, and is eminently suited as an accompaniment, in terms of both its content and its tone. The people then jump down and rearrange themselves into a giant 'X', which reminds us of the Halifax (Figures 6.2 and 6.3).

Figure 6.2

Figure 6.3

The voiceover says, in the middle of the film and towards the end, something about having helped over a million people in the past five years to find the right mortgage scheme, and how the advertiser has lent more money to more people for more mortgages than anyone else. 'So if you want to get into a new home, you'll know who to talk to.' We do not perhaps listen closely to it, but take out an overall reassuring feeling that the Halifax is *big/experienced* and *nice/caring*. This message combination is interesting not least because it includes elements of both *attribute* and *attitude*.

The structural headings I use – *brand, proposition, vehicle* and *execution* – are not new. They are all concepts familiar to those who work with ads or in advertising itself. I then try to identify what each is, or is made of. What is different is that in that process I attempt to examine the extent to which they are consonant, or contained within each other. My contention is that the closer-knit they are in terms of association and meaning (i.e. their capacity to represent significant aspects of each other) the more likely is the ad to communicate well. The model, it should be said, does not seem to fit *every* type of commercial – testimony to the very diversity of creativity – but it seems to illuminate this one well.

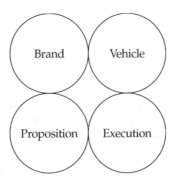

Figure 6.4 A Venn Diagram

The presence or absence of relationship between these structural components (although not the degrees to which these occur) can be shown quite dramatically using a type of Venn Diagram, which simply has four circles. I arrange them as in Figure 6.4. Fairly obviously, where a meaningful interrelationship in terms of what viewers perceive seems to exist, I show the circles overlapping, and where none seems to exist there is no overlap. It follows from this that the most robustly structured scripts will manifest as four overlapping circles, which create a 'flower' shape in the middle. In fact, this is a cruelly stringent 'test' of the ostensible 'efficiency' of a commercial, and very few actually achieve this degree of tightness. The Halifax 'House' ad, however, seems to be one which does (Figure 6.5).

The Execution elements are powerfully interrelated with the others, as well as bringing tonal values of their own which are constructive to the whole:

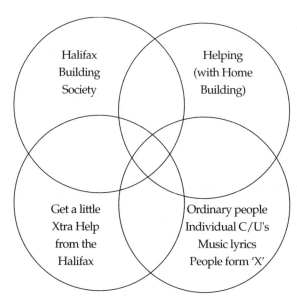

Figure 6.5 The overlapping circles of the Halifax 'House' ad

- The people are ordinary, like you and me. We can relate to them.
- The direction chooses to focus in on them in close-up, and this creates a feeling of the celebration of the individual. We are facilitated in one of our favourite pastimes – people-watching. It is greatly charming, and indicative of a corporate attitude which acknowledges people as individuals.
- The music, as well as being melodic and quite well known (especially if you are over 35!), is lyrically apt for the communicative intention. It is tonally cosy and reassuring. And it ends with the line 'Now everything is easy 'cos of you', just in time for the sign-off to imply ownership of the second-person pronoun.
- The people (still a living example of cooperation) form themselves into the 'X' – the (long-ago) well-chosen brand logo.

The overall piece emerges with a reassuring tonality, along with a nobility of spirit and an elegant simplicity of form. All the four component areas contain something meaningful of each other, giving rise to a superbly consistent communication both of the proposition and of positioning through felt brand values.

Conclusion

What I hope I have shown in this chapter is that analysing and interpreting qualitative data is both more complex and potentially more fun than many might think. It is also more essential than some seem to believe. As opposed simply to occurring after the fieldwork, the interpretative process begins with the first contact from the client or agency and continues throughout, taking in project and sample design, content briefing, the interviewing itself, as well as the subsequent sifting and sorting of the data.

Hypotheses which you intuit at the outset, and which you then develop, refine or reject, are a core part of the process. The more questions you ask yourself, and the more hypotheses you try out, the richer will be your relationship with what happens in the interviews and, ultimately, the more robust will be your conclusions.

There is no satisfactory substitute for immersing yourself thoroughly in the data – tapes, transcripts, notes and thoughts of your own and of any skilled and briefed observers. Different researchers find different methods best for them. It's a personal thing.

Often there is not enough time to undertake all the procedures I have discussed here, but in 'short-cutting' we should always be aware that that is what we've done and by how much we've done it.

That said, it is equally important to develop an ability to rise above the data once they are sifted, sorted and differentiated. The ability to make intuitive leaps with confidence once the data *patterns* have been assimilated is a crucial part of the interpretative process, and one which takes time and experience to grow into. In interpreting qualitative data in this way, you should be courageous. You should trust yourself, and believe in your own experience.

The responses in the tapes and transcripts are only *part* of the overall process. They do *not* provide the conceptual frameworks, but they do give clues about the dimensions which are important in such frameworks, and they do give indications as to where problems appear to lie.

Interrogating the 'Client's Thing' in terms of its structures both before fieldwork (hypothesis generation) and in light of responses is vital, for two reasons:

1 As qualitative researchers our job is not simply one of trying to understand people alone. We seek to illuminate the *relationships* between people and brands, advertisements, packs, markets, etc. So why be satisfied with only one side of the story?

2 By achieving and communicating the required understanding in terms of *supply-side* structures we are enhancing the usefulness of the research to the client. It then explains what is happening *in terms of* the client's end of things. It provides explanations, diagnoses and guidelines in terms of the structure of the 'Client's Thing' – and that is what he or she is able to change, not the people. It's in a *user-friendly* language, and may not involve the mention of specific responses at all.

Lastly, what I hope I have *not* said is that if you don't do all of this you're not doing it well. That isn't necessarily so. It behoves us all, however, to be aware of by how far we fall short of the rigorous professional ideal when yet again we are faced with the need to deliver in three days findings which in academia might be felt to need three months.

References

Gordon, W. (1983), Paper given at The Analysis of Qualitative Data, AQRP One-Day Event.

Gordon, W. and Langmaid, R. (1988), *Qualitative Market Research. A Practitioner's and Buyer's Guide*, Gower: Aldershot.

Hedges, A. (1983), Paper given at The Analysis of Qualitative Data, AQRP One-Day Event.

Robson, S. and Foster, A. (eds) (1989), *Qualitative Research in Action*, Edward Arnold: London.

Wells, S. (1991), Wet towels and whetted appetites or a wet blanket? The role of analysis in qualitative research. *Journal of the Market Research Society*, **33**, (1), January.

Overview: Chapter 7

The advertising development process within the agency resembles a communications 'relay race'. The creative brief represents a pivotal phase in the chain, marking the point where the strategic understanding gleaned by the account team is passed on. It is the point at which the understanding of the client's problem becomes distilled into a form that makes it clear what the advertising solution is required to achieve and provides inspiration for the creative team. It therefore represents the single most important contribution the account team can make to influencing the power and creativity of the advertising.

Creative people have to generate original ideas on the back of thinking done by other people. They must turn the thinking in the brief into a piece of communication that solves the problem. A successful campaign idea is the result of inspiration, intuition, and experimentation built on the foundation of logical analysis and the footholds for inspiration the brief provides.

The value of the brief is defined entirely by how useful it is to the creative team. To maximize value the brief needs two key properties: directionality, and inspiration. The directional elements are those which elucidate the nature of the problem the advertising is trying to solve and what it needs to achieve. The inspirational elements are those which provide a foothold, a place to start the process of creative generation.

This chapter examines some real creative briefs and discusses the issues encountered in writing briefs in real life. It also highlights the role of the briefing and the context of working relationships between account team and creative team which maximize the chances of a successful outcome. This chapter, originally presented on the IPA Stage 2 course (Campaign Planning) in 1990, is an excellent and well-argued point of view (from the perspective of one of the UK's most highly regarded planners) of the fulcrum of the advertising process.

Chapter 7

Creative briefing

Gary Duckworth

Briefing in the advertising process

Client companies employ and pay advertising agencies because they enable them to solve brand problems and exploit brand opportunities. Advertising is a functional instrument, designed to achieve specific objectives, as earlier chapters on strategy have outlined. The reason the brief is so important is because much money is going to be spent on the campaign that emerges from it. So the agency has both the opportunity to create something that works and the responsibility to ensure that it does.

You can consider the advertising development process as a kind of relay race (Figure 7.1). The essential job of the first part of the chain – let's call it strategic development – is to take an understanding of the client's business, their consumers, their marketplace, their brand, etc. and from all this come up with a clearly defined role for advertising to play in building their client's success.

Creative briefing is pivotal because it represents the stage in the advertising development process where the strategic understanding developed by the account team reaches the people whose job it is to really crack the creative problem. But this strategic understanding has to be transmuted into a form the

Figure 7.1 The relay race

creative people can use, so that it becomes a useful tool and inspiration for the creative team. The essence of creative briefing is that the initial understanding must now be distilled, and then passed on in a way that provides a foundation and the beginnings of inspiration for a solution.

Archimedes and the lever

Archimedes said: 'Give me a place to stand and I can move the world'. He was explaining the concept of leverage, whereby a small force exerted at the right point is magnified through distance to move an immense object. The brief is the place the account team gives the creative team to stand in their quest to move the world – i.e. to shape the decisions and perceptions of the target group out there in the real world (Figure 7.2).

People outside advertising often make the erroneous assumption that all advertising works. The truth is that some works and some doesn't. Some creates an enduring brand asset but some offers a few fleeting seconds of entertainment and is then forgotten forever. In this respect, creative briefing is the pivot of a process that may or may not end up producing a satisfactory result. It marks the point at which the understanding of the problem becomes distilled into a form that makes it clear what the solution is required to achieve and provides some inspiration for the creative mind to work with. It is the point where the account team exert the maximum leverage on the eventual advertising outcome because the briefing represents a *passing on* of understanding and of ownership of the problem from one part of the agency to the other. Someone else is taking over the bus.

From here on, it is going to be the responsibility of the creative team to devise a campaign which, when it finally emerges, will do the job it is

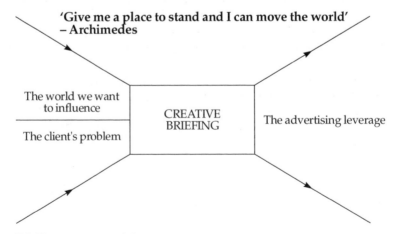

Figure 7.2 The creative team's leverage

supposed to do. Many other people, further along the process, will play a role in shaping the campaign – planners and researchers, media and production people. But it is the creative team who will *originate* the solution.

So the briefing represents the single most important contribution the account team can make to influence the power and creativity of the advertising. Two important consequences follow:

1 *The rudder and the supertanker*   The rudder on a tanker is only a relatively small part of the ship, but a few degrees change of trim in the bearing of the rudder to port or starboard can make an immense difference to where the supertanker ends up over the course of a voyage. Similarly with a brief, a steer to the team that is off-course can make an immense difference to the eventual creative outcome.
2 *The oil and the engine*   I have observed that the brief represents a passing on. The brief is a tool for the benefit of the creative people: an instrument to make the job of the agency's most valued and talented people as easy as it can possibly be for them to exercise those talents. The lubrication in a car makes it possible for the engine to work to its best ability – its value is defined entirely by how well it enables the engine to do its job. The value of the briefing is defined entirely by the value it provides to the creative team in originating an advertising solution.

I hope this point seems obvious. The fact is, sometimes there is an unhealthy tendency for account teams, and especially planners, to 'fetishize' the brief. The brief becomes treated as some precious, almost mystical object, filled with intellectual cleverness or obscurely written guidance. It becomes treated as something important in its own right, an end in itself.

There is the enduring myth of 'The Great Brief', which is apocryphally believed to lie behind great campaigns. I've investigated this issue, and traced backwards to the original brief from some justly famous work.

The brief that originated the Levi's campaign (Figure 7.3) that ran for many years was:

What must the advertising say?

501s from Levi's are the right look and the only label.

And why should the consumer believe it?

Because they represent the way jeans should be worn today; and because they are the original jean, indelibly associated with the birth of teenage culture in the 1950s, and its finest expressions since

Tone of voice

Heroic
Highly charged
American (but 'period')

Figure 7.3 One of the first commercials in the long-running Levi's campaign

The brief that originated the 'Heineken Refreshes the Parts' campaign was 'refreshment'.

What is interesting about both of these briefs is that they are simple and to the point. But I don't think either could be accused of expressing some profound philosophical insight. And though you can see in both cases how the campaign emerged from the brief, you can't see the campaign idea in it. The brief is a start – a vital start, but only a start.

Wittgenstein observed that the study of philosophy was like a ladder: you climbed it to reach a certain point of enlightenment, but once you had attained that point you could throw the ladder away. All briefs end up in the bin.

Principles of a good brief

I'm going to start distinguishing here between the *brief* – i.e. the written communication which goes to the creative team, and the *briefing* – i.e. the context of dialogue and discussion that goes on around it when the briefing meeting takes place (Figure 7.4).

Figure 7.4 The difference between the brief and the briefing

So what is a good brief?

People often say that advertising is a blunt instrument. Imagine a brief for a blunt instrument – it wouldn't run to many pages. It would say something like: 'About two feet long, wider at one end than the other, made of wood.' Whereas a brief for knitting a jumper is a complex of tiny elements that reveal the end result slowly as we follow it, a creative brief needs to give the big picture quickly and directly.

So it has to be clear and simple if we are to stand a chance of producing effective communication. There are two key properties it needs: to be *directional* and *inspirational* (Figure 7.5):

- A creative brief gives guidance to a team who are going to produce a piece of communication that *does* something, something that will intervene in the external world. The directional elements of the brief are those which define the task – what the advertising needs to achieve, the problem it is trying to solve. Plus the kind of people it is talking to, how they think, feel and behave. In a nutshell, the directional elements of the brief are those which give the creative team a clear understanding of the problem.
- The inspirational elements are those which give the creative team a springboard, a jumping-off point for originating the campaign idea. They include the 'tone of voice' elements, the kind of 'feel' which the advertising needs to have – soft and cuddly, or cold and sharp, etc.

Every agency has its own creative brief form, as part of its working processes, and each designs the brief in different ways, giving the sections different names because each agency likes to think it is unique and special, but

Direction

Inspiration

Figure 7.5 The two key properties of effective communication

the essential components nonetheless bear a strong family resemblance (Figures 7.6 and 7.7).

The sections of the brief fall roughly into these two areas (Figure 7.8):

- **Why are we advertising?** Role of advertising. What is the advertising doing? What do we want people to think?
- **Who are we talking to?** Target group. Type and outlook of person, not just demographics. Their behaviour with respect to our objective.
- **What are we saying?** Proposition/main thought plus support.
- **How are we saying it?** Tone of voice, brand identity.
- **Executional guidelines** Things to avoid. Things you must do.
- **Requirement** Media consideration/requirements. Timing.

Giving clear directions

If the advertising the creative team produce is to shape the perceptual aspect of our world, we must begin by giving them a picture of how it is currently shaped and the shift in perception the advertising needs to achieve. Let's pull the focus back here and examine the concept of giving clear directions – how directions can be helpful or unhelpful. Suppose you're lost on your way to visit some friends who have recently moved. You stop the car and ask directions from somebody passing by. Here are two different replies you might receive:

- **Reply I** 'Moreton Road. You definitely mean Moreton Road not Marsham Road? Okay. You're not far away. Continue straight along here about 400 metres and take

Bartle Bogle Hegarty

Creative Brief

CLIENT _____

BRAND _____

THE PRODUCT IS:

THE BRAND IS:

1. THE ROLE OF ADVERTISING:-

A. WHAT DO WE WANT PEOPLE TO DO AS A RESULT OF SEEING THIS ADVERTISING?

B. HOW DO WE BELIEVE THE ADVERTISING WILL WORK TO ACHIEVE THIS?

2. WHO ARE WE TALKING TO?

3. **WHAT IS THE SINGLE MOST IMPORTANT THING THIS ADVERTISING SHOULD CONVEY?**

4. WHY SHOULD PEOPLE BELIEVE THIS?

5. WHAT PRACTICAL CONSIDERATIONS ARE THERE?

DATE
JOB NO.
1ST REVIEW
FINAL SIGN OFF
CREATIVE DIRECTOR
TEAM LEADER
BUDGET ESTIMATE £
MEDIA

Figure 7.6 A creative brief form

DUCKWORTH FINN GRUBB WATERS

41 Great Pulteney Street, London W1R 3DE. Telephone: (0171) 734 5888.
Facsimile: (0171) 734 3716. E-mail: dfgw@dfgw.com

BRIEF

What is this brand called?

What is this brand's DNA?

Who do we want to buy it?

Why should people buy this brand?

Requirement

Signature   Date   Traffic   Date

Duckworth, Finn, Grubb, Waters Limited registered in England number 2377231.
Registered Office: 41 Great Pulteney Street, London W1R 3DE.

Figure 7.7 Another creative brief form

**DIRECTION
GIVING**

**INSPIRATION
GIVING**

Figure 7.8 Interaction of the two key properties of effective briefing

the left after the Red Lion pub. Continue straight on over a narrow bridge and just continue. Eventually you get to another main road with traffic lights – turn right, and it's first on your left.'

■ **Reply 2** 'Moreton Road? Moreton Road. Now let me think. Funny you know, I've lived round here all my life – yeees, I know. It's the one near where they built the new school my daughter goes to. If I'm not mistaken. You'll need … Now wait a minute so go right after the school. Wait a minute. That's Marsham Road. Moreton, Moreton, No, I tell a lie, go along until you … take the second right … or is it the third? Anyway it's on the right somewhere then … Or maybe there's a quicker way altogether. If I'm right…'.

Reply 1 is clear, crisp, and highly functional. It establishes the goal, briefly sets the context and then provides clear directions so the person hearing it knows unambiguously the right thing to do. Reply 2 is well intentioned but that is about all that can be said in its favour: it rambles, it adds detail completely unrelated to the task in hand. It goes off on a completely misleading tack: it considers alternatives, but fails to opt in favour of any one in particular. The person receiving it is no better off than when they started; in fact they may be worse off because they are more confused. Bad creative briefs can have the same effect.

Here's a real-life example of directions, where people have paid attention to clarity, because these are for a situation that could be critical: these directions used to be on cards in London Underground trains:

What to do if you see a suspicious unattended package

1 Don't panic
2 Pull the red emergency handle at the next station.
3 Get your fellow passengers off the train. Alert a member of staff.

Here is what the card does *not* say:

What to do if you see a suspicious unattended package

It is quite possible that a tumult of conflicting emotions will course through your mind: concern for your own safety, your loved ones, regret that you'll never finish those dining-room shelves. However, research and years of experience have shown that the optimum response is – don't panic, rend your garments or vent your resentment at God's vindictive capriciousness, etc., etc.

Can you explain it to your mum?

So the writer of the brief has to do all the homework, understand the problem in depth, then simplify and distil, so the directions become clear. If you put too much in, people will get lost. One simple test I apply when I'm engaged in this exercise is to ask myself if I can put the problem in three short sentences. Can I express it in a way (and using language) that my mum would understand?

Here's an example of just the direction element of a brief I wrote for a campaign for the Sunday newspaper *The People*.

Why are we advertising?
People don't think of buying *The People* because it's very low profile. If they do think of it they assume it's a less sleazy version of the *News of the World*, or have no clear picture.

We need to put the paper back on the Sunday newspaper map and give it an attractive identity which reflects the paper as it is today.

The issue of language

The passage above is deliberately written in ordinary language. It's very important, as the distillation of our strategic thinking reaches the team whose job it is to 'translate' it into a piece of communication, that the language we use changes and doesn't use 'marketing speak'.

For example I could have written the same kind of directions for *The People* brief, but in this kind of language:

Why are we advertising?
The product has a severe saliency deficiency so it does not get into the target's consideration set. The leading brand sets the category values and our brand is perceived as a 'me-too' because of these dominant associations. Alternatively, a proportion of the target segment have a dissociated perceptual set with respect to the brand.

The campaign objective is to increase saliency and to communicate a brand identity which is motivating and more appropriate to the product's experiential manifestation.

Some people find this kind of language tempting because they feel it sounds 'clever', in just the same way many academics write using obscure jargon because they feel it helps their career advancement if they have an intellectual image among their peers. To a greater or lesser extent all professional disciplines develop their own language, and there is a value to this because they need words for concepts that are not part of our everyday discourse.

If you work in the marketing or advertising business you may be able to remember the shock you had when you first saw an example of 'marketing speak', e.g. 'The everyday cheese that meets your needs for mildness with flavour.' After a few months you forgot how weird this language is because you learned to use it habitually as a working tool. While this may be fine for certain professional purposes, the danger is that if we get wrapped up in the cleverness of our own words, we run the risk of a breakdown in the communication process because the creative teams do not generally use this kind of language. Nor indeed does anyone else.

A similar kind of issue often arises with the description of the target group. Because we have so many tools for analysing people's behaviour in markets, all of which use 'code', there is a tendency to be sloppy and to continue to describe the target group in this code in the creative brief, without translating it back into something more recognizable:

Target group
The target group are 30–45 BCI adults, 80:20 men:women. Living in Acorn areas J–K, and with a median income of £30,000 pa. Attitudinally they are achievers and secure conservatives.

The difficulty with this is you don't feel you know the people you are trying to reach. Here's an ordinary-language example from a brief for Pharmaton:

Why are we advertising?
To position Pharmaton as a capsule taken to combat everyday tiredness, far superior to traditional vitamins, minerals and dietary supplements.

Target group

Men and women, between 30 and 50, who feel tired because of the demands of today's lifestyle, e.g. stressed jobs, going out a lot, a heavy sports routine or the juggling act of a family. These demands can take control and leave them feeling drained. Despite suffering from everyday exhaustion, they have never thought of doing something about it and thus do not treat the symptoms as they might a headache. They tend to feel tired particularly mid-afternoon and early evening; it is at these moments that some resort to alternative measures for a quick boost of energy such as alcohol, coffee or a chocolate bar. These people are not overly concerned with their health but, because of the lifestyle they lead, they feel they should be doing something to maintain a level of general well-being.

The more we use language rooted in the real, ordinary world, the better equipped the creative team will be to communicate with it in our campaign.

The structure of the brief

Just because the brief is written in ordinary language does not mean it is mundane or prosaic. On the contrary, it is a highly structured set of instructions and ideas.

The centrepiece of every brief is the 'proposition' or main thought which describes the essence of what we want to communicate. The key to good proposition writing is to keep the proposition brief, single-minded and simple. As a rule of thumb, once you've written it, you need to look at it and ask yourself: 'Could I write an ad from that?' – just a simple, straightforward idea of what your proposition might just look like when turned into an advert. So you can work out if what you've ended up with is a useful working tool for a creative person. If *you* can't write an ad from it, it's unlikely anyone else can.

The role of the proposition is to encapsulate the *main* thing you want to communicate, not to contain everything you want to say:

- Do say: The Honda Banzai is the family coupé with great performance.
- Don't say: The Honda Banzai coupé combines performance, reliability, economy and cat-like roadholding with sporty good looks and room for a family of five.

It is important to take the responsibility for the brief being single-minded. If your strategy development has left you in an ambiguous position, and you are not sure what the core communication needs to be, it is not acceptable to use the proposition as some kind of selection box for the creative team to make their own choice. If you can't agree with your client whether the proposition is 'thickness' or 'a range of flavours' you need to do more strategic homework and distillation to get to a resolution. If you put 'A range of thick flavours' all you are in effect doing is avoiding the decision and dumping the responsibility for the strategy on the creative team.

I'm a great believer in giving people a concrete thought rather than an abstract one, because an abstract one can so easily end up just being vague. This is a particular issue with brands built on emotional imagery – for example, fashion, perfumes, cosmetics, or confectionery. You don't necessarily have to have a 'fact' to be concrete.

A perfume example
Do say: The essence of the East.
Don't say: Floating and beautiful.

A confectionery example
Do say: Private moment.
Don't say: A unique taste experience, full of indulgence.

A snack example
Do say: Big crunch in a neat, light gold square.
Don't say: A totally different kind of crisp.

I've had a lot of discussions with creative teams about 'Can you express the proposition as a headline?', 'Should it be creative?' and so on. I've had mixed views back. In fact I now work with one creative director who finds this helpful, and one who doesn't.

Here's the same brief, for Granada TV Rental, so you and your creative team can make up your own minds. The proposition is written in two different ways, but the support doesn't change:

'Creative' version of proposition
Why buy a millstone when you can rent a milestone?

Support
If you rent from Granada you can stay always up to date. For example, widescreen and digital.

Plain vanilla version of proposition
Renting from Granada is more sensible than owning.

Support
If you rent from Granada you can stay always up to date. For example, widescreen and digital.

The support

If the proposition represents the kind of understanding or conclusion we want the target group to come to, then it needs to be backed by evidence – the support for the proposition. This should be one of the most inspirational elements of the brief, because it gives the creative team ideas or product points that can be dramatized creatively. It's an area where doing your homework into the brand and its performance or history can unearth some really interesting fact or 'nugget' and give the creative team a really powerful jumping-off point.

> *Proposition*
> If you suffer from daily fatigue, now you can do something about it with Pharmaton.
>
> *Support*
> Pharmaton is a balanced combination of vitamins, minerals and trace elements as well as specially purified ginseng. It is this powerful combination that makes it particularly effective (Figure 7.9).
>   Because Pharmaton is one of the few dietary supplements to carry out studies into tiredness and exhaustion, we know that most people will start feeling the effects after 5 weeks.
>
> *Tone*
> Calm, adult to adult.

Tone

The 'tone paragraph' is there is to give guidance on the 'feel' of the advertising – the tonal ambience of the communication. Should it be 'short and sharp' or 'soft and seductive'? I'm using clichés here deliberately to illustrate the point, but in reality the tone paragraph aims to be specific to the circumstances and needs of the brand.

I always try to give myself a rule that you can only use two words for tone. Even one will do fine as long as it's well chosen. So what you don't write is:

> *Tone*
> Warm, reassuring, yet jaunty and audacious.

Because it is nonsense.

The awful example

I've made up bad examples so far to illustrate my points, but here's a fine example of true-life waffle which led to a TV campaign that spent a significant sum of money and vanished without trace. The brand has been disguised to protect the guilty.

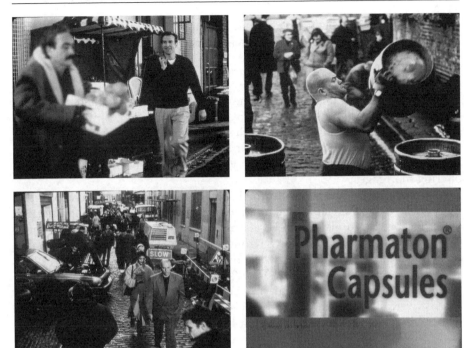

Figure 7.9 Pharmaton's power to relieve tiredness is dramatized by a man who walks at normal speed through an urban landscape where everyone else is in slow motion

Proposition
Brand X ground coffee. Its distinctive character stands out from the rest.

Brand character
X is the sort of character everyone admires – he's warm, friendly, sociable and approachable, yet retains a distinctive style so that he stands out from the crowd.

Tone
A distinctive and different treatment from any other ground coffee advertising that gives contemporary relevance to the brand in the real lives of our primary audience.

This brief gives us some classic guidelines on how not to do it. The proposition is hackneyed. There is no support given as to why we should believe it. It sounds like it could apply to a lot of products, rather than specifically a coffee brand (there appears to be nothing relevant to coffee in it). Language is used portentously but unhelpfully ('distinctive and different'). It employs the kind of phrase-making ('contemporary relevance') that nobody apart from people writing creative briefs ever uses. We all make mistakes.

Mandatories

Sometimes you need this section in the brief – essentially it's there to set out what the advertising must include. A mandatory might be a genre convention where the received wisdom suggests that some creative element is essential to success – for example, a beautiful hair shot in a shampoo commercial. Or it might be the regulatory financial rubric you have to show in a commercial offering mortgages.

Alternatively, you may have learned something that has to be avoided. For example, in a commercial for the London Fire Brigade which had the objective of getting people to install smoke alarms, we had a mandatory not to show children in the ad because research strongly suggested that those in households without children – e.g. the elderly – were likely to interpret the message as 'not aimed at me'. Their response was 'That's right – people with children at home should definitely get a smoke alarm'. Yet statistical analysis showed that the elderly were in fact one of the highest risk groups, whereas smoke alarm ownership was most advanced among homes with children.

The requirement

This is where you specify what format the campaign needs to take. And it is important to be clear. There's no use in your creative team producing a brilliant script for a 60-second TV commercial if the media budget will only support 30 seconds. Giving the creative team a clear idea of the number of executions you need in press or posters helps them to focus their minds on the task.

More complex brands, still simple briefs

Different advertising problems emerge over time as new types of brand owners come to the marketplace. Twenty years ago we had largely FMCG brand problems to solve – yoghurt, frozen peas, crisps, detergents, etc. Now we have retailers, TV channels, telecoms companies, banks, airlines, and cars as well. These often present more tricky problems to analyse because understanding what the advertising needs to do (i.e. understanding the directional element of the brief) is tougher. It remains just as important to stick with the distillation process, but sometimes the structure of the brief needs to change slightly.

To launch Daewoo cars in the UK we had an overall positioning we wanted the advertising to achieve: 'The most customer-focused car company.' There were a very large number of differences between what Daewoo offered and what other car manufacturers provided. None of these differences was in its own right big enough to build the entire brand on, but taken together they added up to something very distinctive. This kind of brand has been well

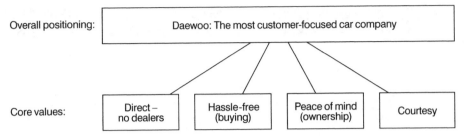

Figure 7.10 The structure of the Daewoo brand

described by John dalla Costa (in *Admap*, January 1996) as a 'Velcro' brand because it has a lot of little 'hooks' which add up to an overall 'perspective'.

To simplify the communication task for the creative brief, we divided all this list of brand differences into four primary categories (we called them core values – Figure 7.10). When we devise a new campaign phase, each execution exemplifies a core value. Figure 7.11 is a 'hassle-free buying' brief, Figure 7.12 shows the result.

Guidance versus rigidity

The best way to describe the brief is as a kind of structural pattern. While it is a set of instructions, it is not like a knitting pattern code that gives an exact and complete guide to the final garment.

The brief offers guidance, but falls short (or should fall short) of prescription. This is because it needs to allow the creative team the latitude to exercise their insights and creative imagination. A brief which is too rigid, and requires the creative work to be a literal translation of what it says, is likely to lead to advertising which fails because it is dull and uninspiring.

It is the power of the creative idea which bring the proposition to life and dramatizes it to us so that we have the chance to interest the target group in what we have to say. The creative team originate the solution, not the brief writers. After all, if writing the brief solved the problem, we wouldn't need creative teams. But someone has to actually do it. And it is in this that the risk and challenge of the advertising process lies.

The briefing

Creative people: what are the target group like?

Given the brief is designed to communicate with the creative team, they are in fact the target group for the brief. Creative people have different orientations to

DUCKWORTH FINN GRUBB WATERS

41 Great Pulteney Street, London W1R 3DE. Telephone: (0171) 734 5888.
Facsimile: (0171) 734 3716. E-mail: dfgw@dfgw.com

BRIEF

What is this brand called?
Daewoo Cars

What is this brand's DNA?
Customer Focus For Real

Who do we want to buy it?
New car buyers aged 35-54 who are disenchanted with the current car buying and owning process.
They tend to feel that this is the norm for car manufacturers and that there is very little they can do
about it. They also tend not to be car crazy so don't read every motoring magazine going and are
not particularly interested in traditional car advertising.
The motoring problems they have tend to relate less to the actual car than to the poor service they
have experienced at both the buying stage and during the ownership period. When we asked these
people about some of the biggest problems they have with the car buying and owning process lots of
them said that they had felt pressurised by car salesman to buy a car and that this had actually put
them off buying the car. We want them to feel that they will never be pressurised by Daewoo into
doing anything they don't want to do.

Why should people buy this brand?
Unlike other car manufacturers Daewoo never put pressure on you when you are buying a car.

Support:

Because we deal direct the whole approach to buying a car is unpressurised and enjoyable with non-
commissioned customer advisers, clear fixed pricing (no haggling), inclusive pricing (no hidden
extras), family friendly showrooms, interactive information units.

Their customer service policy is never to hassle customers on anything.
N.B. 67% of car buyers who responded to the dialogue campaign have been put off from buying a
car because they felt pressurised and 18% of them had actually been pressurised into buying a car
they didn't want.

Requirement
1 x 30 sec TV

N.B. Beautiful looking car!

Signature	Date	Traffic	Date

Dave 11/8/98 A.T 11/8/98.

Present to Client- w/c 7 Sept   Brendan/Paul   Si/Tim.

Duckworth, Finn, Grubb, Waters Limited registered in England number 2377231.
Registered Office: 41 Great Pulteney Street, London W1R 3DE

Figure 7.11 Daewoo 'hassle-free' execution brief

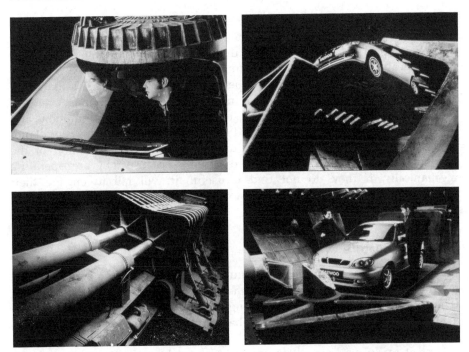

Figure 7.12 The execution of the 'hassle-free' brief – the idea that with Daewoo cars buyers are 'protected' from pressure dramatized by showing them going through a car crusher which collapses, leaving them unscathed. 'Pressure-free car buying? That'll be the Daewoo.'

their work. They are conscious of what their peer group will think. They know their work will be on show in public. Imagine how you would feel about your own work if you knew it was going to be widely publicized, there for everyone to see. It is a very different feeling from the feelings of those earlier in the advertising development chain.

Another important difference is that far more of what they actually produce comes from the self. If you are an account planner you have the raw material of research to work from, you have your spreadsheets and models. If you are an account manager you have a process to manage, a team to coordinate, and a client to look after. If you are a creative person you start with a brief, you own life experiences, and a blank piece of paper.

Anyone who has ever been on a creative role-reversal course (I recommend it) will know how difficult it is to produce an original advertising idea in response to a brief. Briefs come from the logical, analytical area of life, but advertising communication is a process that goes beyond the rational, that uses symbols and emotional understanding, so a good advertising idea inherently uses non-logical processes.

A good idea emerges out of the brief, synthesizes it, and goes beyond it. Creative people have to generate original ideas on the back of thinking done by other people. They must turn the thinking in the brief into a piece of communication that solves the problem. A successful campaign idea is the end result of inspiration, intuition, and experimentation built on the foundation of logical analysis and the footholds for inspiration the brief provides.

Because their work comes from the self, from their intuitions, emotions and hunches, they have to be committed or these creative processes will not operate. If they do not find in the brief a convincing explanation of the problem, they will tend to produce dull work because they are operating mechanically. If they do not find it useful, it will fail to engage their imagination, and they will tend to ignore it.

The critical nature of the briefing

Because the creatives' emotional commitment and morale is so important, the briefing – i.e. the context in which the brief is delivered – is all-important (Figure 7.13). To create the right working environment for the briefing there are a number of circumstantial factors that significantly influence whether the briefing is likely to be productive.

First, it really makes a difference to have good relationships between the people who write the briefs – account planners and/or account managers and the creative department. If the agency culture is cluttered with unhelpful stereotypes – e.g. planners are 'boffins', creatives are 'prima donnas' – it is very difficult for both sides to have the mutual respect needed for a successful

Figure 7.13 The importance of the briefing – the context in which the brief is delivered

outcome, because everyone will be in their corner emotionally, defending their egos (not to mention living up to their stereotypes).

Second, do you, the brief writer, know your creative team as people? Do you talk to them outside of the work context about music, football, ads they admire and so on? How can you brief someone effectively if you don't know the people you are talking to? More to the point, the chances are that you can communicate with them better and they will trust you, the more you know them. Just like in real life.

Always remember, *you* haven't cracked it, *they* are the ones who originate the solution.

Making the briefing interesting

Let's start with a question here. Why should your advertising be interesting if your briefing isn't? Ever been inspired by hearing something really dull? It may only be for a trade ad, but every brief is important given that it has a job to do.

I once heard of an account director who was asked to brief the creative team on a DIY product which filled holes in walls. He walked into the briefing with a hammer, smashed a hole in the wall, and then mixed the product in front of them, using it very successfully to mend the hole in the wall. And then walked out. It's a good story. It doesn't really matter if it's true or not, because it illustrates some great insights. First, it was dramatic and entertaining. You wouldn't forget a briefing like that. Second, it gave the creative team a really good idea of what the benefit of the product was. Third, it was a brilliant way to create commitment to the product so the team could feel enthusiastic about solving the advertising problem.

So what can you do to bring it to life? Sadly, not all the things we advertise can be so convincingly demonstrated. Nonetheless, there are lots of ways you can bring things to life. Perhaps a video of people talking about what they like about the product, or how it helps them in their work. Perhaps photographs to show the kind of people the campaign is aimed at, or a few quotes from research of their views.

Maybe you can experience the product directly if it is something like a mobile phone, an airline or car. If it's a bar of chocolate you can always eat it. If it's a store you can wander round and buy something, talk to the staff. Maybe do the briefing in the store or driving along in the car. None of this will necessarily end up directly in the creative work, although it's possible that one of these experiences may spark something off. But the briefing will be more memorable and chances are that the creative team will absorb more.

The briefing gives you the chance to embellish and amplify what you have set down formally in the brief. Don't use it to sneak in extra things that suddenly occur to you, or clutter and ambiguity will rear their heads. A briefing is a performance of an existing script, not a chance to suddenly write a new one.

The team will probably have questions, and you may need to do some more work or thinking. It may be that something they observe helps you understand more than you've got to so far. I've frequently had the experience of talking through a brief with a team, only to find something somebody says gives me the insight to improve it.

And when the creative team have heard enough, don't hassle them about how they're getting on. All of us have had the experience in a briefing situation when you feel you have enough to go on, at least for now, and creative teams need the space to go away and let it all sink in. Maybe they'll want to talk more later. You have to let go of the responsibility for solving the problem and recognize that the baton has been passed on...

Reacting to the work

When you get the campaign idea presented back to you, remember the point about the personal element, so if you have points or criticisms, act sensitively. First, though, just make sure you create a clear visualization of what exactly is supposed to happen in the ad. Creative people, because they have worked hard on the idea and have got so close, sometimes neglect to explain it fully. Ask questions if you need to.

I think you have to start by reacting to it spontaneously – laugh, cry, whatever. Just imagine the ad in a break, or a newspaper. Remember, the people seeing your ad aren't going to be comparing it to the brief you've written. They're just going to be in their everyday lives when suddenly this ad comes up in front of them. What will they take out of it? Even if it's not 'propositionally perfect', it may well still accomplish the task you've defined. If it's not the kind of idea you expected, try to understand its potential.

Make sure you distinguish between the idea and the execution. There's nothing more frustrating for a creative team to take you through their campaign idea, only to find you querying some trivial executional element which is not fundamental to the script.

If you have problems with it, be articulate about your reservations so your views can be as constructive as possible, and if it really isn't right, now in the meeting may not be the best time to say so. Maybe you need to do some more thinking and come back with a more considered view about what needs to be done.

Remember, you are all working together to get a result. When the advertising is right, everybody wins.

And finally

There are no great briefs, only great ads.

There are no great briefs, but there are a lot of bad ones.

A good brief is probably about as good as a brief gets.

Good luck.

Reference

dalla Costa, J. (1996), A new marketing model for a new advertising reality, *Admap*, **358** (January), pp. 31–36).

Overview: Chapter 8

This chapter is essentially concerned with giving suggestions on how to write a creative brief, based on the way it's done at HHCL & Partners, the agency Steve Henry founded in 1987. It is taken from a speech given annually since 1990 on IPA Stage 4 (Better Account Direction), a course aimed at improving the craft skills of account directors with four or five years' experience in the business.

After a general introduction, Steve looks at the concept of 'being different – for the sake of being better'. He goes on to make five suggestions for writing a creative brief:

- Decide which rules in your marketplace can be broken
- Forget the 'USP', and look for the brand personality
- Define the target market so that you like and respect them
- Write creative starters
- Make your brief inspiring.

Steve Henry's style is highly personal, often controversial but always entertaining. Which is probably why his advertising is as successful among the mass market as this chapter is when delivered to the much smaller audience of account directors – who receive its freshness with rapture.

Chapter 8

Creative briefing: the creative perspective

Steve Henry

(If you want to make a difference, make it different)

Introduction

A few years ago, Leslie Butterfield asked me to give a talk at an IPA course, aimed at '4-year-old' account directors, on the subject of writing creative briefs. This was an unusual request for at least two reasons. First, I'm a copywriter by training, not a planner or an account director. So I don't write creative briefs. However, like all writers, I like to think of myself as a strategist manqué, so I thought ... what the hell, I can handle it. (Basically, I believe that if you put enough manqués in front of enough word processors, one of them will eventually write a decent strategy.)

But the second reason was perhaps more interesting. At the time of the request, HHCL enjoyed a unique reputation in the advertising industry. Our work seemed wilfully complex to most people in the industry – 'different for the sake of being different' was probably the most common accusation levelled at us. The fact that clients gave us interesting and increasingly high-profile accounts to work on seemed to puzzle and annoy our critics. Perhaps it was the radical inside Leslie which urged him to invite me to speak; perhaps it was a competitive streak in him – and he merely hoped that I would make a prat of myself in front of some highly impressionable young people. More likely, I think it was just that Leslie recognized that something interesting was going on at HHCL.

Criticism

Because, while we didn't enjoy having criticism levelled at us, we liked the idea of being different. In fact, we felt that you had to be 'different' to survive, and thrive. So we adapted the phrase aimed at us and made it our credo to be 'different – for the sake of being better', and this applied to nearly all the processes of working at HHCL.

However, it's outside the orbit of this chapter to go into all our structures and processes (although, when I was giving the talk, people usually spent a lot of time asking about them). And it is also outside the orbit to discuss fully our agency's beliefs about total marketing, about getting outside the 'advertising box' to produce what we call '3D marketing' solutions. Because the briefs on the course were very clear in being 'advertising-only' projects.

That's realistic ... because quite often briefs are limited like this. But clearly, you can have a lot more fun if you allow yourself to think about all the media available to you, and attempt to solve a marketing problem by exploring all the marketing avenues there are. And, in passing, I would like to say that I hope the terms 'above-' and 'below-the-line' will soon be banished, as agencies face up to the fact that there are a whole range of new opportunities which must be taken for our clients – including amazingly sophisticated direct marketing-, PR- and IT-based solutions.

But enough of the waffle. The purpose of my talk was to pass on five thoughts which we used at HHCL to help our project teams create interesting, inspiring, and distinctive creative briefs when applied to 'advertising-only' projects.

The first suggestion

Find out what everybody else is doing in your marketplace. Then do something different.

When you approach a particular client's problems, take a long look at what the competition is doing. I ask our planners to form a mental picture of what the most typical communication looks like in that marketplace, and then write it down, so that we can all discuss it.

Limiting ourselves to TV advertising, we can all come up with 'typical' images in most markets – here are two current examples.

1 The car market. The received wisdom here seems to be that 'to shift metal, you've got to show metal', and as most cars increasingly come to resemble each other, so too do most car ads – the same low-angle shot of the tyre holding the road, the same three-quarter rear profile (which seems to flatter the common design of most modern cars), the same long and winding road, and probably an interior shot showing the steering wheel as if such an item were a unique luxury in modern cars. Product 'bunny', usually mentioning the ubiquitous 'ABS', is intoned by one of three or four favoured voiceovers. This is a crude overview – but whichever sector of the car market you're working in should throw up several more specific 'rules', which the advertisers feel they must adhere to ... or die.

2 The holiday market. Again, we could probably all write a typical holiday ad – open on a palm-fringed beach and then cut to various cultural clichés – golf course, bit of local archaeology, distant shot of a water-skier, romantic dinner for two, close-up on some scuba diver, and some garnished fish in a pan. Which country, or which company, is being advertised seems less important than everyone in the team getting a good tan. And that is why our work for Thomson Holidays appears so radical. Sure, we use appetite appeal where necessary, but we weren't afraid to launch the campaign in an anonymous British airport. Because what we were talking about – i.e. the question of whether to spend a bit more money to get a better holiday – was a relevant and provocative question.

The sort of questions you might like to ask yourself about your market are these:

- Does everybody do 'funny' ads?
- Does everybody do ads with music in them?
- Does everybody do ads that are deadly serious?
- Is there a typical consumer in the ads?
- Is there a typical way to describe or show the product?

Or (moving away from TV advertising)

- Why does everybody else use TV advertising, and is there another medium we can dominate and make uniquely ours?

For instance, a few years ago we achieved record sales for our client at the time, Mazda, by using interactive posters and press. While everybody else threw money at the TV companies, to create the clichés described above, Mazda went a different way – and, in a very depressed market, achieved a 40 per cent year-on-year sales increase (Figure 8.1). You have to find out the 'rules' – in order to break them. You have to find out what everybody else is doing – and do it differently.

Why should you do this? On a glib level, you're doing it because you're writing a 'creative brief' – and you should be creative. On a much more serious

Figure 8.1

level, you're doing it to grab the high ground for your client. To be competitive for your client. And to help your client to win.

Most briefs, in most agencies, simply describe the status quo. And that, by definition, is where everybody else is. At HHCL we describe the status quo as follows:

What is = what was.

Anita Roddick once said something similar. She described conventional research as being like a rear-view mirror. It told her where she'd been. It couldn't tell her where to go next.

So, find out how the marketplace is currently 'working'. Then grab the high ground for yourself, by breaking some rules. Not all the rules – at least not all the time. And picking the right rules to break is the key (and most adrenaline-pumping) challenge. But if you play to the rules that exist out there, you're playing on somebody else's pitch. You're automatically at a disadvantage.

Of course, breaking rules requires confidence. And confidence has been at something of a low ebb in the marketing industry recently. But you still have to do it.

If you need any more persuading, look at one very simple, but very frightening, statistic. It's recently been claimed that the average person in Britain is exposed to 1,300 commercial messages a day – from their wake-up breakfast radio station, through the logos on every carrier bag and T-shirt they encounter, to the last commercial on late-night TV before they've finally had enough and close their eyes for the day. And the same research claims that the average Briton remembers only two of these messages. Why should they remember more? A commercial message is asking you to spend money or change a habit. People by and large don't like doing either of these things.

The human brain can adapt to most changing environments – and it's adapted to today's highly commercial environment by learning how to screen out our messages. In research groups, people might say they *like* certain ads – a typically funny lager ad, or a celebrity endorsement which tickles them – but really getting through to people takes a lot more than this. People no longer just ignore advertising – they've learned how to 'pigeon-hole' our messages so that the brain absorbs, then ignores, our expensively produced efforts. You have to get under people's defences. And the best way to do this is to do something unexpected.

Of course, it still has to be palatable – you have to check that people want to come with you to this new place. But it can't be overemphasized how important it is that your message is distinctive. (For those of you who want to know the provenance of that alarming statistic, I'm afraid I can't help. I can only remember that I read it somewhere! But advertising can never be a scientific endeavour; you just know that what I'm saying makes sense. Don't you?)

As an addendum, beware of people who are 'brave in hindsight', by which I mean the kind of people who say things like 'Hey, I love that Tango work – let's do a Tango for our brand'. This sounds brave – but it's the opposite, because it's copying a formula that's out there, and the most it can expect to do is a percentage of what the original work did.

It's like in Hollywood (where the writer William Goldman said that the golden rule is that 'Nobody Knows Anything'). To counteract the fear involved in launching any new film, most executives will fall into the seductive trap of commissioning a sequel. ('Hey, that worked. Let's do it again.') But the money people in Hollywood finally figured out that sequels usually only gross (at tops) about 60 per cent of the original film. Number 3 in the sequence grosses 60 per cent of that, and so on. Of course, that still makes sequels attractive – but are you happy to create an effect in the marketplace that is just 60 per cent of what your competitor has already achieved? If you do, please leave the room and allow me to cry quietly for a moment.

Incidentally, I now know what to say to clients who ask us to do 'another Tango'. First, I tell them that they deserve something unique. And second, I take them through the process which Tony Hillyer (our original Britvic client) went through in buying (or rather co-creating, since his involvement was so crucial) the original work. He looked at a brand which was selling a million cans a day, and decided he could make a difference to this figure. (There's confidence for you.) Then he looked with us at the typical soft-drinks advertising of the time (which could be summed up in the visual image of boy meets girl on American street while sun shines and *fire hydrant goes off*) and decided to reject nearly all the rules therein. In other words, he decided to break the rules of the marketplace, and grab the high ground for his brand. Together, we created an advertising campaign that used street-credible, British humour for the first time in soft-drinks' advertising (Figure 8.2). We also tried

Figure 8.2

to avoid showing fire hydrants, wherever possible. We were rewarded by an increased sales figure of one-and-a-third million cans. A day.

The second suggestion

Forget the logical proposition. And find the personality of the brand instead.

There used to be something in advertising called the Unique Selling Proposition, which necessitated going down a list of the brand's qualities until you found something unique and then concentrating on that. This led to such advertising claims as 'Treats – they melt in your mouth, not in your hand'. Unfortunately, a lot of people in the business still believe in this approach. And it's a mistake. Which is not to say that it was always a mistake, because, despite the almost transcendent meaninglessness of the Treats claim, the USP was a useful approach at one time.

But those times have changed, because competitive insulation is now more or less dead. That's what we said when we launched our agency in 1987, and one of our very first clients was able to confirm this for us, with an amazing story.

Aiwa, the Japanese electronics company, invented DAT – Digital Audio Tape – and were copied within six hours. If they'd briefed us to tell people about the 'USP' of DAT, it would have been *unique* for less than a morning.

Lead times in the fashion industry, to take another example, are down to less than half-an-hour.

These days, if you invent a better mouse-trap, the world probably won't beat a path to your door. The chances are that someone like Alan Sugar will copy it, put it on the market at half-price, and the path to your door will remain woefully overgrown, like the 'before' half of a hedge-trimmer advertisement. If your client has a competitive advantage, it will be copied.

But this is a tricky area. Every time I said these words to my class of 4-year-olds, some of them would look worried. It feels comfortable to put in a logical proposition. It's something concrete to hang your hat on, or rest your case on. (There's a mixed metaphor for you!) It helps to make the whole business feel more objective and quasi-scientific (which is very reassuring, in a world of unknowns and unknowables).

Also, clients take pride in their product 'breakthroughs'. 'Aha', you can hear the brand manager exclaim, 'we've finally got chocolate that won't melt in your hand. Let's see those other companies copy *that*.' But if consumers want non-hand-melty chocolate, your competitors *will* copy it. I'm sorry, but they will.

Lots of people have coined their own versions of the USP. One very memorable expression of it was the phrase 'interrogating the product until it confessed to its strengths'. At one time I felt that this was a brilliant concept, but I believe that it is no longer as relevant as it once was. What consumers are really motivated by now is the personality of the brand.

At this point of the speech, I always used to ask my audience how they chose their company cars (assuming they were allowed that luxury and that latitude). I know how I chose my first one. I did my homework. I read the trade mags, and discovered that

Car X was faster 0–60.
Car Y was better on head-room.
Car Z was best on fuel economy.

But I soon got bored and confused with all this, and bought a Volkswagen Golf, the one with the red line round the radiator. Because that was the early 1980s, and that was a great yuppie car to have. The personality of the car was absolutely right for me (and other sad proto-pseudo-yuppies) at that time.

I believe that great car advertising has always realized this. Look at the brand personalities built by, at various times, Volkswagen, Volvo, and Audi or, even more relevantly, BMW. A fabulous campaign, which has been built on a whole host of logical propositions. But I would argue that what is really being sold in every BMW ad is the *personality of the brand* – in this case, a personality which cared passionately about every detail of its engineering.

For further proof, look at the distinct lack of logical propositions in some other brilliant campaigns. Look at clients as different as Oxo, Diesel Jeans and Pot Noodle, or the original work for First Direct.

First Direct was launched almost as you would launch a fashion label. The bank had no high street presence, and 'existed' only in terms of the perception created by its advertising. We created a personality that was quirky, provocative, individualistic – and appealed to our target market of 'early-adopters' in such a way that we attracted 100,000 accounts in our first year. This was the target set by First Direct's parent company, Midland Bank, and it seemed at the time an almost impossible target because we were dealing with a bank that had no high street branches, and we knew that only 300,000 people switched bank accounts each year. But we achieved that target – by creating a unique brand personality (Figure 8.3). And when the same clients turned up to launch a direct bank for the Prudential, we helped them create Egg – another unique brand personality.

banking without branches. it's extraordinary.

first direct
0800 22 2000

Figure 8.3

So that's what we look for in our creative briefs – a description of what we christened the Unique Selling Persona. (Actually, as a piece of neologism, this was a bit of a cock-up. By using the same initials as the Unique Selling Proposition, we made sure that our term wouldn't stand out as the strategic breakthrough it surely was. But never mind. These things happen ... At least it stopped the rest of the industry from catching on quite so quickly.)

So, if you follow this reasoning, you'll see that

The hops in the beer don't matter
The stitching on the T-shirt doesn't matter
The interest rates in the bank don't matter.

Of course, your client has to get those things right – that's the hygiene factor. And you can sprinkle a bit of logical argument over your concoction – but don't believe that a logical proposition is going to sell your product by itself. Put all the stuff about interest rates etc. in if you want to. But make it subservient to the personality of the brand. That's what you're really selling.

This seems to me so crucial that I think it constitutes a definition of what we are all doing in this industry. I believe we are in the business of creating distinctive, appropriate, impactful *tones of voice* for our clients – and each one has to be different for each brand we work on. That tone of voice can then be used across all the client's marketing communications – from the trade brochure through to their web-site. Another client we've worked with demonstrates this point further.

When we won the Martini account, we realized that they already had a very distinctive tone of voice – but that it was no longer deemed appropriate for modern drinkers. Searching for a logical proposition was never part of the

Figure 8.4

game. But by concentrating on their brand personality, we were able to understand the root of the problem. What we had to do was reframe their existing (and inescapable) tone of voice in a way that motivated a new generation.

We took their heritage – the drink of the 'beautiful people' – and put a modern twist on it. By saying that you had to be beautiful to drink Martini – and, moreover, by suggesting that most people would require cosmetic surgery to achieve the desired level of pulchritude – we effectively owned and mocked our property at the same time (Figure 8.4).

The marketing generated enormous amounts of PR – but what did it do for sales? At the time of the appointment, our client said that we would be performing a miracle if we slowed down the sales decrease which had been happening for the previous fifteen years. In fact, once the advertising began, sales increased 10 per cent. We all rubbed our eyes in disbelief when the figures first came in.

But, as I say, this *is* a tricky area. Increasingly, more and more agencies have understood the importance of a brand personality over a logical proposition (which means that I've got into fewer and fewer arguments with the 4-year-olds listening to me telling them this). As a result of this, I've started to think that maybe it's time to push the pendulum back again. Maybe we should revert to logical propositions – to be different.

Who knows? Everything I'm saying here will only be right for a small period of time, before the world turns again.

The third suggestion

Except possibly suggestion number three, which will always be true. *Define the 'target market' so that you like and respect them.*

David Ogilvy once said 'the consumer is not a moron. The consumer is your wife'. I'm going to ignore the inherent sexism in that remark, because I believe it was just a product of the time he was working in. The point is that this is a fabulous piece of advice – and one of the most crucial things for everybody in marketing to think about.

For a long time, the advertising industry has defined its 'target market' using ghastly, patronizing jargon, like

The consumer is a C2 housewife, living at home, with two kids.

or

The consumer is a young professional, age 25–30, living in a flat in London Docklands.

The point about both these descriptions is that you don't *like* the people involved. Even the small pen portraits sometimes offered up are no better – they're usually attempts to pigeon-hole and somehow belittle the people you're interested in communicating with. You cannot advertise to people you don't like and respect.

This seems such an obvious point, I'm amazed more people haven't clocked onto it. Think about your personal experience. If you're at a party, and you find yourself talking to someone you're not interested in, how effective are you at communicating with them?

Incidentally, I think this is one of the reasons why it is now so difficult to advertise to a large section of the population – a group of people you might call 'Middle England'. These people, usually middle-class, often women, are responsible for buying millions of pounds' worth of products every day. The advertising industry has patronized them for so long that they're not interested in having a conversation with us any more. Try to talk to them in research groups about moving the advertising on, and they're like bored partners who can't be bothered to talk over the cornflakes any more. Too many years of men in white coats talking down to them about meaningless 'secret' ingredients has rendered them so fed up with advertising, they don't think we're ever going to change. But we can change. And the key is to treat every sector of the marketplace with respect.

Incidentally, it's worth looking at the terminology we tend to use about the people we want to talk to. The phrase 'target market' is inherently hostile, aggressive. The term 'consumer' is more than a little derogatory – it's only one step up from the very insulting 'punter'.

At HHCL we try to use the word 'customer' as often as we can – as a term of respect. (But I must admit that old habits die hard, and I often find myself still using terms like 'target market' and 'consumer' because they're so well-recognized. But that's just because I'm lazy – and there's really no excuse for it …) The point is that this area constitutes probably the biggest mistake the advertising industry makes. By patronizing the people we want to talk to, we've created, in a large number of market sectors, a fundamental breakdown in communication.

Let's take another difficult market sector – business people. In traditional research (done one-on-one because they're all far too important to join any group!) they'll tell you that they like to be treated with respect and with a businesslike tone of voice. Hence the deadly boringness of most business-to-business advertising. But if you do sensitive research among business people, you find that – surprise, surprise – they have the same sense of humour as the rest of us

At HHCL we like to do media-based research with our audience. Because if you find out which TV programmes and films they like, and which newspapers and magazines they read, two things happen. First, you know the media to employ when you want to talk to them. Second, they become more human and more interesting. Personally, I also like to know which books they read, what music they prefer, and if there are any other cultural things they get into – because then I can rip those off for the creative execution. So find out what makes them laugh. What makes them cry. What they think about current affairs. The point I am making is to treat your customers – both clients and 'end-consumers' – with respect.

When I first got into the industry, one analogy was always being used about our profession. It was said that we were like lawyers, being paid to put the best case forward for our clients. But that's so defensive. It has the effect of making the client look like some poor, bent, second-hand car salesman, clasping his sweaty hands in the dock.

I prefer a different analogy for our business. It's like when you're giving a dinner party, and you want to introduce people to each other who've never met before. You find something which you know they both share an interest in – whether it be the music of Van Morrison, the short stories of Raymond Carver, or even (God help us) the difficulty of finding a good school for the kids. And once you find that topic, you can leave them to get on with it, knowing that there's a good chance that they'll get on.

Incidentally – this may sound like an argument for precision targeting and up to a point, it is. But I would also like to say that I agree with Jeremy Bulmore's argument that, for an ambitious brand, being overheard is always good – that there is much less 'wastage' than people may suppose in using mass media.

But I am straying from the point, so let's move on to the fourth suggestion.

The fourth suggestion

Put in creative starters, i.e. write your own creative ideas to your own creative brief. It only needs to be a sentence or two for each idea to describe how your strategy might look in its final medium. Limit yourself to about seven creative starters at the most. Some people at HHCL get a bit carried away at this point and write up thirty creative starters. But that's just showing off. Doing this is a good test of how interesting and actionable your strategy is. It's also a good test of how collaborative your creative team is, because a lot of them will reject anybody else's ideas – and I think that's stupid.

It can't be overemphasized, throughout this process, how important it is to be collaborative with your client and with the rest of your agency team. Try not to be too possessive about your role in the process – and encourage other people not to be too possessive about their roles either.

To give you one example from HHCL. It was actually an art director who came up with the final wording of the strategic breakthrough on the AA, rechristening them 'the fourth Emergency Service'. In this instance, the planner was able to enjoy the traditional creative director's role – saying 'that sounds great, let's do it' and then enjoying a lot of reflected kudos. In this case the reflected kudos consisted of a client enjoying record levels of recruitment because they were brave enough to go with such a bold repositioning. Membership levels rose from 7 million to just on 9.5 million four years later.

This is a great strategic idea – and it could have come from anyone in the team. Similarly, with creative ideas. If you're creative enough to write a brief, you're creative enough to write creative ideas, and that plethora of the word 'creative' in this sentence says something itself. Everybody in this industry is 'creative'; we really need a new word to describe the people who are charged with coming up with proposed conceptions and then executing them. Any suggestions, gratefully received.

But meanwhile, onto suggestion number five. The final suggestion.

The fifth suggestion

Make it inspiring. Make your brief inspiring. Believe in the power of the brief, which is to address fundamentally important business issues in a creative, innovative way. What I *don't* mean is this – don't shove in loads of jokes, or write it in some 'funny' dialect. Don't try to disguise a boring piece of thinking by dressing it up in funky clothes. (Incidentally, I would also beware of too many diagrams. Sometimes they're incredibly valuable and insightful, but more often they're just a way of jazzing up the obvious. Planners as a breed seem to have an undue fondness for some of the geometrical shapes available on the Powerpoint program. I don't know how many other writers in this book have had recourse to this method of communication, so I hope this doesn't come across as a cheap dig).

Don't make your enthusiasm shallow. I recently saw a brief from another agency which included, as its proposition, the line 'PHWOOOARR, they don't half taste good'. It looks enthusiastic, but actually it's just very poor camouflage for the most boring proposition there ever was.

Derive your energy from the challenge of making your thinking fresh. If (following suggestion number one) you can show the creative team how to break the rules – and which rules you can break – they'll love you for it. That's what good creatives want to do, not out of some unreconstructed infantile desire to break things in general (at least, hopefully not) but because they instinctively know that that is how you get through to people.

Be ambitious. Be confident. Believe that you can really change the marketplace. Hopefully, your clients will also share your enthusiasm. The best ones will – and they're the ones you should be working with, if you're bright enough to buy the very important, nay seminal, piece of work you've got in your hands right now!

Let me summarize some of the things I've said in this chapter.

1 Find out what everybody else is doing in your marketplace – and decide how you are going to do it differently.
2 Don't look for logical propositions – look for and describe a brand personality.
3 Describe the 'target market' in non-patronizing ways, so that you like and respect them.
4 Put in creative starters – to demonstrate how actionable your brief is.
5 Make the brief inspiring – by making your thinking fresh and unexpected.

That's probably the most important point of all. If I wanted to sum up everything I wanted to say in one sentence, it would be contained in point five. Another way of expressing point five is to say this:

Write the brief with the intention of changing the world.

Overview: Chapter 9

If you haven't seen Richard Hytner present in person, you've missed a good show from a great professional.

Richard's experience of running people businesses qualifies him well to speak (and write) on the subject of managing personal relationships and he does so with verve and enthusiasm.

In this chapter, he strips away the pomposity of some advertising agency management styles – and sets out in their place some practical tips as to how employers and employees can construct a positive and cooperative approach that is every bit as effective as the traditional 'command and control' structures.

Richard's style is disarmingly modest, but that should not obscure the value of the learning to be gained from this most accomplished of agency managers.

This chapter first saw the light of day in May 1998 as a presentation on the IPA Stage 4 course: Excellent Account Direction.

Chapter 9

Getting the best out of people in advertising

Richard Hytner

Introduction

The following chapter is different from all others in this book: it is riddled with personal prejudice; it is a data-free zone; and at least half the bosses running today's leading advertising agencies may dismiss it as fluffy nonsense (there is statistically no substantiation for this claim but I know there are detractors out there – typically male, Western, autocratic).

Its central argument is that you can only get the best out of the people for whom you are responsible if you understand yourself and the effect of your behaviour on them. This applies to all businesses (and extends far beyond) but my attempt is to dramatize why I believe it to be particularly important for those in a leadership role in advertising. If your understanding is not just confined to yourself but also embraces the aspirations of your agency and its (note, not *your*) clients, you stand a good chance of getting the best out of the team you lead.

A few personal prejudices

To dispense with some personal prejudices...

■ Despite doomed attempts to prove the contrary, agencies and clients badly need account directors. Not simply in the stereotypical sense to resolve the differing ambitions of prescriptive clients and truculent creatives but, more importantly, to set a context and a tone for every interaction between client and agency.

- Clients do not wish to be 'handled'. Precious cargo is handled, as are dogs. Clients are human.
- Creatives operate in a world of commerce and are remunerated accordingly. They should not be indulged. They deserve respect, of course, if they have the talent to create ideas of sustainable value to clients' brands. But they should be valued and nurtured like all other agency talent. No more, no less. Treat people with kid gloves and they'll behave like kids. The very best creatives with whom I've had the privilege to work want no special favours – simply the opportunity to do their job brilliantly. This usually demands an inspired piece of thinking on which both client and agency agree and a constructive business relationship with the client born of mutual respect in which a great idea can be developed.
- Account direction is about leadership. It is a journey not a stopping-off point. Irrespective of what fancy titles appear on your business cards, you never stop being an account director.
- There is no one proven model for successful leadership in advertising. Account direction allows you the chance to develop, refine and practise your own model until you leave the business.
- Clients appoint agencies to access the combined talents of a mixed discipline team. Phrases like 'my client' or 'my account' should trigger a Yellow Card for a first offence and a Red Card for persistent repetition.

The Brits are made of sterner stuff

Psychometric testing and other techniques to enhance self-awareness are easy to dismiss as a bit of self-indulgence. Particularly by the healthily sceptical British. It's the stuff of shrinks and, as such, not really for us. The net result is that we are, within the context of our professional lives at least, hopeless at understanding ourselves and, therefore, every bit as hopeless at understanding the effect of our behaviour on others.

We hire people in our industry on the basis of two or three 45-minute interviews; we construct teams on client business without ever consciously

Figure 9.1

assessing the different personalities of the team members and their cumulative effect; and the most feedback we get is invariably when we're in receipt of a P45 ('things haven't worked out') or a car parking space ('you could go all the way'). Those who ask for feedback are seen to be insecure and inappropriate for the cut and thrust of account direction. To test this hypothesis, I asked the delegates on IPA Stage 4 four simple questions:

- **Question 1:** How many of you have concrete measurable objectives for the next 90 days agreed with your line manager?
- **Question 2:** How many of you have had a formal appraisal in the last six months?
- **Question 3:** How many of you, until this course, have had any kind of personality profiling or psychometric testing?
- **Question 4:** How many of you know how your career is to be developed, say, over the next two years and have an active development programme agreed with your company?

The poor show of hands confirmed that few had experienced that which in our client companies would be seen as routine entitlement.

Rather than wait for yet another training initiative to be taken by yet another management team, here are a few practical tips that are guaranteed to give you the clarity you deserve:

Practical Tip No. 1: Write your own measurable objectives, book a meeting with your boss and agree them. At that meeting, book a follow-up in 90 days to talk through what you achieved. Politely request to see their objectives.

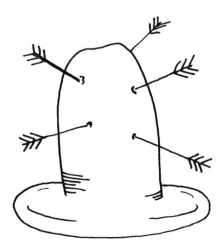

Figure 9.2

Practical Tip No. 2: Get your boss to spend no more than 30 minutes, answering the following three questions:

1 What behaviour would you like me to stop?
2 What behaviour would you like me to continue?
3 What behaviour would you like me to start?

Then ask them if they would value your answers to the same three questions. Some of the giggling by the Stage 4 delegates implied a potential difficulty in approaching this question with their bosses. Just try it. A boss who shows no interest is a boss not worth having.

Practical Tip No. 3: Take responsibility for your own development. Put simply, it is unwise to leave your career wholly in the hands of an advertising executive, who, in assessing your future potential, is as likely to be influenced by a casual remark made by a client than to form their own opinion.

You will get the most out of your agency if you get the most out of you and, importantly, if you own the responsibility for getting the most out of you.

Know thine agency

Getting the most out of your agency doesn't just rely, however, on knowing thyself. It also relies on knowing thine agency.

Like it or not, with a few honourable exceptions, advertising agencies are hopelessly lacking in perceived differentiation. Spontaneous awareness of agencies amongst the client community is remarkably low. They are either big or small, domestic or international, creatively-driven or client-driven. Despite this (or principally because of it), the real source of distinction lies in the 'softer' value system enshrined by the people running the agency and perpetuated by the people choosing to work for the agency. Only when you are clear about the values that pertain to your particular agency can you be held accountable for directing the agency's resources in pursuit of the agency's intent.

Practical Tip No. 4: Ask your agency management the following question: 'If our agency didn't exist tomorrow, what would the world be missing?'

This might get you (and probably them) to a closer understanding of what it is your agency is actually trying to achieve.

It may, for example, be committed to the single-minded pursuit of more D&AD yellow pencils for its reception. Alternatively, it may want to double in size to break into the UK Top Ten. In either case, the rules of engagement for an account director become clear. Life, of course, is not that simple and most agency leaders will expect you to resolve some of the contradictions inherent in achieving more than one goal.

Your agency's clients

In any event, you will better serve your agency if you fully understand your agency's clients. Others more qualified than I offer guidance in this book on how best to get to grips with clients' businesses. Suffice to say, you will doubtless have noticed how saturated are their markets; how the IT revolution is transforming their channels of distribution and their operations; and how their competitive sets are being redefined for them by both region and category.

Figure 9.3

There is an abundance of published data (take my word for it, I promised a data-free zone) which demonstrates that, against this backdrop, our clients want value for money, creativity and strategic guidance (in that order) and that none of us should envy the position in which clients find themselves.

Some post-recession research by management consultants, Coopers & Lybrand, predicted the current gloom for marketing:

The marketing department is critically ill. When any business catches a cold, the marketing department catches pneumonia.

A more recent study by Synesis was undertaken to explore how marketing was perceived by other key functions in a business. According to those in IT, Logistics, HR, Finance, and Sales, marketeers are 'flashy, unrealistic, financially naive, emotionally volatile and poor at communicating internally'.

They are *our* clients! Little wonder that they need help from their agencies and that, against their key requirements, they feel that they are being short-changed.

According to a study by Harris Research into the images and reputations of the top 25 agencies, there is dramatic room for improvement from all agencies on all dimensions from creativity to value for money, from client service to business understanding. Even the top six agencies are performing well below that which the market is demanding.

Practical Tip No. 5: You can only get the best out of your agency if you constantly focus the agency team on the client need. Focus on the context in which your client colleagues are operating and on the company's real business problem or challenge.

One tip you should not ignore

By now I hope you will have gleaned why the functional tasks of an account director are certainly the least valuable part of the job. One way to focus your mind on the essential part of the job is to ask yourself the following question:

Practical Tip No. 6 (and certainly the one you'll remember): What will trigger my next pay rise? And how can I double my current salary as quickly as possible?

Figure 9.4

Will it be by being the peerless administrator or the quickest issuer of call reports known to man? Doubtful. Will it be by writing your boss's presentations and showing them how to use Powerpoint? More likely, but still a long shot. Or will it be by solving a client's business problem using the talent of the agency to create an idea which builds sales, generates revenue and increases profitability? Still no guarantees because a good idea has many fathers (and, being a good account director, you won't claim any paternity rights). But after you develop a bit of a track record, the odds against a salary hike should shorten considerably.

In all seriousness, why would an agency, commercial ventures as they are, despite appearances to the contrary, pay an account director more than a head teacher responsible for 600 children at the pinnacle of their career? To persuade creative teams that a particularly unrewarding client brief merits their attention or to let them down gently after a withering research debrief on their work? To jolly clients along when the tracking study demonstrates a campaign is underperforming, as if a lunch could possibly pull the wool over their eyes? The only justification for an account director's handsome reward is the delivery of an outstanding performance from the teams which they lead.

Alternative models for getting the best out of people in advertising

And so to my 'alternative models for getting the best out of people in advertising'. Please do not take my own preferred, somewhat pious, model as gospel or my condemnation of others' models as a reason not to test or apply them for yourself. What works for Alex Ferguson may not for Arsène Wenger. The models are the result of almost invasive observation of others but legal training has encouraged me to disguise the real characters on whom the models are drawn. I hope nevertheless you can identify an exponent of each approach from within your own agency.

The tyrant

You will know if Rule by Fear is a model given credence within your agency: grown up men and women stand up to take a telephone call from their chairman or chief executive. The words 'yes' and 'I agree' are used liberally when 'no' and 'I disagree' seem a more obvious answer. A sudden exuberance breaks out in the corridors when it becomes known that the tyrant has gone on holiday. But the tyrannical behaviour passes down the line and is mimicked by the ambitious account director. There are advantages to cultures which rely on fear: there tends to be a clarity of purpose; meetings are kept short; and phones

Figure 9.5

get answered. You can certainly build a viable business this way. Sustaining it, however, might prove more troublesome because, in my view, the ultimate sanction – 'you're fired' – holds no fear for good people.

The reluctant go-between

Hallmarks you might recognize include the oft repeated remarks to creatives, 'I totally agree, but the client wouldn't have it', and to clients, 'I totally agree but the creatives wouldn't have it'. The account director who avoids conflict of any kind, is nice to everybody and who sits on the fence may win the popularity prize but is really no use to anyone. It is the account director's responsibility to create an environment in which constructive conflict is encouraged, valued and allowed to flourish. A significant pitch during 1998 which we did not win acts as a permanent if painful reminder to me on this key dimension of an account director's job. The night before the final presentation, we had two campaigns on the table. One which large numbers of people had painstakingly developed over an eight–week period, the other a very late entrant from one very talented individual. The former had been shared with

Figure 9.6

the client, and with some caveats had got some encouragement. The latter was higher risk but, in my view, was also a more surprising and creative campaign. By presenting both campaigns, we offended nobody in the agency but also showed the client no firm resolve. Did this mistake cost us the pitch? Probably not. Do I still feel bad about this limp-wristed leadership? Yes.

The in-house client

Playing the role of client within the agency has been for years a workable strategy for many an account director. The evangelists have tended to be those charged with international responsibilities. You can spot them an air mile away. They fuel the client's natural suspicion that, but for their account director, the agency would sell them down the river, thus securing their own tenure on the

Figure 9.7

account. When the client says 'Jump', the account director asks 'How high?'; When the creative director says, 'Jump', the account director says, 'My client hasn't asked me to'. A first-class strategy for improving your golf handicap but not so effective for inspiring others. Certainly after the fourth great campaign idea gets sacrificed to reinforce the account director's conspiracy of mediocrity with the client, no creative team worth their pencil will ever take a brief from you again. And clients do move on.

The best job you can do for your agency is to increase the client's dependency (by legal means) on the agency. Encouraging reliance on you individually is a cheap and unworthy pursuit.

The arch manipulator

Exponents of this highly skilled technique are not so easy to identify. Search for those who do not give each of their team members the same set of facts. They

Figure 9.8

are somewhat sparing in their dispensation of the truth. We had an account director who returned from a creative presentation informing us that the client had insisted we use an alternative endline of the client's invention. Never averse to ideas from clients, we caught the culprit when we discussed with the client 'his' idea, only to discover it was the account director's own recommendation. We gave him ten out of ten for thinking creatively and a telling off for his duplicity. If you believe manipulation is an attractive option, perfect the technique by breaking the odd promise. Create a few wholly unnecessary problems which you can then very loudly and publicly solve. It can certainly work for those whose bosses are too naive to spot it or too lazy to do anything about it, but it might lead you into hazardous waters if those being manipulated rumble the tactic and don't take kindly to it.

The e-mailer

Here I commend you *The Corporate Infighter's Handbook* (Davis, 1984) and the chapter on the inter-office memo. Presumably it will be updated to reflect the even greater significance of the e-mail. I quote:

> The memorandum is one of the most useful weapons in the corporate infighter's armoury. Newcomers to the battlefront tend to assume, naively, that the main function of memos is to pass on information and assignments. This, of course, is nonsense. They are sent for a wide range of other reasons.

It goes on to document other uses for the memo, all of which pertain to the e-mail: the account director quick on the e-mail is using it as a substitute for action, as a means of self-protection, as a tool for self-promotion and, indeed, as a weapon against rivals. All useful, if somewhat cowardly. Just by way of example, creatives and others in the team would prefer to hear news first hand, however unpalatable.

Figure 9.9

You will have gathered by now that I am not recommending any one model thus far described, though to the more sophisticated operators, there are times when fear is entirely appropriate (my good friend and former Chairman at Lintas, Anthony Simonds-Gooding, taught me that fear and vision were the only management tools at one's disposal. The skill is knowing which to dispense, when and to whom); there are times when it is healthy to win the hearts of one's team members; times, too, to represent firmly the client's agenda within the agency. To be clear, however, in my view, the arch manipulator has nothing to commend them (fibbing is not a legitimate management technique) and e-mails and memos have little value in creating vibrant relationships.

One final model, I hope, is worthy of your consideration, though it is offered tentatively. To some it will be deemed sanctimonious. To others it will hold no surprises.

The respected and self-respecting account director

Most self-respecting professionals value the respect of others. For an account director, generating respect is a tall order. It involves:

Knowing the client's business

Seemingly a statement of the blindingly obvious but often ignored. So much of the account director's ability to influence rests on the trust they are able to engender. Why would a client trust an account director and act on their advice if it is apparently without foundation? The account director (not the planner, in my view) should be expert in the client's business – its objectives, its drivers, its category and its performance – historical and current.

You don't need an MBA to be an outstanding account director. But you will never be an outstanding account director without an intellectual curiosity for the client's business and an enthusiasm to identify how communications can help. I have seen the most sceptical, even antagonistic, client rendered mute with admiration by an account director's obvious, detailed grasp of that client's competitors.

Having an opinion

No comment, no account director. More than anybody else in the agency, you must listen. Only the arrogant do not. But when everybody else has voiced their view (in a climate which you have created to encourage the open airing of conflicting views), you must offer your own, however uncomfortable that is. You go to a doctor with a problem. He asks you to describe the symptoms. He probes, he listens – intently – he thinks, he asks some more questions, he pauses and he says, 'Well, what do you think?' Never. He comes up with a theory which either merits immediate treatment or more rigorous testing. He will, however, have a view.

Adapting to change

Much hot air has been generated by advertising agencies over the great integrated debate. 'Are we an advertising agency or a communications consultancy?' is a question that's fuelled many a management away-day. Suffice to say, in my view, no self-respecting and respected account director can limit their sphere of influence to the conventional channels by which a client is able to reach their consumers. Agencies do not have to be able to implement ideas in all media. But account directors should whet the agency's appetite to explore new territory and to adapt to the changing communications landscape. It's simply impossible to have an informed opinion about a client's business – its competitive set, its distribution, its potential – without first-hand experience of buying something on the internet or subscribing to digital interactive television. Creatives may harbour a reluctance to get involved, fearing their advertising craft skills may not transfer (they do, of course), but for an account director not to master their new brief is gutless.

Accepting responsibility

Take ownership of the problem – be it the client's business problem or the problem of resolving a debate between the client and agency or between agency team members. Never let the client resolve a conflict that you should have resolved back at the agency. A crass example: If you think the logo should be bigger, don't leave it to the client to demand the increase in point size. A more common example: if the proposition in the client brief does not appear to address the client's business objectives, have the debate at the outset. Leaving it to the creative work for a resolution will cause frustration internally as well as with the client.

Being an energy source, not an energy drain

In ASDA's words, a Zapper not a Sapper. There is nothing more demotivating to a team than its leader spreading doom and gloom: 'It looks like we're going to lose the business'; 'The client's sales are dreadful, they'll have to cut the budget'; 'We haven't won much new business recently'; 'You've no idea how many people have got their CVs out at the moment'. Weather reporting feeds the insecurities of others and reduces people's desire and ability to perform. It should be a fireable offence for an account director. (An additional dimension to this is that once you're an account director, don't expect anybody else to energize you. Accept responsibility for replenishing your own energy supplies.)

Using your EQ not your IQ

Daniel Goleman's book, *Emotional Intelligence* (1996), argues that our emotions do (and should) play a far greater role in decision-making and team performance:

> Whenever people come together to collaborate, there is a very real sense in which they have a group IQ, the sum total of the talents and skills of all those involved. And how well they accomplish their task will be determined by how high that IQ is. The single most important element in group intelligence, it turns out, is not the average IQ in the academic sense, but rather in terms of emotional intelligence.

He quotes a psychologist at Harvard Business School:

> The jungle fighter symbolizes where the corporation has been; the virtuoso in interpersonal skills is the corporate future.

For all their strategic insight, their detailed knowledge of the client business and their grip on the changing world of communications, account directors will really add value if they develop and draw on their emotional intelligence. Agencies are full of brilliant, driven, ambitious individuals. They are, at times, selfish, egotistical, insecure, unpredictable. The account director's core competence should be an ability not to lead by domination but to lead by emotional savvy.

Conclusion

It has often been said that the job of an account director is the worst in an advertising agency. Defined functionally, one has to concur – the dull fodder of administration, the tight deadlines, the financial accountability without necessarily the full responsibility. The job is only worth doing (and then it really is worth doing) if the role is extended to that of leadership. This involves providing vision to the team of people you are charged to lead – whither the client's business, how can communications help – and providing energy and an operating environment in which all disciplines within the agency (and with the client) can flourish.

A long, hard look at yourself, particularly in relation to others, is as good a place as any to start perfecting your own leadership model.

Which brings me to the final tip.

Practical Tip No. 7: For your next appraisal, preferably self-appraisal, ask yourself and your colleagues the following questions, then document an exhaustive set of responses. The answers may surprise you.

To do your job brilliantly:

Who should you interact with?
What does each expect of you?
How can you help each of them?
What do you expect of each?
How can each of them help you?
What do you need from the agency in support?

In the view of Peter Drucker (1988), one of the greatest contributors to thinking on management and leadership, it is simply not enough to have a 'talent for people' or to trade in warm feelings and pleasant words. The key in a work-focused and task-focused relationship is to concentrate on performance and achievement. It is the prime responsibility of the account director to extract from the team, individually and collectively, the best possible performance. An understanding of one's own contribution and one's behaviour relative to others is one of the best tools you have. Use your 'emotional intelligence' sensitively and often. It is far more useful than some of the less legitimate and less effective methods all too prevalent in today's advertising agency industry.

References

Davis, W. (1984), *The Corporate Infighter's Handbook*, Sidgewick & Jackson.
Drucker, P. (1988), *Management*, Butterworth-Heinemann: Oxford
Goleman, D. (1996), *Emotional Intelligence*, Bloomsbury Publishing: London.

Overview: Chapter 10

Andy Tilley is one of the 'big thinkers' in the world of media. He and his colleagues at Unity came from one of the finest full-service agency backgrounds: BMP DDB. Perhaps this is what gives Andy the breadth of perspective and depth of insight that sets his thinking apart from so many of the 'commodity' attitudes prevalent in this area.

This chapter illustrates that intelligence perfectly. Andy looks at the macro issues, rather than the more familiar buying skills, and gives us a rich picture of one of the most dynamic parts of the advertising industry.

This chapter was originally presented on the IPA's Stage 4 course – Excellent Account Direction – in 1998.

Chapter 10

The strategic importance of media

Andy Tilley

Introduction

This chapter started life as a presentation on IPA 4. The purpose of the presentation was to provide a media perspective on strategy development for a group of account directors and account planners from some of London's top agencies. As a result the content focused on the relationship between media and account planning, identifying a strategic role for media in the communication process. This will be continued here.

This is also very much a personal view, and like much in advertising and marketing it is but one route to a solution. Nevertheless, there is a central thread to the chapter and it is this: that we need to move media planning more centre-stage in the communications process if we are to make the step change in effectiveness that is now possible in a changed media landscape.

Media's changing role

In Monty Python's *Life of Brian* there is a memorable scene featuring the late, great, Graham Chapman ('He's not the Messiah, he's a very naughty boy!') and the streetwise, stall-holding Eric Idle. In an attempt to disguise himself from the pursuing Roman soldiers, Chapman tries to buy a beard – I know this loses much in the telling but it is Monty Python – and ends up with a lesson in haggling. At the completion of the deal, as Chapman exits clutching a particularly gaudy, orange, ill-fitting specimen, a very satisfied Eric Idle concludes, 'Ah well, there's one born every minute'.

Haggling over price, and avoiding 'being had' by armies of media-owning Eric Idles, has been the popular view of 'what media does' until relatively recently. And whilst this function is still important it is but one part of the overall role of the media professional in today's communication industry. In fact, in less than two decades the role of media strategy has changed dramatically, due largely to the increasing dynamism of the media landscape, and a desire amongst clients to improve the effectiveness of their media investment against an increasingly over-choiced and indifferent public.

In the last year alone, some of the UK's largest advertisers, including Procter & Gamble, BT and Unilever, have taken the decision to put media at the heart of their communications strategy.

So how can media contribute to strategy development? And how can it help to improve both the relevance and effectiveness of communication?

The purpose of this chapter is to consider these issues and to examine in more detail the ways in which we might achieve such ambitions. After all, the business of media strategy is really very simple. At its heart lie four basic questions: who are we trying to reach, and how, when, and where should we reach them? It is just that these four questions have become so much more difficult to answer comprehensively, as the media landscape has evolved.

The changing media landscape

In order to understand why there is a real need for media strategy to contribute to the development of the overall communication strategy, we need to pause for a moment, survey the media landscape, and take stock of the media now available to the consumer (see Figure 10.1).

Up until November 1982 there was only one commercial TV channel available in the UK and that was ITV. It had commercial exclusivity for just

	1982	1999
Commercial TV stations	1 ⟶	100+
Commercial radio stations	28 ⟶	200+
Consumer magazines	1,300 ⟶	2,600+
Business magazines	2,000 ⟶	5,400+
National daily and Sunday papers	21 ⟶	21

Figure 10.1 Big changes in the media world

over 27 years; it was available for roughly twelve hours a day and closed down around midnight. At the same time there were 28 commercial radio stations broadcasting locally across the UK, some 1,300 consumer magazines, around 2,000 business magazines and 21 national daily and Sunday newspapers.

By the beginning of 1999 the picture had changed somewhat, with over 100 commercial TV channels available to the consumer, many broadcasting for 24 hours a day. Both analogue and digital satellite and cable, together with digital terrestrial television, have launched in the last six months and look set to push the choice even higher across a much larger cross-section of the population.

The number of commercial radio stations has grown to over 200, offering a range of formats from speech to sport, from golden oldies to garage, on both FM and AM on a local, regional or national basis.

Consumer and business magazines have more than doubled in number, with births, deaths and marriages in the sector making it one of the most dynamic in the UK. Overall, circulation has grown with many of the newer arrivals, particularly in the men's and women's magazine sectors, gaining ground at the expense of the older, more generalist weekly publications.

The national daily and Sunday newspaper market has seen a number of launches and closures since 1982 and yet by the beginning of 1999 the number of titles available was the same as in 1982. *Today, News on Sunday,* and the *Sunday Correspondent,* all came and went, and in the last few months the *Sporting Life* finally closed. However, it has proved to be a highly competitive sector and despite the proliferation of price cuts, supplements, extra sections, magazines, band-ons, wrap-arounds and so forth, catering for a wealth of consumer interests and family needs, circulation decline has become the norm rather than the exception.

Cinema audiences, although way below their golden years prior to the widespread growth of television, have shown significant growth in recent years, and outdoor, whilst a little harder to measure, has continued to benefit from the increasing mobility of consumers. As the number of cars within the population has grown dramatically over the last ten years, the average speed within most city centres has fallen, providing far greater visibility for the medium.

Add to these more conventional offerings, the dramatic growth of new media, particularly the internet, the host of other screen-based activities, the arrival of ambient media, including everything from shopping trolleys and floor tiles to take-away lids and petrol pump ads, and you have a bewilderment of opportunities battling for consumer attention.

Understanding the consumer viewpoint

As a result of the dramatic expansion of media choice, the consumer–media relationship – the way in which consumers choose and use the media and their attitudes to it – has also changed.

At its most basic, with increased choice, the portfolio of media that an individual experiences – their 'Personal Media Network' – is far greater than it was in 1982. At the same time, the time available to actively consume media, whether that is reading, listening to radio, or watching TV, has fallen. Leisure time has not increased as was forecast in the mid-eighties, which has made us a nation of experience-hungry and time-poor individuals.

As a result, consumers, now armed with an increasing array of technology and information, actively edit their own media environment. Gone are the days when the TV set stayed tuned to the same channel, all night, every night. The remote control, and to a lesser extent the VCR and the growth of multi-set households, have made the creation of the 'personal schedule' an everyday occurrence. And this is something that will soon be made broader as well as easier, via the Electronic Programme Guide (EPG) and the advent of digital services. Push-button and search/seek tuning on radios, particularly in cars, has made the radio listener more promiscuous in station choice, and the sectionalization of newspapers and specialist focus of magazines has made the selective consumption of print both easier and more commonplace.

One outcome of these behavioural shifts is that, in general, audiences across most media have fragmented. And whilst audiences to commercial television in total have grown – largely due to the penetration of satellite and cable – the share of audience by channel has fallen. The same dynamic can be seen in other markets, and across most media, with particular editorial environments, irrespective of whether they are broadcast or print, attracting individuals with particular interests, needs or beliefs.

And here lies the opportunity. The concentration of like-minded individuals should allow us to segment our audiences far more accurately: to reach individuals that have a unity of belief or a unity of behaviour irrespective of the size of that audience. If we can create relevant content for such groups then there should be a trade-off between a large, indifferent audience and a smaller, more interested one. We need to stop thinking about headcount and start thinking about effectiveness, and central to this is the need to define brand audiences in a more relevant and meaningful way, rather than be shackled by the safety of simple demographics. And if we were to apply this principle across media then we might well be getting somewhere.

However, what we need to consider in this regard is the reality of production costs. The creation of a variety of different advertising executions to suit the environments in which they are placed will almost certainly improve both relevance and cut-through. However, whilst this may be feasible in certain cases – print for example – the cost of producing a range of television or cinema executions is a different matter. And whilst this may change in the future with the application of digital technology and computer-based origination, at present it requires a value judgement about increased investment in this area against the potential return from improved communication.

If we are to improve both the interest and involvement of consumers in commercial communication, then we need to ensure that whatever we create is of greater relevance to them. To achieve this we need to add to our understanding of the ways in which consumers choose and use their media. We need to put more effort, time and resources into building greater understanding of the attitudes, needs and beliefs of consumers and how they relate to the media they consume. We need to examine more closely the mood and mind-set that different consumers experience with different media at different moments. Only armed with a better understanding of this relationship can we hope to break through the wall of indifference to commercial messages that exists amongst consumers.

These more qualitative elements are inextricably linked to what consumers see, hear and experience all the time. Their trust, enjoyment, interests and desires are influenced, challenged, reinforced and satisfied on a day-to-day basis by the media around them. And if we are to make the most of the new media environment for commercial communication, then we need to understand and exploit this understanding more fully.

So how do we do it?

Changing the way we work

Despite the increased complexity of the media landscape and the subsequent shifts in consumers' media behaviour, the changes that brought us to where we are today have been more evolutionary than revolutionary. As a result we seem to be showing more and more symptoms of what has been termed 'Dead Frog Syndrome'. Let me try to enlighten you.

If you drop a frog into a pot of boiling water it is likely that it will leap out and save its skin. But if you put a frog into a pot of lukewarm water and gradually turn up the heat to boiling point, the frog will not realize what is being done until it is too late. Result: a dead frog!

The problem the communications industry faces is that over the last two decades the temperature in our particular pot has been rising. The consumer–media relationship has evolved beyond all recognition, and yet the way in which we develop communication strategy, and in particular advertising strategy, has remained much the same since the early eighties. Unless we are prepared to recognize this dynamic, change the way we work, and use consumer–media understanding much earlier in the process, then Dead Frog Syndrome will reach epidemic proportions!

In my view what we need to do is foster a closer working relationship between account planners and media planners and create a true strategic centre. As the overlap in the tasks undertaken by the two disciplines has grown over time, each needs to work more closely with the other. This has nothing whatsoever to do with agency geography, and everything to do with a working philosophy. In fact, so important is this working relationship that we must ensure that the disciplines don't grow apart. Both look at different sides of the strategic development process and yet pursue a single outcome – a meaningful communication strategy.

What we need is a fresh approach to strategy development: one that makes the most of the skills and data available and encourages specialist input, cross-discipline teamwork and complementarity.

Diamonds are forever (the sequel)

Leslie Butterfield, in his chapter on strategy development in the first edition of this book, characterized the framework for strategic analysis as a diamond. The sequence he described and the actions taken at each stage, with suitable amendments, provides an excellent framework for the media role in strategy development and its relationship with other disciplines, particularly account planning (see Figure 10.2).

Butterfield's diamond shape, as a framework for strategic analysis, was quite deliberate. The vertical dimension approximates to the sequence of steps involved in the process from top to bottom. The horizontal dimension, the width of the diamond at various points, represents the breadth of consideration, analysis and research implicit in those steps. It does, as described above, start and finish as a point. But it does also cast the net wide towards the middle of the process. It moves from the specific to the general and then back to the specific again.

Much of the remainder of this chapter will be given over to exploration of the sequence outlined in this framework, the requirements of the media planner at each stage and the opportunities for cooperation and collaboration.

First steps

Up until a few years ago I was the proud owner of a very crumpled England's Glory matchbox. On the back of this matchbox was one of those wonderful thought-provoking one-liners: 'The art of good conversation is to know something about everything and everything about something.' And for me the art of good media planning is exactly the same.

Despite some views to the contrary, I firmly believe that it is essential for the media planner to know the 'something about everything' – the answers to some of the 'big' questions – in order to frame their approach (see Chapters 4

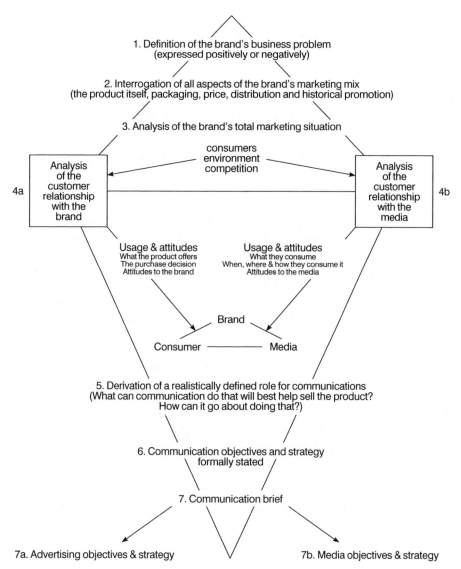

Figure 10.2

and 5 for a more in-depth analysis). Otherwise how on earth can they hope to make a meaningful contribution if they are working in a strategic vacuum? At the same time as understanding the bigger picture they also need to know the 'everything about something' – that being media planning and buying.

So let's start with the bigger picture and some of the bigger questions. Here are a few worthy of consideration:

- What is the client's business problem?
- How did the brand, product or service come to be in the situation it is today?
- Where could the brand be?
- How can we get there?
- What is the competitive situation in the marketplace?
- How has the product or service's individual characteristics influenced the above?
- What has been the role of packaging, pricing, distribution, or historical promotion on the above?

Whilst the above is critical to an understanding of what has gone before, we need to move analysis from the past and look to the future if we are to recommend on strategy. In this regard an understanding of the brand's total marketing situation is essential. The media strategist should seek to understand the likely environmental, social, political, and technological influences that could affect both the brand and the market in which it operates, but in turn should bring an informed view of the media future to the table at this point.

New media opportunities and new routes to the consumer resulting in lower entry costs to the media marketplace may well be of significant importance to future strategy. This information is of particular use when competitive communications activity, including the quantitative and qualitative assessment of a competitor's delivery against our own target audience, is viewed in this context.

Having considered in some detail the 'something about everything' element of planning, the media planner must now turn his or her attention to their own area of specialism. It is at this stage that the 'everything about something' element of the process must come to the fore, and an investigation of the consumer–media relationship must begin (Step 4b of our diamond).

At this stage of the process we will concern ourselves with the consumer and how he or she chooses and uses media. Once this has been completed, we will then be in a position to consider how this impacts upon the consumer–brand relationship, and vice versa, and how we follow this understanding through to its execution, either in terms of media buying, PR, direct marketing or other channels.

The consumer–media relationship

The contribution to the understanding of a brand's customers is where media can begin to add substantially to the analysis, and provide a unique insight into a substantial slice of consumer behaviour. More importantly, it is a slice of consumer life that will be absolutely key, if and when it is decided to use communication as the solution to the client's business problem.

In Simon Clemmow's chapter (Chapter 4), he identifies at least sixteen potential routes to the consumer of which above-the-line advertising is but one.

By analysing and understanding the consumer's relationship with the many media available to them (using the term in its broadest sense) the most appropriate routes may be more readily identified.

Exploring and understanding the consumer's relationship with the media is probably the most time-consuming and the most rewarding part of the process. Running in parallel with account planning's investigation of the consumer–brand relationship (Step 4a of the diamond), this should be a time of greatest dialogue between the two disciplines: each helping the other to shape their approach; each contributing to the other's knowledge of the 'something about everything'.

It is at this point that the media planner must begin to flesh out the core elements of the media contribution. Almost certainly this will require a combination of research, analysis, and the creation of a set of hypotheses, which will in turn need to be re-researched and analysed. Once a healthy sprinkling of common sense and gut-feel have been added then we might be ready to proceed.

However, this is not a process conducted in isolation at a computer terminal – this is real life! It is essential that ideas are debated and tested with anyone who you believe may be able to provide a useful insight. It may be that structured research is required, or it may be that a simple conversation with your family, friends, or members of the public is sufficient (I always found cab drivers to be willing to commit themselves on just about any subject!). What is necessary though, is that we take the investigation beyond the confines of a desk and get under the skin of the problem.

In order to do this our line of inquiry will need to consider many elements and although there is no one way of doing this I have always found the following to be a useful structure for the investigation, given the questions we need to answer.

Who?

- What is the brand audience and how can we best define them?
- Can media refine the definition? Embellish or colour it?
- Can media **be** the audience definition (see Figure 10.3).

How, when and where?

- How should we reach our audience? Which media do they prefer and how do they consume it?
- How does each medium interact or relate to another?
- How many people do we need to reach and how often?
- When, where and under what circumstances do they consume these media?

So let's start with the definition of precisely who we are seeking to target.

'News and sports fans'

Appointment to view

News (BBC 9 O'Clock/ITN News)
Current Affairs (esp *Newsnight*)
Dispatches
Horizon
All Football!
C4 Friday Comedy
BBC2 Comedy
Paramount/VH1/MTV

Appointment to listen

Radio 4 *Today*
Radio 4 6.30 Comedy Slot
Virgin (occasionally)

Must read

Guardian
Independent
Times
Observer
Independent on Sunday
Q
The Week

Buy for sport

Sunday Mirror / *News of the World*
Monday *Sun*
Racing Post

Mid Thirties - Mid Forties
(Think they are Late Twenties!)
Professional Males

Figure 10.3

The brand audience

Far too frequently the brand audience definition is either stated or set in stone long before media has become involved. More worryingly it is almost always described in terms of age, class, or sex with little or no ancillary information at all.

As far as I'm concerned, this is worse than useless. It is a habit we have sunk into due, in the main, to the restrictions of syndicated research, developed at a time when mass audiences were delivered by the media, and when socio-demography was a far more accurate barometer of both behaviour and belief. And it has been perpetuated because media buying has demanded that audiences be translated into a standard buying currency, and because the briefing process has demanded a one-line definition in order to get everything onto one page!

The thing is that not one of these has anything whatsoever to do with consumer reality. Demographics are an increasingly blunt tool when predicting consumer behaviour, particularly at a time when composite lifestyles – those with atypical product consumption or behaviour patterns, such as the professional couple who eat takeaway fish and chips with a bottle of Moet & Chandon – are far more commonplace. What we need at this stage of the process is a far more meaningful definition of the brand audience that everyone can relate to, and there is so much more information we could use. What we really need is the equivalent of a colour photo, a curriculum vitae, and the notes from an interview, rather than one line of socio-demographic algebra!

It is possible to define audiences in a number of meaningful ways. For example one might use:

- Attitude or market sophistication (e.g. green consumers/technophiles)
- Nature of product usage or ownership (e.g. regular buyers/occasional users/bitter drinkers/PC owners)
- Geodemography (e.g. affluent urbanites; older suburbia)
- Media consumption (e.g. *Daily Mail* readers/'news and sports fans'/heavy radio listeners).

There is a raft of techniques available that allows us to manipulate existing data in ways that we would never have believed possible twenty years ago. Correspondence analysis, and cluster analysis, have allowed us to use single source data like TGI, to create far more accurate definitions of a target audience and relate product consumption to both attitude and media preference. The same techniques are as applicable to proprietary data and have been used successfully in markets as diverse as lager, mayonnaise, telecommunications and insurance.

Whilst attitude, lifestyle and market sophistication definitions of target consumers are increasing in popularity, product usage definitions, such as 'occasional users of margarine', or 'heavy users of mayonnaise', are far less common. This is rather surprising as in many cases it offers the most precise definition of a category user, or a competitor's consumer, which one could hope for. There are many other ways in which to describe or define a target audience, and a whole industry has grown up based upon the categorization and provision of information on the UK consumer, using everything from product guarantee cards to census data. Geodemography – a 'you are where you live' approach to targeting, and its derivative classifications – have proved to be a popular means of defining consumers using this type of data, with ACORN, Mosaic and Super Profiles just some of the databases available to the planner.

However, it is my belief that one of the most potent ways in which to define an audience is in terms of what they read, watch, and listen to. Media consumption, as a means of segmenting a target audience, is extremely powerful. It has the benefit of being understandable, using a tangible acceptable language, and of cutting out the middleman by providing a definition of an audience that is closest to implementation. Let me give you an example.

A few years ago when working on a BT campaign to sell answer phones and cordless phones to a younger, professional, technophile audience, we were given the demographic descriptor of ABC1 adults 25–44 as the core consumer target. Through a combination of quantitative and qualitative research we discovered that the media consumption patterns of potential purchasers gave us a far more accurate definition of their behaviour than socio-demographics alone. Their interest in technology, and their desire and ability to purchase high-ticket items, was as important as their busy social lives and their need to keep 'in touch', in defining their behaviour.

Recruiting discussion groups using a combination of these criteria provided us with the opportunity to do some in-depth research of their media consumption behaviour. What we found provided us with an in-depth understanding of their media consumption patterns, as well as a far more readily understood definition of the people we were after.

The 'C4 FriGOS' (Friday-Night-Channel 4-*Guardian-Observer*-Sunday-night drama) as they became known, were typically hard-working couples and singles in metropolitan areas. After a long week at work they would often go out for drinks on Friday evening, returning home around 8–9 p.m. They would then settle down with their partner, often with the takeaway meal and a bottle of wine, to their favourite session on Channel 4. On Saturday morning they would get up later; they tended to buy *The Guardian*, *The Independent* or *The Times* which they read at their leisure over an early brunch, and they enjoyed playing or watching sport, or shopping in the afternoon. They all admitted to watching *Blind Date* or *Man o' Man* – although industry quantitative research would have you believe that this was not the case – before going out with friends drinking, clubbing, or for dinner on a Saturday evening. On Sunday morning some would listen to *The Archers*, and most would read either *The Observer* or *The Sunday Times*. Sunday lunch was a real treat, whilst in the evening they settled down to watch ITV quality drama before work on a Monday morning.

This 'Audience Media Network' approach provided considerable insight into both the interests and character of a target audience. Notwithstanding the obvious benefits to the media strategist, it proved particularly useful in the development of the creative ideas. It made the audience tangible and 'human'; it brought them to life, and it provided the creative teams with a clear understanding of precisely who they were writing for and how they should create and combine messages in a multi-media context. Steve Henry (see Chapter 8) sees this as a particularly important part of the creative briefing process.

It would appear that there is a real benefit in using media to define, as well as refine, an audience definition. It can add colour, substance and depth to our understanding of precisely who we should be targeting, and it can help to forge creative links between the chosen communication channels.

Media consumption

Building an understanding of the media consumption patterns of a particular brand audience – providing the material to answer the remaining how, when, and where questions – requires a combination of hard work, imagination, and investigative research. The media planner will need to consider all of the relevant available research that they can lay their hands on. The amount of industry research, and of published proprietary research (much of it produced by agencies and media owners), has grown considerably in the last ten years. Both quantitative and qualitative in nature, these studies have added much to our understanding of the role of media in consumers' lives.

However, in many cases there will be a requirement to design and execute tailor-made research in order to build an understanding of the media behaviour of a specific target audience. The application of qualitative research techniques, referred to in the earlier BT example, has added much to our understanding of consumers' media behaviour (see Chapter 6), although in my experience it is a combination of both quantitative and qualitative data that provides the most compelling evidence in media decision-making.

There is a wealth of industry data available that allows us to build what might be termed the quantity surveyor's view of media consumption. It allows us to make some judgements about the scale of the audience delivered by a medium, or part of that medium such as a particular programme, newspaper section or broadcast time band. In certain cases it allows us to gain some understanding of the level of interest an individual shows in a particular medium in comparison to the whole population, and occasionally it allows us to link attitude or product consumption information to each of these. However, in the main, industry research has failed to keep pace with the dramatic changes we have witnessed in the media landscape and has a number of shortcomings when used at this stage of the strategy development process.

The definition of a reader, listener or viewer is often of limited use when considering in detail precisely *how* an individual consumes a particular medium. For example, a viewer is simply defined as someone who is present in the room with a television set switched on. 'Viewing' starts from the moment the person records their presence, provided that the 'viewing' to a channel persists for a minimum of 15 seconds! Whilst 'viewing' is reported on a minute-by-minute basis, it is worth noting that the term 'in the room' covers anything from attentive watching to a casual glance while undertaking some other activity.

And as for 'reading', the National Readership Survey's definition of Average Issue Readership (AIR) is an estimate of the number of people who claim to have read or looked at one or more copies of a given publication for at least two minutes during a period dating back from the date of interviewing equal to the interval at which the publication appears.

Now forget for one moment, if you can, the research-speak, and let a couple of things sink in. 'Reading' or 'looking' can mean anything from a quick flip through to total engrossment – not much difference there, then. And two minutes is about the time it took you, dear reader, to plough through this stuff from the start of the Media Consumption section! So if you consider any of the Sunday broadsheets in this context, the number and nature of their many sections, and the way in which they are likely to be read, one begins to question the usefulness of such research for strategic purposes.

As a result of this lowest common denominator, currency-driven approach, more and more agencies are using bespoke research studies to gain a more detailed understanding of an audience's media consumption. At the same time, media owners, having recognized both the need and the potency of such an approach, have continued to commit considerable amounts of time and money to their own research investigations, many of which have proved to be landmark studies in consumer–media–brand understanding.

At my own company, Unity, we have developed a Media Usage and Attitudes study (U&A) for precisely this purpose. Using a combination of proprietary quantitative and qualitative research as well as published/industry sources, we produce an Audience Media Network analysis for a particular brand audience. This document, a cross between a diary, a debrief and a database, attempts to detail all of the elements of consumer–media behaviour that fall within the sphere of 'Who, How, When and Where?' This includes:

- What is the consumer's habitual media activity across a particular time frame (e.g. a day; a weekend; week, etc.), including both commercial and non-commercial opportunities?
- What are the 'must-listen-to', 'must-read', and 'must-view' appointments of the day?
- How are they consumed?
- Where do they take place and in whose company?
- What frame of mind is the consumer in?
- Are they in active (search) mode or passive (receive) mode?
- Are they time-rich or time-poor?
- How do they feel about each medium?(Trust? Respect? Believe?)
- Why do they use each medium? (Enjoyment? Information?)

- What other elements of their behaviour may be of interest to us?
- Where do they spend their leisure time?
- What are their interests, and hobbies?
- Where do they shop? Eat out?
- What other media opportunities could we use, conventional or otherwise, to reach them?

Having built up a detailed knowledge of the consumer's relationship with their media, we are now in a position to combine this with the consumer–brand understanding developed in parallel. And it is at this point that the real brand–consumer–media insight should emerge.

So let's just recap. In conjunction with our account planning colleagues we should now have identified the issues facing the brand; the strategic goals in both the short and medium term, and a comprehensive understanding of the brand audience. We must now decide whether there is a role for communication; whether advertising and media have a part to play, and if so what it should be (Step 5 of the diamond). In a growing number of campaigns that we have been involved with in recent years the decision has not been an either/or decision about one particular route to the consumer versus another, but more a case of which combination.

Assuming that there is a role for both communications in general and media in particular, we need a more formalized statement of what the role should be (Steps 6 and 7b).

The media objectives and strategy

Whilst much that has gone before has been about a different way of doing things, the final stage is more about following a tried and tested route, albeit armed with much more detailed information about the consumer–media–brand relationship. The creation of the media strategy and its ultimate execution (normally through media buying, although other channels such as sponsorship, PR or events should not be discounted) is an iterative process, requiring both collaboration and discussion.

In most cases the media objectives and media strategy should be derived from an understanding of what a particular communications route, such as advertising, is trying to achieve and how it is expected to work. If media planning has been involved as recommended earlier, then this becomes a seamless, logical extension of the process. However, there will be occasions when such involvement is absent and in these cases it will be necessary to immerse the media agency in an understanding of the brand, its current position, and the problem that we are seeking to redress.

Media objectives and media strategy are, in effect, an extension of the advertising objectives and strategy. And yet far too often we see the same media objectives trotted out for a whole range of different campaigns. I have lost count of the number of times I have seen 'to build coverage' as the objective, and 'by identifying high rating programmes' as the strategy. Surely there is more to media than such tautological twaddle?

Let us consider a hypothetical case. If the advertising objective for a brand of packet soup targeted at busy working mums is 'to demonstrate its versatility', and the advertising strategy is 'by giving examples of usage opportunities', the media objective would almost certainly be the same as the advertising objective. 'To demonstrate the brand's versatility' is equally applicable in both cases. The media strategy, based upon all of the work that has now been undertaken, could be formally stated as 'by using high interest, high involvement environments where busy mums seek ideas'.

At this stage the media planner may have a clear idea of precisely which media are appropriate for the task, but needs to work closely with the specialist buyers to explore both the brief and its marketplace realities. In the case of our packet soup brand, one would need to explore the implications of, say, a magazine route versus a daytime and satellite TV route. One would need to consider:

- The findings of the Media U&A, particularly information on attention, interest and the desire of our audience to seek out information within the prospective media
- The scale of the audience, and its build and delivery over time
- The loyalty of the audience and its likelihood for repeat exposure
- The costs of media and production in both media (particularly given the need for multiple executions)
- The budget available (whether stated or task-oriented)
- Any seasonal or regional influences
- Other add-ons or incentives such as production facilities, text services, the opportunity to create promotional videos, access to mailing lists, recipe cards, etc.

There will come a point when one needs to exercise judgement, based upon all of the analysis that has gone before; the business and marketing needs of the brand; the stated objectives and strategy, and perhaps most importantly, the flash of inspiration that will make the campaign look and feel different to the consumer. It is at this point that we need to construct a buying brief – a blueprint for the media architecture – on which to build an effective communications strategy.

It is vitally important that such a brief is descriptive rather than prescriptive, collaborative rather than instructional, and encourages creativity, flair, innovation and discussion.

At the same time there needs to be an ongoing dialogue with the account team and the creative department in order to ensure that discussions on media context and the development of the creative content remain in harmony.

Overview and conclusion

The dramatic changes in the media landscape over the last two decades have made a significant impact upon consumer behaviour. One only has to think about the activities of a normal day to realize that the media in one form or another are interwoven with most of the things that people see, hear or experience, most of the time. If not by choice, then often by chance, the consumer is assailed by commercial communication.

One piece of 'research' I have often heard quoted, but as yet have failed to discover the source, suggests that 'yer average Londoner' (a segmentation term from the Cabbie School of research) encounters over 1,000 brand messages a day. Now even if this is 100 per cent exaggerated – and given all of the potential sources, I sort of feel that it is not – how on earth can we ensure that we nudge up the odds in favour of our clients' messages getting through over and above everyone else's? How can we break through the clutter, overcome the subconscious filtering by the human brain and really communicate?

The answer is to ensure that we reach:

the right people
in the right place
at the right time
with the right message.

In effect, we need to provide in-depth answers to the four basic questions posed at the start of this chapter: who, where, when, and how? And it is my contention that consumer–media understanding has a significant role to play in all four of these elements.

The right people

As we have seen, media consumption information can help to define, humanize, colour or embellish a brand audience definition. It can bring an audience to life for both the client and the creative teams and, with the increasing potency of media as a segmentation tool for audiences, it can actually *become* the audience definition in its own right.

The right place ... the right time

Building an understanding of a particular 'Audience Media Network' which does not just consider the conventional media but allows for all potential consumer contact opportunities is critical. Knowing both the quantitative and qualitative dimensions of this network – how the consumer relates to each element; how each element relates to the other in both time and space; the particular mood and mind-set of consumers at the time of each media experience, including how this relates to the brand in question – are just some of the essential elements that should help to shape....

The right message

The creation of relevant content is the key to consumer interest and involvement. By understanding a consumer's likely frame of mind, his or her needs, beliefs, and attitudes at the time of exposure, we can begin to shape the content accordingly and improve both the relevance and effectiveness of communication.

At the start of this chapter I set out to demonstrate how media planning (or media strategy: the terms have become synonymous in this context) could contribute to strategy development, and how it might help to improve both the relevance and overall effectiveness of communication. The approach I have proposed is neither radical nor revolutionary: it is simply common sense. To ignore such a significant body of useful and useable information about the media – the ultimate point of contact for the communication and the consumer – seems heretical.

In the 60s, 70s, and early 80s, media was a bit like Postman Pat. It turned up, delivered its messages then went on its way to feed the cat. Nowadays things are different. There are a whole host of Postmen, each with their own charm and personality lining up at the gate to deliver their messages. We now do have a choice and can decide which of the Postmen to allow up the garden path to deliver their missive. However, the very act of choosing empowers post-modern Pat to make it up the path, through the front door, and to sit down for a nice cup of tea and a chat! And if we use this opportunity wisely we can make the experience so much more fulfilling for both Pat and his customer by influencing what is said over the cup of tea. What we have done is change Pat's job specification. We have made it more of a two-way process: dialogue rather than delivery. In effect we have started to treat media as a salesman not as a postman.

As a result we need to start thinking about how our knowledge of potential customers should influence the salesman's pitch and patter, rather than simply counting the number of houses he has visited. We need to think about how we might help to customize and personalize the approach to take account of the product, the proposition and the purchaser. And we need to be involved much earlier in the creation of the sales approach and scripts, if this understanding is to be of any use.

Media, I believe, has much to offer in terms of its strategic contribution. As we move into a world of increasing interactivity, the need for greater relevance can only increase. And in a world where the active reception of messages rather than selective reception will become critical, the strategic role of media can only grow in importance.

Reference

National Readership Survey (1998), Volume 1, Appendix H, Definitions Used.

Overview: Chapter 11

As the demand for accountability within the marketing and advertising industries continues to grow (almost exponentially it seems sometimes), so the temptation is often to turn to the latest, simplest, 'hardest' or most quantifiable research technique.

In this chapter, Tim Broadbent takes an intelligent and wide-ranging view of those techniques, and the temptations behind them.

He shows how the pursuit of simplicity and certainty in this area can be either futile or misleading or both – and, instead, points us towards composite models of advertising effect that may lead to better tailor-made measures.

The evidence for and content of some of these approaches exists, Tim argues, within the IPA's database of Effectiveness Awards cases.

This chapter was first presented in November 1997 on the IPA's course on Evaluating Advertising.

Chapter 11

Evaluating advertising

Tim Broadbent

Introduction

In the 1970s some people thought advertising's effectiveness could not be measured. They argued that so many other factors affect consumer demand for a brand – such as its price, product quality, distribution and so on – that advertising's specific contribution could not be isolated. For example, Bob Jones, one of the founders of BMP, wrote a book in 1973 called *The Business of Advertising* which said, 'The effect of advertising is largely immeasurable . . . Advertising makes an unknown contribution to selling goods.'

Small wonder that some clients lost confidence in advertising. If its effects are so thoroughly swamped by the other elements of the marketing mix as to be 'immeasurable', they can only be small effects at best. And small effects can only be worth small money.

Ad agencies lost boardroom clout as advertising budgets were switched to other communication channels. Direct mail might produce low response rates, but at least clients can measure what they get for their money. Advertising, from being the leader, became just one voice in the communication chorus.

The IPA Advertising Effectiveness Awards were set up in the late 1970s to challenge what Charles Channon called the 'myth of advertising's ineffectiveness'. The objective was to publish case histories which demonstrated, with greater rigour than had been attempted before, that advertising contributed to sales and profit. Since 1980 some 700 case histories, covering almost every advertised category, have been collected. The Awards Databank is available for inspection via the IPA website at www.ipa.co.uk. The learning they represent has made the UK the global centre of excellence for advertising evaluation.

In addition to showing that advertising *works*, the Databank casts new light on *how* it works. An ad agency might expound a theory that reflects its own creative philosophy, or a research company might promote its own method-ology, but the Awards have no commercial axe to grind. The Databank is theory-neutral.

In the following sections, we shall review the two main theories of how advertising works, namely the Recall and Persuasion models. Both theories have influenced how the majority of ads are currently pre-tested and tracked. Understanding the thinking behind these research techniques helps make sense of the data and suggests when they are, and are not, appropriate. We then review contemporary alternatives to these models.

How advertising researchers think advertising works

Most quantitative researchers have a theory about how to make ads more effective. The problem for advertisers is that researchers disagree. Since the 1930s ad researchers have pretty much split into the main sects. There are those who worship at the house of recall, and then there are those who consider persuasion the true religion.

Acolytes of recall bend the knee to George Gallup. In the 1920s he was professor of advertising and journalism at Northwestern University. He hit on the notion of conducting large quantitative surveys to find out which parts of newspapers were read by the audience – how many read the lead editorial, the sports reports, the cartoons and so on.

In 1931 he applied a similar research technique to ads. He started with the advertising input. He cut out all the ads from four magazines, organized them into ten broad categories based on their general selling message, then counted how many ads there were in each category. Economy was the most often used appeal (e.g. 'costs less', 'lasts longer'), while sex and vanity were the least often used. Then his researchers rang 15,000 doorbells. Which ads had the readers of these magazines actually noticed?

It turned out that ads based on sex and vanity were the best recalled, even though there were fewer of them. Clearly consumers were processing ad messages according to what they saw as important to themselves, not passively absorbing them. What might seem a competitive advantage to an advertiser was not necessarily seen as worth remembering by the audience. This conclusion may seem pretty obvious, but it caused a great stir in the advertising circles of the day, and the lesson has still not been fully assimilated. Stephen King, one of the founders of account planning, had to argue forty years later that a basic principle of effective advertising was to set advertising strategy in terms of consumer response – JWT's T-Plan creative briefing document 'was based not on what ought to *go into* the advertising, but what ought to be the consumer's *responses* to the brand as a result'.

One reason this case still needs to be argued, even today, is because of an ex-army psychologist called Horace Schwerin, who developed an alternative view of how advertising works. Who cares whether an ad is recalled or not, so long as it is obeyed? Researchers can ignore intermediate measures such as ad recall. The only thing that really matters is how many consumers become persuaded to buy the advertised brand.

Schwerin's methodology, known as ARS Persuasion®, is to show people a basket of grocery brands and ask which ones they want. Then they are exposed to an ad. Then it's the basket again, and people say which brands they want now. The difference between the before and after scores shows how persuasive the ad is.

On first acquaintance, this seems quite a sensible approach. But over time, having tested thousands of ads on this system, it has become known that only a certain type of ad will pass this test. What matters, according to ARS Persuasion, is what goes *into* an ad. To pass the test, ads must:

- Demonstrate the product in use
- Have the product on-screen for more than one-third of the commercial
- Make the product benefit the main message
- Demonstrate the results of use.

This requirement explains the construction of many American soap-powder-style commercials. Persuasion testing has been out of favour for so long in Britain that most advertisers have forgotten why they dropped it. One reason was a devastating analysis published by Fothergill and Ehrenberg in 1965. This showed that the technique is fundamentally flawed. Random numbers fed into the model produced a correlation of 0.6, compared to the correlation for observed data of 0.7. If many people choose a brand at the pre stage, there are fewer available to be persuaded at the post stage. So this model has a built-in systematic bias against large brands.

Other criticisms are that persuasion testing focuses exclusively on product advantages and ignores advertising's effects on the brand; and that it just tests individual executions, ignoring the effect of long-running campaigns or repeated viewing of the same ad. By contrast, in Britain, 60 to 70 of the 100 largest advertisers use Millward Brown to track recall or to pre-test ads in order to predict how noticeable they will be. Nevertheless, we cannot ignore persuasion testing, because it is still the orthodoxy in America. Four of the six largest American pre-testing research agencies (and of course their clients) still use and recommend it. As advertising becomes more global, which in practice means more American, persuasion testing has been returning to Britain recently, even though it was thought to be dead and buried.

ιs been given a new impetus by the 'discovery' of STAS (Short Term Αϋνϵιtising Strength), described in Professor John Philip Jones's latest book, *When Ads Work*. This shows that ads can work in a matter of days, which an advertiser who only tracked sales via a monthly retail audit would not know (though of course retailers have always known about short-term responses). The STAS methodology is to use household scanners to record weekly purchases, together with metered TV sets to record household ad exposure. Thus one can compare purchases amongst households exposed to ads against households which didn't get ads. If the ad-exposed bought more, the ad gets a positive STAS score. A negative score could mean that competitive ads in the category were stronger.

Jones found that about 70 per cent of US ads produced positive STAS scores. This proportion appears to be normal. Colin Macdonald found virtually the same in Britain, 73 per cent, when he looked at the old Central TV Adlab panel data, and Burckhard Brandes found 71 per cent from German Nielsen data. So far, so good: most ads work quickly. But recently Jones has gone further. He now claims that ARS Persuasion scores are good predictors of STAS. He says, 'The higher the score, the higher the sales'. Improved predictions will mean an end to 'a waste of resources that can be measured in scores or even hundreds of billions of dollars spent on campaigns that do not work'.

In slightly smaller print, however, Jones acknowledges that persuasion scores did not predict STAS accurately in all cases. Some predictions were off because competitors had rather unsportingly cut their prices or used promotions, which 'contaminated' the data. Other predictions were off because the brands were large, and large brands 'typically score below the ARS Persuasion mean' (for the reason explained earlier). Besides, whatever the pre-test score, advertising strength is a *relative* matter: you would still end up with negative STAS in the market if a competitor has a better ad than you have.

So the vision of sure and certain predictions via ARS Persuasion testing applies only to certain advertisers in certain circumstances. It only applies to you if you have a small brand, *and* if your competitors don't cut prices or use promotions, *and* if they can be trusted to do weak ads. It is hard to think of many advertisers in this happy position. For example, price competition seems a feature of all markets. Besides, the recall church has its own miracle sales correlations as well. The graphs in Figure 11.1 show the correlations between sales and pre-testing scores. One can see that Millward Brown's correlation between recall and sales, at 0.9, appears to be better than that between ARS Persuasion and sales, which is still at 0.7.

While superficially impressive, these charts leave many questions unanswered. They give the impression that advertising is the only influence on sales growth, which is not the case. A full assessment of advertising's effects must include and allow for the influence of price, distribution, product quality, competitive activity, communications other than advertising, etc. Correlation is not the same as causality.

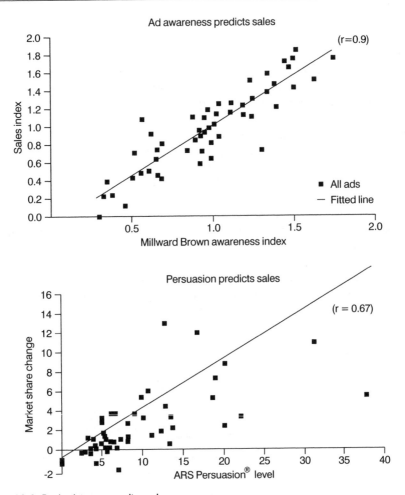

Figure 11.1 Both claim to predict sales

1990s researchers no longer look for a single magic number that will explain and predict how advertising works. Rather than a simple model, they offer more complex models, acknowledging that different ads for different brands will have different roles to play. Two techniques illustrate this more sophisticated approach, from Hall & Partners and from the HPI Research Group.

Hall & Partners classify ads into four main types: sales response, persuasion, involvement and salience. According to which category your ad falls into, different pre-testing and tracking questions will be appropriate.

■ **Sales response** advertising is typically promotional advertising (e.g. 'This week's special offer'), with a coupon or phone number. Research needs to measure whether target consumers find the offer interesting and worth doing something about urgently.

- **Persuasion** advertising is similar to the original model that still sometimes applies today: where brand commitment is built because people believe there's a product-based 'reason why' the brand works better. Research needs to measure how well the advertising communicates a unique selling proposition in a credible and convincing way, by testing purchase intention.
- **Involvement** advertising is relevant where brand commitment is driven less by belief in product superiority than by people identifying with brand values that make the brand 'mean more' to them. To get this feeling about the brand, people have to get into the advertising, so research needs to measure how well the ad involves them.
- **Salience** advertising makes the brand stand out. Sheer currency and leadership behaviour can be enough to drive brand commitment, so research needs to measure the extent to which the advertising itself is seen as different and distinctive.

The HPI Group offer an inclusive model of what advertising does, involving the easily-remembered ABCD checklist of Appreciation, Branding, Communication and Desired effect on the brand (Figure 11.2).

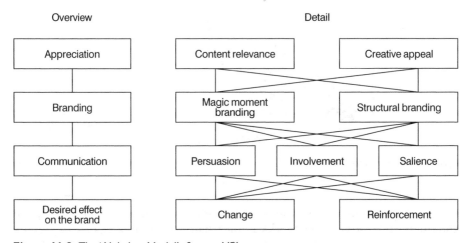

Figure 11.2 The 'Alphabet Model'. *Source*: HPI

Note that the communication tasks are also defined as either persuasion, involvement or salience.

A benefit of approaches such as these is that client and agency are more or less obliged to discuss and agree *how* they expect the ad to work before doing the pre-testing or tracking research. All advertising research rests on an assumption about how ads work, which may or may not be made explicit but is invariably there. Without shared agreement on the model beforehand, interpreting research findings will be a chancy business.

However, these newer approaches also have their critics. Three models of how advertising works are better than one, but why stop at three? Advertising is, in fact, used to do many different things: to defend a brand against own label growth, to slow or reverse a sales decline, to maintain premium pricing, to increase recruitment efficiency, to stop line extensions cannibalizing existing sales of the main brand, to launch new products, to raise awareness of the dangers of drug use, to raise money for charity, to change perceptions of a corporation or a whole industry ... the list goes on. (These are some actual examples taken from the 1998 IPA Advertising Effectiveness Awards.)

Each of the objectives requires different pre-testing and tracking questions. For example, defending against own label growth needs measures of customer loyalty. Increasing recruitment efficiency needs measures of how attractive the job is to quality applicants and how the fainthearted are dissuaded. Changing perceptions of a corporation needs research amongst all stakeholders, such as employees and shareholders, not solely amongst consumers. And so on.

A second criticism is that the three types of advertising (persuasion, involvement and salience) are not alternatives. Effective ads may well use all three together. Salience is often a prerequisite, in order to cut through commercial clutter. Involvement is necessary as ads are seldom screened just once, and rewarding the viewer for repeated viewings maintains their attention. And most ads have some product message in there somewhere. Rather than there being three distinct types of ads as the model implies, each ad will often contain all three objectives in different proportions.

In the late 1990s, some researchers are offering tailor-made rather than one-size-fits-all systems. For example, The Research Business International has a pre-testing system called Vision^{TM}. Each ad is evaluated against its particular objectives. TRBI says:

> We don't try to force an ad into a research straitjacket based on one model of how advertising works (or even a limited number). Instead, we set out with you to identify the desired consumer response, and then tailor-make a questionnaire that's going to fathom how often this occurs.

Designing research around an ad's objectives may not seem a big step. But it has taken some of the research industry 70 years to get there!

The underlying issues

Disagreements about research techniques are the superficial manifestations of a deeper issue – the froth which shows which way the current is running, not the underlying cause of the tides.

On the one hand, there are advertising agencies. Their commercial future depends on making ads that sell on their clients' behalf. For the most part they welcome research – agencies originated the ideas of the marketing department and the research department. (Of course some individual creatives have to be dragged to consumer realities kicking and screaming, but at a deeper level one of advertising agencies' core functions is to mediate between producers and markets.) Stanley Pollitt founded BMP on the idea that a trained researcher should become an integral part of the agency's central decision-making unit (creative and account handler, plus this new animal, the account planner), in order to 'get the advertising right'. That means using the right research in the right way.

Ad agencies therefore tend to resist attempts to force all ads into oversimplified research models which do not reflect the actual strategy of particular ads. Just because something can easily be measured does not make it the right thing to measure. A recent letter in *The Times* from the professor of Mathematical Studies at the University of Southampton put the case in a nutshell:

> The proposal reflects the well-known tendency to assess people and organisations by counting something, even if that something is somewhat irrelevant. The reason? Counting is easier than thinking.

On the other hand, clients are busy people and advertising is only a small part of what a company does. Global clients in particular may need to evaluate twenty or more different ads for a brand produced in twenty or more different markets. Consistent research measures make their lives easier, and conventional techniques allow them to justify spending decisions up the line more simply.

This tension, I believe, is what really lies behind the debate over methodologies. Agencies want research that is aligned around each ad's objectives. Clients may have different priorities: measuring all ads in the same way has cost and time advantages for them.

It may be presumptuous to suggest that the IPA Effectiveness Awards resolve this debate, but that is exactly what we will suggest in the next section. The idea we will be proposing is that conventional research may have drastically understated advertising's commercial benefits. The total returns that advertising brings may be much larger than was dreamt of in Gallup's or Schwerin's philosophies. If this is indeed the case, the higher costs of tailor-made research can more easily be justified.

The manifold ways advertising contributes to profit

The early papers in the IPA Effectiveness Awards typically showed advertising's contribution to sales growth. Their great achievement was to show that, despite the 'noise' in the marketplace, it was possible to estimate what advertising in particular had contributed over and above other marketing activities. But this focus on sales contained an unexpected trap: Simon Broadbent wrote in 1988 that:

> Unfortunately, the objective most often chosen to demonstrate that advertising works, is in the short term and on sales volume. Nothing wrong with that. But managers . . . come to believe there are no other objectives. A particular objective, achievement of short-term volume return, is seen as all there is.

Accordingly, the Awards set out to encourage a new type of entry, about advertising's longer and broader effects. Paul Feldwick, the Convenor in 1990, wrote that 'The Awards have not shown all the ways advertising can be a serious business proposition. Future competitors might like to consider the challenge of how advertising *adds value*'.

Some classic papers have demonstrated that the return advertisers get from adding value to the brand dwarfs the return from short-term volume increases. For example, the PG Tips paper quantified the financial contribution of 20 years of the chimps campaign. The paper shows that a media spend of £86m produced extra sales worth about £2,000m. The BMW paper quantified the financial contribution of 15 years of the 'Ultimate Driving Machine' campaign. This showed that a media spend of £91m produced extra sales worth about £3,000m. In these cases the decisive contribution advertising made to profit was in creating and maintaining premium prices, not just volumes.

This is a world away from the short-term increases in product sales measured by persuasion testing. Short-term sales returns are often not profitable. Millward Brown recently reported on econometric tests on 300 ads from the UK, the Continent and the USA. They found that the average ad generated £1,300 extra turnover per GRP in the short term. Unfortunately, however, the cost of the average GRP is £2,000. Therefore, if all that advertising is judged on is short-term volume, advertising is a waste of money, and the industry might as well fold its tents and steal away silently into the night.

Brand-building, however, can be seriously profitable. Often the brand is a company's most valuable asset. For example, Diageo's brand portfolio was valued in its 1996 balance sheet at £2,800m, 74 per cent of total shareholder funds. Strongly branded companies also tend to have more valuable shares. An analysis by Citibank and Interbrand has shown that over the long term (1980 to 1997), heavily branded companies outperformed the FTSE 350 by about 20 per cent.

An explanation for this stronger financial performance has been given in Young & Rubicam's proprietorial research study, the Brand Asset Valuator™. This is a very large database of consumer perceptions of brand strength. The study includes, to date, 95,000 consumer interviews into 13,000 different brands. Each brand is ranked on 55 measures of brand equity.

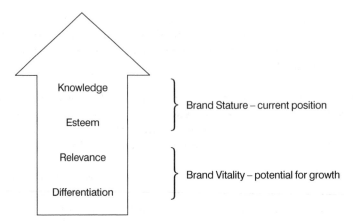

Figure 11.3

According to the BAV™, there are four primary pillars of brand strength, which are combined into two key factors (Figure 11.3).

A unique feature of the survey is that each brand is ranked against every other brand in the survey, not just against other brands in the same product category. Thus the survey plots each brand against the whole national brandscape. Comparing brand strength against established brands' financial performance has shown a correlation between brand vitality and average operating margins, shown in Figure 11.4.

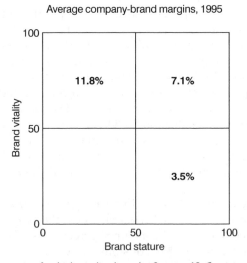

Figure 11.4 Higher margins for high-vitality brands. *Source: 63 Company-brands, USA,* Y&R

New brands start in the bottom left quadrant. As they grow, they move into the top left quadrant. Here we find strong niche brands, which make the highest margins. As brands grow from niche to mass-market, they move into the top right quadrant. Here margins per unit are typically lower than for niche brands, but they sell more units. Less differentiated brands, though still high in stature, are found in the bottom right quadrant. Such brands have to compete on price rather than on brand values, which reduces margins. It can be seen that the source of high margins is high perceived vitality, rather than stature.

While any O-level marketing textbook will say that relevant differentiation is crucial for consumer preference, very few market research departments or agencies measure the extent to which advertising differentiates the brand. Yet differentiation is the foundation of consumer choice. Highly differentiated brands are at less risk from competitive inroads because consumers believe they offer something that other brands do not, so they are less easily substituted. Thus differentiation creates premium prices and sustainable long-term incomes for the company. Increased differentiation is the engine of profit growth, as is shown in Figure 11.5.

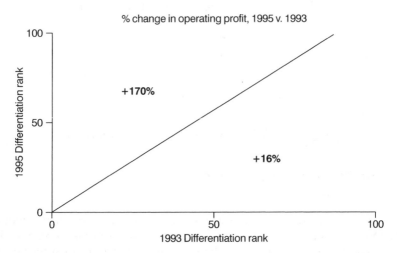

Figure 11.5 Increased differentiation = increased operating profit. *Source: 63 Company-brands, USA,* Y&R

Brands to the left of the diagonal line increased in perceived differentiation between 1993 and 1995, while brands to the right of the line were seen as less highly differentiated. The effect on profit growth is remarkable.

The history of the IPA Awards can be thought of as the progressive revelation of advertising's profitable effects, from short-term sales volume to long-term brand differentiation. However, a company's commercial success depends on more than just consumer demand. Successful companies also acquire, retain and motivate the right people; have good investor relations; build strong partnerships; develop winning new products; etc. Since 1998, the IPA Awards have encouraged entrants to consider advertising's influences on these non-consumer audiences too.

Unlike other marketing communications, advertising reaches multiple audiences simultaneously, aligning them around a common understanding of the brand. Advertising aimed at consumers is 'overheard' by staff, by the trade, and by the City. The benefit of these effects, though real and substantial, has been invisible to consumer research. For example, the Orange case history in the 1998 Awards showed the benefit of consumer advertising on the City audience. The paper described a Lehman Brothers analysis which showed that, without consumer advertising, Orange's share price would have been 279p, compared to its actual price of 528p. The difference amounted to extra shareholder value of £3,000m, over and above any extra consumer sales due to the ads. Conventional pre-testing techniques ignore these returns.

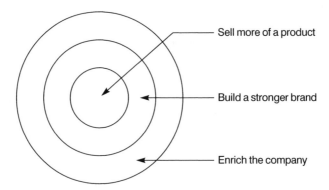

Figure 11.6 Showing advertising's total effects

What we're learning from these new papers is that advertising works in many more ways than conventional research attempts to measure, and that it enriches companies in more ways than just by stimulating consumer demand (Figure 11.6). There is a new world of advertising effects out there, which we know exists but have only started to map. We need new research thinking that will break out of the sterile debates of the past and help us to explore advertising's influences on new audiences.

References

Blair, M. (1995), *An Emerging Renaissance in Advertising Through a TQ Approach for Maximising Productivity*, RSC, (March).

Brandes, B. (1996), *How Advertising Works*, European Advertising Effectiveness Symposium, Lisbon, May 1996.

Broadbent, S. (1988), *Marketing Magazine*, (June).

Fothergill, J. and Ehrenberg, A. (1965), On the Schwerin analysis of advertising effectiveness, *Journal of Market Research*, (August).

Jones, J. P. (1995), *When Ads Work*. Lexington Books.

Jones, J. P. (1996), Look before you leap, *Admap* (November).

Jones, R. W. (1973), *The Business of Advertising*, Longman.

King, S. (1964),quoted in J. Treasure, The Origins of Account Planning, *Admap* (March 1985).

Landsberg, P. (1999), Faculty of Mathematical Studies, University of Southampton, *The Times*, (22 February).

McDonald, C. (1996), How frequently should you advertise? *Admap* (July/August).

The Millward Brown Link Tests (1993), Millward Brown.

Prue, T. (1998), An all-embracing theory of how advertising works, *Admap* (February).

Vision™ Pre-testing, TRBI (1998).

Overview: Chapter 12

'Integration' was one of the buzz words in the advertising world for much of the 1990s. It described some agencies' response to the growth in importance of media other than traditional 'above the line' advertising.

Cynics might say it was also a 'wrapper' within which agencies could offer those services from under one roof!

Either way, the agenda has moved on – and now it is clients who are driving the 'joined-up thinking' in this area.

'Total communications' describes the strategic attitude that many enlightened clients are now adopting towards the ever-expanding portfolio of communications mechanisms.

In this chapter, Tim Pile, one of those very much in the vanguard of this thinking, takes a hard but impassioned look at how clients are doing it – and how agencies are (or are not) responding.

As is his style, Tim doesn't pull any punches here! Neither did he when he first presented this paper as a speech on the IPA/ISBA course on Total Communication Strategy in 1998.

Chapter 12

Total communications strategy

Tim Pile

Introduction – the Percy syndrome

Do you remember the scene in *Blackadder* where Lord Percy, in pursuit of creating the purest gold, inadvertently creates the purest green and is devastated to learn that it is not nearly so valuable? We are in a similar position with regard to delivering a 'Total Communications Strategy'. We know instinctively that it would be a good thing. Unfortunately nobody has as yet, told us what it looks like, or how to do it.

We understand that many benefits flow from informational coherence. We know that our brands will be greatly enhanced by such a strategy and that it could even make us the darlings of institutional stockholders. We might even find out which half of the advertising budget is being wasted (if that was ever true) and make the whole add up to more than the sum of the parts. The logic for pursuing the total communications route is inarguable and unassailable but it seems to be as seductive as yesterday's curry.

There are no training courses or models. A view of the marketing industry can be entirely conditioned by where someone enters it and whether or not they are ever offered the opportunity to look at the totality of disciplines involved in the creation and maintenance of a brand. We are myopic. This is not so in other walks of life where the business landscape is littered with management colleges of one kind or another. In the armed forces, there comes a point where, regardless of specialization, future leaders are selected to go to staff college so that they can gain the wider picture. We have no such institution. We have no focused training. There are no rewards or motivators and there is precious little literature on the subject and even less media interest. Even our organizational structures have to be bent to fit the requirements of total communications.

We are in pretty poor shape and yet, we know, really know deep down, that a total communications strategy is central to the delivery of a powerful, effective and efficient brand offer.

The brand: why bother?

Increasingly, the brand is the last point of differentiation in a world where it can seem as if everybody can 'do' everything. Virgin can fly you to the States, or sell you a PEP, or perhaps make you wait for a train. Any of the major retailers can very quickly enter any of the service industries and sell anything from medical insurance to cut-price holidays. A company which possesses a solid body of customer data, a distribution channel and the product knowledge – inherent or bought-in – can compete directly for 'your' customer. It is possible that the internet, or its progeny, will alter the manufacturer–retailer–customer paradigm forever and yet much of our industry continues to ignore the trend. As they say in Chicago – 'If the future gets you, it won't be in the temple. You'll get it right between the eyes and you should have seen it coming.'

Interestingly, the new players, especially the internet-based ones, realize the power and importance of brands in a world characterized as increasingly fragmented, full of multiple choice and stunning speed of change. In fact, they realize this truth more so than the supposed established players.

Financial services

Over the last ten years, the financial services sector has become perhaps the most intense battleground and one which illustrates the previous point most clearly. In that time, building societies became banks. Retailers began to sell savings products and if you went into a bank branch to cash a cheque, you might well have left as the proud owner of some form of insurance. And the increased competition meant that customers (remember them?) inevitably became better informed and began to pick and choose their products from a wide range of financial institutions.

The concept of 'customer for life' died, unmourned by the consumer. The banks entered new product distribution channels – in addition to having branches on every high street: telephone, direct mail and off-the-page sales became widely accepted by the public as convenient alternatives. There was a completely new ballgame being played: one which had been created by a conspiracy of trends. One which affected hugely the role of the brand and the role of communications. And it is a conspiracy that we would do well to examine.

Some key trends

- Legislation, regulators, technology and the media have combined to give the customer such power that the major financial services companies, in trying to defend their margins and market shares, have drawn up completely new rules of engagement, or rules that are new to them at least.
- Tactical alignments, which often place companies simultaneously in the roles of competitor, supplier and partner, are the order of the day.
- Although there have been a number of consolidations amongst traditional brands in the form of mergers, still the net result is that there are more overall brands in play. New entrants, empowered by technology and using the banks as suppliers of raw material, are pouring over the, now very low, barriers to market entry. And they know that there are equally low barriers to exit!
- Unquestionably, financial services is the single most competitive market you can play in: mergers; new entrants; old entrants; brand extensions; price wars; cost of search decreasing; product copying and proliferation; huge marketing spends, etc.
- Power is in the hands of the consumer. Armed with widely available information – which is now written in accessible language – and with an almost limitless product choice, the customer 'cherry picks'. Whereas customers used to be selected by a bank and would content themselves with whatever was on that financial menu, their fiscal needs are now satisfied by a number of different financial and some not very financial concerns.
- A large cake is now being sliced very small indeed. In an already crowded field, there has been an explosion of media; for some classes of product, direct marketing is now the most significant delivery channel; one-to-one marketing, enabled by advances in technology and segmentation techniques, is now a practical reality.
- In this fragmenting marketplace, the brand is still central, but its role is changing so that it is becoming an umbrella of values, under which shelter a wide range of different propositions.

If the financial services model is a guide, then brands will change into much more complex animals, with multi-point access and a number of layers, where individual products can spin off into service offerings. The umbrella's construction will allow it to stretch over a number of different products and that in turn will have implications for how specific the brand promise can be. For instance, British Gas now sells electricity and the electricity companies sell gas. The 'winning' strategy will be to build and sustain long-term, profitable customer relationships. The winners will be those companies who gain the customer's attention through owning the communication; owning the customer interface; owning the customer knowledge; and, most importantly, the brand.

The brand

What is a brand?

This is the 'meaning of life' question beloved of all advertising agencies and we have all listened to countless expositions on the nature and shape of a brand, so please do not imagine that you are about to receive the definitive answer here. However, we should be clear that a brand exists only in the collective mind of the consumer. It is a personality or an identity which is described in the collective perception of the consumer and like any other personality, it is unique because it is made up of promises fulfilled and a discrete set of values. Its character is communicated by a very large number of tangible and intangible experiences, and when the various elements fuse together well, a brand is unmistakably different from every other 'similar' product or service.

Now you know!

Any experience of the brand either subtracts from, or reinforces, the brand proposition – and I do mean *any* experience. The list of possible experiences is of course endless and is dictated by the product or service in question, but you might consider:

■ Performance
■ Packaging
■ Fulfilment
■ Advertising
■ Staff
■ Community role
■ Premises
■ Service
■ And on and on and on . . .

If I am giving you the impression that a brand is a volatile, easily bruised creature, I do not mean to. Certainly, even the longest established brands can be damaged, as Hoover knows only too well, but 'brandicide' is hard to commit.

Erosion through neglect (just think of some well-known retail brands) is much more likely and in a market that is rapidly changing, where customers have increasing choice and price begins to rule the earth, even the strongest brands require constant attention. The faster the change, the more important it is to build or maintain the brand, if only because a customer is two and a half times more likely to purchase a familiar brand than an unfamiliar one.

There are, of course, a number of other advantages such as:

■ Ability to sustain price premiums
■ Stable, less risky, income streams
■ Longevity and loyalty

- Easier cross sales and extensions
- Greater potential for growth
- The brand can be a barrier to competitive market entry
- Organizational focus
- New product launches, new channels and direct business.

The foregoing list is not exhaustive and it ignores the most significant competitive advantage that can be delivered by a brand:

- *A strong brand is not copyable – even when everything else about your product or service is.*

A new(ish) brand model

There are as many types of brands as there are definitions:

- The 'classic' customer, single-need, single-delivery brand like Macleans toothpaste
- 'Spoke' brands which depend on a core competency and deliver it across all the branded products like Black and Decker
- 'Ripple' brands like Cadbury Schweppes.

But, increasingly, the new brand model is the 'super', or 'master' brand. All-encompassing and driven at CEO level, it sidesteps the usual core customer benefits and relegates them to product level. It relies on PR, sponsorship, mass communications and media management to give it a 'hard' edge. Its individual products, whilst having clear parentage, are sold through a widely fragmented series of routes selected by data, by channel and by customer. A world of increasingly discrete propositions (driven by data and interactive media) from the same brand to different sets of customers. The whole enterprise, whilst retaining its shape and personality, seems to present an ever-changing variety of faces.

In this model, the brand is not in the packaging, although the packaging is important, and TV is the very last thing to worry about. The essence of this brand is the daily customer experience. And to control that, you need a strong, clear strategy and some very robust rules.

Brand communication strategy

The road to total communications

Successful brand communications depend upon seven key factors which, happily, all begin with 'C'. Actually there are eight, but in these presentations the established mantra is always to say seven!

■ **Clarity**   As they almost say about computers, 'clarity in – clarity out'. Unless the offer is clear and there is a clear sense of purpose as well as position, the brand's personality will be indistinct. The vision must not be obscured. A clearly defined brand also provides a beacon of light to consumers and staff alike.

■ **Coherence**   The brand is the sum total of all communication and from staff uniforms to television, from customer enquiry lines to sales promotion: *everything* communicates. Self-evidently, therefore, they must all communicate the same brand idea, in the same tone of voice. If you are to create or maintain a strong brand, then the integration of all these possible brand signals must become an obsession.

'One brand. One voice'. Otherwise, if there are many voices, then the brand will come tumbling down, in the same way that the Tower of Babel had a bit of a problem of biblical proportions when the workers spoke with different tongues. Again the more cohesion you put in (like all these rules, input/output is the game) the more cohesion you get out.

■ **Consistency**   If you have a single, coherent message then it follows that you must deliver it consistently across time, across geography, across media, across distribution channels and across products. In the face of tumultuous change and stop-start management, the brand must be a fixed and unchanging point of reference.

■ **Control**   I have argued that the brand is the last point of competitive advantage. Ironically it is also the only competitive weapon over which we have real control – it is genuinely within our gift to deliver; it is genuinely within our control. Most other levers such as price or product originality aren't to the same degree.

Control of the brand is too important to be left to the agency, because only the owner is at the centre of the spider's web. It is also too important to be left solely to the marketing team, who should concentrate their efforts on leading the players and orchestrating brand activity. Control must be vested at the highest corporate level, if only because there are structural implications which can only be resolved at that level, and the brand needs a patron with the authority to stare down potential 'blockers' within the organization.

And then there is the ultimate paradox: given that the brand is defined by everything that we do – it is the experience and the staff embody it – then the more marketing try to control and own the responsibility for the brand, the more likely it is to fail. Marketing has to let go and lead and champion and inspire and persuade. Not keep *it* within the marketing department and send out missives every now and then!

■ **Commitment**   Good brand management is an attitude of mind. It is obsessional and it does not permit seasonality, lack of focus or automatic running. Achieving the necessary level of commitment requires extremely hard work by everybody connected with the brand, because the brand promise must be real, provable and inherent at all levels throughout the value chain. Brands must have real substance and that requires commitment: provable and real commitment. Brand management is company management and the ultimate brand manager can only be the chief executive officer.

- **Contact**   The brand must be managed across all the diverse points of customer contact and communication, many of which do not fall within the marketing aegis. Forms design, uniforms, till receipts, the way the sales force behave and the manner in which the telephone is answered all count. Every customer contact either adds to, or subtracts from, the brand's reputation. *Every* contact.
- **Customer driven**   This last 'C' is from the Ministry of the Obvious. The brand must be customer driven. Full stop. This point should not need expansion!
- The mystery eighth 'C' is, of course, **Communicate**. Communicate internally to sell the spirit of the brand. Internalize in order to externalize. And then communicate externally to frame consumer expectation without over-promising and to ensure that there are no surprises except pleasant ones.

There are, perversely, two more Cs. As in the two contained within the word success! Crucial to any brand strategy is the continued momentum of success. It is crucial that the brand is internally and externally perceived to be successful. That will then give the room to breathe and grow and the credibility to move on to the next stage of brand development – and brands *are* living things that grow and change. The alternative to such change is fairly final!

Like all the other elements of the seven Cs, there is a perpetual motion machine of input and output. OK it is not friction free and truly perpetual (far from it in a highly competitive and exposed world) but if the right ingredients help build success or cohesion or clarity or commitment, then you will get these values out of the 'machine' in spades. And the momentum then increases – but cannot be left untended.

So much for my seven Cs, but if they are all so obvious when I spell them out, and indeed they are, why do so many companies fail to build strong brands through total communications? There are a number of reasons and they are not mutually exclusive, so you can expect to find them operating in any number of interesting combinations. Often, companies do not understand either what a brand is, or the rules of whole brand management, and even when they do they do not apply the rules consistently because to do so is a difficult and unglamorous business. They think that brands are things you 'do' on TV and do not understand that they need to be nurtured holistically, with passion and commitment. The people who care and have the courage to implement best practice are in such demand that they rarely stay anywhere long enough to make a real difference.

The marketing structure is so often peopled by marketers who live in the silos of their own disciplines and who possess the narrowness of vision such habitation affords.

Integration

The levers to pull

There are a wide number of tools available to assist in the delivery of total communications. Some, like research and measurement, are purely diagnostic. Budget control is, of course, a great lever to ensure real total communications.

Unfortunately one seldom controls the budget for everything – but that is exactly what needs to be integrated – everything. TV or telephone. Sales promotion or sales force. Direct mail or the physical distribution. And so on. Anyone in a hugely complex and competitive industry knows that it is vital that *you speak in a clear, unmistakable voice, which delivers a consistency of message and personality. One brand; One voice; One creative message; One customer.*

This does not mean slavishly copying all previous campaigns – indeed, a fixation with typefaces, headlines and imagery might well prove counter-productive and result in all our campaigns looking the same. Try to ensure a consistency of 'feel', logic and proposition without becoming, or remaining, committed to a particular executional strategy. A great communications idea deserves the most appropriate medium and expression.

Integrating is not about the execution. Not about taking a TV ad and putting the still on a poster. But it is about having a strong idea that both transcends and is expressed in different ways in different media.

And in my experience the integration – the responsibility for total communications – cannot be delegated to the agency. Only the client has the total picture; the ability to influence all aspects of the brand; the accountability.

The blockers

There are people who will not or cannot see the big picture. This myopia can be caused by the 'silo' phenomenon mentioned earlier, or by simple ignorance on the part of people who, through specializing exclusively in their own field, do not understand that there *is* a big picture. For instance, short-termists who think that tactical behaviour is a bit long term and want results tomorrow without the capability of seeing the end game; and agencies who can only recommend strategies driven by their own profit motives.

Other hurdles to be climbed include those which cannot be described as the failings of individuals. A corporate alliance may mitigate against the coherence of brand communications and, all too easily, internal departments of the same company can, mysteriously, start to sing from different hymn sheets.

Fragmenting media can result in a fragmenting message, but there are ways of overcoming the problem:

■ Only a strong idea can survive, so stress test the brainwave to see if it has life beyond television

- The idea must have substance and be born of the product or service, or be engineered into it
- Integrate the idea as far across media as possible, consistent with maintaining the core customer proposition
- Remember all the points of customer contact
- Lead from the front by taking personal responsibility and by organizing all your resources – agency, human and financial – to optimize success.

Structures and relationships

Having said that strategy dictates structure, we know that the perfect structure cannot exist, because any organization composed of people is dynamic and hence is in a continual process of change. Change is the new status quo. All structures are incompetent – it is just that some are more so than others which should not, of course, prevent anyone from trying to design the optimum one for your purpose. There are, however, some issues which should be borne in mind. Advertising agencies often believe that the client thinks of little else but mainstream advertising. The reality is that advertising plays only a small part in the client's total responsibilities and that the largest part of his day is taken up with trivial 'stuff' like trying not to get de-listed by a major retail chain, or maintaining profit differentials!

The typical advertising agency has to be a shape-changer, because it knows that it cannot be all things to all men and that its mix of skills will never match exactly the requirements of all its clients. No 'client' has the right structure and no agency has all the right skills, but if you wait for all the auguries to come good, you will wait forever.

Before we examine how these two disparate organizations can form a profitable and productive relationship, we should be aware of the different kinds of individual structures that can be involved.

Client structures

- The classical brand management structure, where each brand is managed as a totality, with the brand manager being responsible for all aspects of brand communications. This is a highly focused style. It is unaffected and undiluted by global issues.
- The central marketing department structure, where communications, customers, products and channels are managed together. Communications are managed by discipline or by product. This structure lends itself to consistency in the brand message.
- The SBU or strategic business unit manages all aspects of the product or brand including HR, finance and marketing. It is the only structure with a truly holistic view, but may be the least flexible or reactive. And if product-based, might fight the brand.

Agency structures

- The single discipline agency which will have formed loose alliances with other agencies of different skills. As a stand-alone agency, it is expert in one field only.
- The integrated communications agency where a range of disciplines coexist under one roof and one management. It should be the ideal structure for managing brand communications, but somehow the sum of the parts always seems to add up to less than the whole.
- The 'family of experts' structure where a number of single discipline agencies exist under the same corporate banner – like Omnicom or WPP. Although this sounds like the ideal structure, in practice the different agencies rarely communicate with each other and frequently compete against each other.
- The management consultancy approach, which is based on the theory advanced by Mike Sommers among others, that the further up the strategic chain the agency can go, the more it can charge.

Agency–client relationships

There are many different variations on this theme and they are not limited to the fifteen possible permutations that spring from the structures above. I will however address myself here only to those which I know work, or can be made to work. My favourite top five are:

- À la carte
- All for one and one for all
- Product total
- Discipline total
- Virtual.

I À la carte

This is probably the least disciplined overall relationship, encompassing as it does a number of different agencies, of different disciplines, reporting to different people. It can also provide brilliant work because the client's players – whether they are in the SBU, brand managers, or marketing managers – choose agencies with whose work and personnel they are already familiar. It works best with the brand management structure.

2 All for one and one for all

Here, a single agency delivers everything the client needs. Whilst this relationship is declining in popularity in an age of increasing specialization, it works very well for some clients, typically those with a single brand or channel or product. Within the limits of practicality, it aids integration and coherence, but it can be undermined if the client begins to delegate responsibility for the brand's management to the agency. Some clients have been known to put the whole business – multiproduct, multichannel, multidiscipline – into one agency.

3 Product total

In this scenario each product or brand has its own agency, responsible for all marketing activity. The agencies employed in this way are individually strong in the most appropriate discipline for the product, but also offer the other necessary disciplines. Although each agency offers a 'total' solution and is responsible for campaign integration, the client restricts them to a single product and the client retains the responsibility for the alignment of all products or brands.

4 Discipline total

Here, each agency is responsible for a single medium such as direct marketing, TV, or sales promotion, and manages the requirements of all the client's products or brands within its specialist field. The client accepts responsibility for campaign integration and each campaign's alignment across the product/ brand mix. This route can deliver both consistency and coherence.

You have to decide whether the client will be responsible for integrating the brand between the products and leave the individual product campaign integration to the agency; or take responsibility for managing integration across the product campaigns and leave the discipline (e.g. TV) brand integration to the agency.

5 Virtual

I have cheated here, because this relationship is not truly a relationship at all. The client simply picks a panel of experts and invites them to work together. There is no agency structure and the client's internal structures are dominated by strong, centralized management. The 'experts' come unencumbered by agency baggage and are free to exchange ideas and best practices. The big communications idea is delivered in this forum and executed by the most appropriate and best qualified supplier.

Sometimes this can work. Whether it can work on a day in day out basis...

There is, of course, no 'right' structure/relationship and often what seems to fit today will be clearly unwearable in six months. It is an absolute truth that all clients' internal marketing structures are always in the process of change. Equally, their aligned agencies train their antennae on the client's likely future shape and try to adapt to it before it excludes them. The architecture of the client–agency relationship is created as much by a combination of circumstances, experience and history, as by marketing strategy or global alignments.

However, if you want to achieve effective total communication you might want to score the communication structures available to you against some or all of the following criteria – which themselves must be ranked in order of importance to your business. FMCG companies, for instance, will score them differently from service industries. Which structure will give you the most in terms of:

- Campaign integration and effectiveness?
- Excellence of ideas?
- And excellence of execution?
- Brand consistency and clarity?
- Cost-efficiency?
- Speed of implementation?
- Which structure motivates best?
- How much will the in-house team do?
- Are there global issues involved?
- Can the structure grow with us?

Research and discussion that I have carried out indicates a strong preference amongst marketers towards structure 3 or 4 as the most effective way to deliver total communications.

In summary

The issues and challenges

We recognize the value of integrating brand communications, but there are lots of hurdles. Whilst individual disciplines such as direct marketing and advertising provide training courses for all levels of experience, nobody is teaching the totality of integrated communications. Even worse, tunnel vision can make it seem to be against the self-interest of agencies and, as total communication is company management, if the top team do not perceive it as important or beneficial it is not going to receive a high priority.

There is very little hard evidence to support evangelists like me and faith alone does not move financial directors. Research into corporate 'familiarity and favourability' is of some help, but where is the media or customer research? How do we measure synergy – and if we cannot, who will value it and how will we preach it to our staff?

Change, in everything from agency relationships to client structures, from corporate mergers to the careers of the key drivers, mitigates against the single-minded pursuit of total communications, and change is endemic in our business. In these shifting sands, who will be accountable?

Some final rules for achieving total communications

- Adopt the agency relationship structure that works for your brand.
- Bear in mind that the brand is an *idea* which must be at the centre of every activity from customer care to packaging.
- Integration is central, but it means different things and has different degrees of importance in different spheres of communications. Whilst there may be advantages in making the brochure carry the same images as the TV and direct mail, they are perhaps less important than ensuring that the customer has a consistently good experience wherever he or she touches your brand.
- Centralize and build internal influence over every aspect of brand communications. Remember that total communications is company management.
- Apply the seven Cs and remember the eighth.
- Work, work and work to build a real brand. One that is total, genuine and dynamic – not simply a name backed up by some 'telly'.
- Love and nurture the brand and its expression – God really is in the detail.

In the context of accelerating change, total communications is only achieved through commitment and belief. Only by continually describing the vision, will you persuade others to see it and share it.

Overview: Chapter 13

Andrew Crosthwaite's chapter sets out to explore the business benefits that are derived from having a loyal customer base, relative to the competition.

It explores different ways in which loyalty can be measured, over and above pure customer share of category sales, looking in particular at how consumer attitudes can act as indicators of brand or company strength.

Finally it reviews the way in which advertising, relative to other communication, can help to crystallize commitment to a brand and illustrates this with three examples taken from the IPA's databank of award-winning case histories.

Although never presented on an IPA training course, this paper first saw the light of day in the Spring of 1999 as part of the IPA's 'AdValue' series – a 'partwork' of general proofs of advertising effectiveness.

Andrew's style and rigorous approach to the hot topic of loyalty make this an important new contribution to the second edition of this book.

Chapter 13

Is there a role for advertising as a driver of loyalty?

Andrew Crosthwaite

Why companies gain from having a loyal consumer base

> Relative retention explains profits better than market share, scale, cost position, or any of the other variables usually associated with competitive advantage.
>
> (*Source*: Bain & Co., quoted in *The Loyalty Effect*, Reichheld)

It is hard to argue with a drive for greater customer loyalty – no one wants a disloyal customer, a business contact that is seen today and gone forever – but what are the specific benefits that can be gained commercially?

Greater customer loyalty leads to greater future certainty. Business plans can be written predicting future sales and profits with a higher level of confidence.

Superior customer loyalty will provide the basis for more realistic brand valuation. The worth of a brand only lies in future potential, not past performance. Above sector-average loyalty allows the analyst to put a value on likely *future* performance and the probable ability of a brand or company to defend against new market entries or competitive initiatives.

More loyal customers make the business easier to administer. The relative costs of obtaining new customers against servicing old ones have been well documented – estimates range from five- to twenty-fold, depending on the market category. Repeat purchasers need to be told less – they 'know the ropes'. They are more forgiving of service lapses or failures.

A repeat user of a hotel costs less than a new one on a per stay basis – check-in is faster and smoother for all parties, the guest is less demanding of the hotel infrastructure for information and so on.

In a world where extension tends to outweigh innovation as a path to growth, a brand with a bigger loyal core can be more confident of quicker take-up of a new variant or range extension by virtue of having a ready-made purchase base. This can be important in product testing (attuned customers who can tell you accurately how you perform against past expectations) and in gaining retail confidence through speed of off-take, with less immediate investment.

The forces lined up against loyalty

However, in most markets the trend is to less close ties between the consumer and brands. Indeed, arguably, when we talk about brand relationships, we should refer to brand acquaintanceships.

A study by the Henley Centre in 1998 identified 'Trust' as the single most important brand or company attribute to foster. The study identified the high level of trust enjoyed by established brands against other institutions.

At the same time, the consumer's willingness to suspend disbelief, to take brand claims at face value, has never been lower. Trust has to be earned by consistent behaviour over time. Speed of communication through traditional mass media and emergent technology means that hard-won trust can swiftly evaporate.

The growth of *individuality* means that to stick rigidly to the same choice can carry pejorative associations – buying the same marque of car, going on holiday to the same destination and so on. The days when someone would describe themselves as 'a Ford man' are long gone.

Table 13.1 Penetration of market leaders 1992–97

Category	Leader penetration 1992 (%)	Leader penetration 1997 (%)
Breakfast cereals	43	34
Sun tan lotion	24	20
Household cleaner	40	29
Toilet tissue	48	42

Source: Target Group Index BMRB International

The plethora of *range extensions* in most FMCG markets means that the segmentation of needs is matched by a growth of options, making purchase patterns more repertoire driven. The segmentation of markets as manufacturers seek to provide higher levels of customization is a double-edged sword – the offer is more specific and personal, but also easier to switch out of when mood and needs show subtle changes.

This can be measured in a wide number of markets. In Table 13.1 the penetration of leader brands is compared between 1992 and 1997. In nearly every case, not only had the user base fallen, but so had the proportion of users having it as their most-often brand.

Brand shift not switch

Because most markets operate on a repertoire basis, changes in behaviour tend to be the result of small changes over a long term. The upside of this is that, except in disastrous circumstances (Perrier, John West, etc.), few suffer cataclysmic falls from grace. The downside is that 'erosion' is often at the margins, imperceptible, and by the time it is detected, reparative action is defensive, expensive and often too late.

Alan Hedges' book, *Testing to Destruction*, recently republished, devotes five pages to showing how, over time, a woman gradually moves from being a loyal user of a fictitious cleaner, Lewis's, to a possible defector to its rivals, Whistle or Glo. The key issue is the myriad of influences that weaken her faith in Lewis's, of which only a minority are advertising-related.

Shifts in preference will come from a wide variety of stimuli:

■ Lack of availability (both inconvenient and a subtle sign that a brand is less 'current')
■ Reduced advertising presence, again denoting diminished popularity (on the whole consumers have a remarkable instinct for which brands are thriving and which are not)
■ Loss of confidence in performance characteristics, whether by experience or undermined by the siren calls of a competitor
■ The lure of sheer 'newness' from a rival
■ Price changes in the market

and be characterized by

■ Repeat trial of an alternative (often sporadic)
■ Changes in share of purchase over time, rather than a one-off, 'Damascus-like' conversion

but also influenced by

- Whether the change is high or low risk (financial, time, reputation)
- Mood and occasion (what my current mindset is, or the influence of 'fitness for purpose').

Figure 13.1 shows a typical map upon which different market sectors can be plotted. At a simplistic level, financial services will have a very different set of dynamics from confectionery.

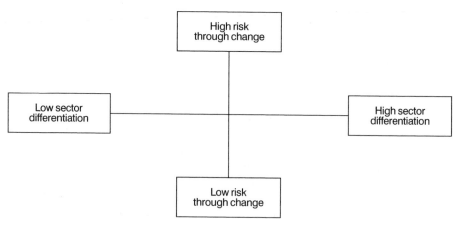

Figure 13.1 A way of mapping your company's risk of loyalty erosion

How can we measure loyalty?

Share of category purchase or usership is one obvious approach and for many companies is the only measure used. The higher the level of an individual's share of category purchase that is accounted for by a particular brand, the stronger, in theory, that brand is.

But we need to be wary.

A loyalty measure that is purely derived from sales may mask some unpalatable truths and be no guide to future performance, or worse, actively misleading. In the 1970s, it was possible for an Italian car marque to have a very high level of repurchase. The reason for this was that problems with corrosion had resulted in such poor resale value that the only way to be able to afford a new car was to trade in to the same franchise.

Many financial services customers are outwardly loyal in their behaviour, but are extremely dissatisfied. It tends to be only the perceived hassle of changing provider or a belief that 'they are all the same' that prevents defection. Research by Millward Brown into the financial services market shows that as many as a fifth of a bank's customers may be attitudinally more positive about a bank other than the one they currently bank with.

However, even in a conservative market like this, disruption can be savage when a compelling product is offered in an innovative way. In 1996 and 1997 First Direct gained a 25 per cent share of all current accounts moved, despite only having 2 per cent of the total market.

What can be confidently assumed is that a brand can be vulnerable to competitive initiative when there are insufficiently strong foundations of goodwill or emotional affinity or belief to fall back onto.

Defining 'true loyalty'

If we accept that behavioural loyalty only demonstrates the symptoms, rather than the cause, there is a need to go deeper to understand the dynamics of behaviour. Rather than being merely observational, we need to get inside the minds of customers and different customer segments to understand not only our brand's real strengths, but also to obtain insights that will help us to maximize them.

One difference between a brand and a mere product is the rich set of beliefs and feelings that people will have towards a brand. Brands, it is often said, do not exist on the shelf, they exist in people's minds.

'True loyalty', then, goes beyond mere behavioural loyalty. It is a measure of the degree of closeness and affinity that customers feel towards brands or companies. This can be assessed in a number of ways.

The BrandDynamics Pyramid

This model (Figure 13.2) has been developed by Millward Brown, based on survey questions which allow the measurement of brand strength and weaknesses at different levels of consumer involvement:

- Presence is the prerequisite for consideration
- Relevance of proposition is a gateway to active consideration
- Performance is an assessment of the brand's fitness to the consumer's needs
- Advantage is the degree to which these needs are met in relation to other options in the repertoire (obviously this will vary according to mood and occasion)
- Bonding is the extent to which these perceptions are carried through to a feeling of closeness or commitment to the brand.

Bonded consumers may only be a small proportion of a brand's customer base – but they are likely to represent a high proportion of the brand's revenue.

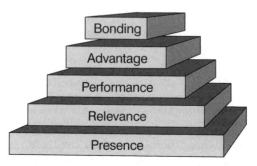

Figure 13.2 The BrandDynamics Pyramid. *Source*: Millward Brown

Figure 13.3 shows the proportion of total revenue accounted for by the bonded consumers in four UK packaged goods categories – tea, coffee, yellow fats and toothpaste.

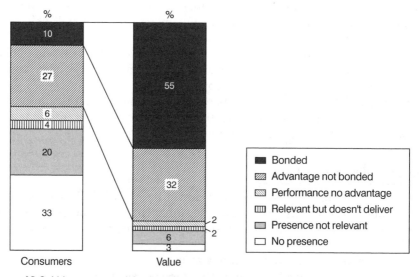

Figure 13.3 Value accounted for by different customer groups. *Source*: Millward Brown

Some of the principal findings from this approach to measuring loyalty include:

■ Brands which gain share over time are likely to be those which currently have more than their fair share of bonded consumers, relative to competitors.

■ Brands which draw a high proportion of their sales from consumers at presence only and don't feel the brand has any particular advantages, rational, emotional or saliency based, will:
  – suffer in the marketplace
  – work hard to justify a price premium
  – be vulnerable to the successful activity of their competitors.

It is possible to calculate whether for its size, familiarity and relevance a brand has more than its fair share at each level of the pyramid.

Brandbuilder

Similar principles are demonstrated by Brandbuilder, a model developed by The NPD Group in the USA (see Figure 13.4)

In this model, those customers in the top right-hand corner exhibit high levels of attitudinal approval of a brand, but relatively low purchase levels. This is based on a study of the 4,000 buyers across 27 brands who were interviewed and segmented into three levels of purchase loyalty levels:

■ high loyals
■ moderate loyals
■ low loyals/non-buyers.

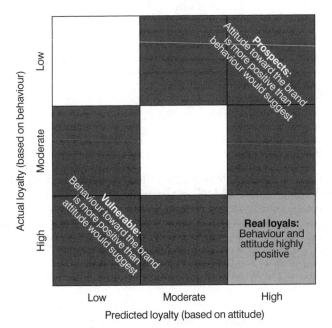

Figure 13.4 Attitudinal and behavioural loyalty model. *Source:* The NPD Group

When recontacted a year later, 60 per cent of the high loyals who demonstrated a *high attitudinal loyalty* to the brand were still loyal, whilst only 25 per cent of those with the same level of purchase behaviour, but a *lower attitudinal level* of respect for it, were still loyal buyers of the brand.

Two groups were then defined: Prospects, whose attitudes to the brand are stronger than their behaviour; Vulnerables, whose behaviour is more committed than their attitudes. In two-thirds of cases, where a brand had more Vulnerables than Prospects, share went down year on year; where more Prospects than Vulnerables, share had gone up.

Another, slightly simpler version of the graphic representation could look like Figure 13.5.

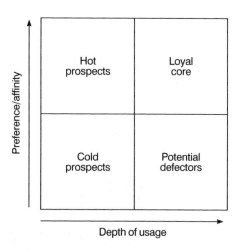

Figure 13.5 Loyalty quadrant

The Conversion Model

A slightly different way of evaluating attitudinal and behavioural loyalty is the Conversion Model (Figure 13.6). Derived from a technique developed in South Africa, designed for measuring religious conversion (hence the name), this process gives a '360 degree picture' of the brand and its market. Fuller examples of its usage can be found in articles in *Admap* by Trevor Richards (March 1997) and Robert Heath (April 1997).

A brand's and its competitors' user base is evaluated according to variables including:

■ The extent of their category involvement
■ The level of satisfaction they have with brands in the current repertoire

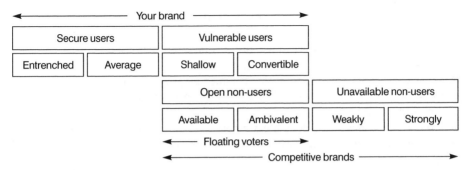

Figure 13.6 The Conversion Model of brand loyalty

- Their attitudes to competitors
- Their own personal characteristics as people.

Consumers are segmented into eight different categories, according to their relationship with the brand or company in question:

Users

- Entrenched – unlikely to change brands in the foreseeable future
- Average – unlikely to change in the short term
- Shallow – lower than average commitment
- Convertible – vulnerable and at the point of making a change.

This last group obviously represents those most at risk for the brand in question and the most likely conquest opportunities for other brands.

Non-users

- Strongly available – users of other brands most likely to be available for 'conversion'
- Ambivalent – non-users who find the brand as attractive as their current ones
- Weakly unavailable – unlikely to become users
- Strongly unavailable – very unlikely to consider the brand.

This enables the marketer to assess the loyalty characteristics of their brands and users, relative to competition, and to identify longer-term opportunities and problems and where they are going to come from.

In particular, the dynamics of the market and brand can be identified, so that a potential gain/loss can be predicted *in advance*, rather than waiting for historical panel or audit data to tell you what went wrong (or right) in the past.

The sort of questions that this approach can be used to answer include:

- What is the profile of my brand (i.e. proportion of my users and the total category fitting into the above typologies)?
- What conclusions can I draw about its future prospects from this?
- What are the market drivers that consolidate my strength or contribute to my potential weakness?
- From which competitors does the greatest level of risk come?
- Conversely, which competitive brands offer the greatest conquest opportunities and why?

Clearly it is also a short step from this to being able to begin to estimate your brand's value, relative to the competition (see also *Understanding the Financial Value of Brands* by Leslie Butterfield and David Haigh).

Importantly, over time, this tool enables the estimation of the contribution of different communication channels to brand loyalty and brand strength, including, of course, advertising.

Advertising, loyalty and other communication

Advertising tends to be viewed by many commentators, not least its practitioners, as a conquest tool, a way of driving awareness, generating trial and establishing personality attributes.

Where promotional activity is often seen as a tangible tool, working hard and producing results (or not, as the case may be), the role of advertising as a loyalty driver can often be undervalued:

> Good general advertising can shape a brand's personality, but only direct marketing can build on-going, durable relationships.

> (*Source: Wunderman*)

Advertising, according to this theory, becomes equated with intangibles, whereas direct marketing and one-to-one activity is at the sharp end, delivering measurable, meaningful payback.

However, many of the widely recognized benefits of an effective advertising campaign impact *directly* onto customer loyalty and hence onto brand performance, brand profitability and brand value.

There are many ways of increasing the *behavioural* loyalty of consumers, although price and other promotional activity has a number of downsides. Functional attributes tend to be changed rather than a richer set of beliefs or associations being developed to sustain a long-term shift of choice, thus limiting payback.

Loyalty is generated to a price point or promotional mechanic, rather than to real or perceived brand benefits. The danger is that markets become offer-led rather than brand value-driven. Tea has gone into a downward spiral of price and on-pack promotion, exacerbating a lack of perceived differentiation by the consumer. The result is that users are buying a promotion with a pack of tea bags attached. The brand becomes only as good as your last banded offer, not your last cup of tea.

The 1990s have seen the launch of a plethora of loyalty cards. 'Loyalty schemes' work only by delivering a benefit tangibly preferable to the competitive offer *and* relevant to the core of the brand offer. Seventy-four per cent of adults own at least one loyalty card, with a quarter of these possessing three or more.

AGB's Superpanel indicates that around a third of all supermarket card holders are no more than 'weakly loyal' to the store in question and although card-holders make more frequent trips on the whole, they do not actually spend more than non-card-holders. (In other words, customers have been given money for doing something that they were already doing.)

More seriously, although consumers perceive that their personal details are being expertly collated, there is scant evidence that companies are currently making active use of much of the data that is collected.

Companies such as Boots who have used their Advantage card as a way of getting customers to spend more and differently are in a minority. (Only 29 per cent of Advantage card-holders are using it to get money off, compared with 68 per cent for supermarket cards; card-holders' expenditure on cosmetics has actually risen by 20 per cent.)

Advertising and the creation of attitudinal loyalty

Bonding and affinity are driven by a variety of factors, and their relative importance varies from category to category. However, many studies, including Brandbuilder, indicate that advertising can have a key role in developing these vital areas:

- Perceived product superiority. It is increasingly difficult for a brand to establish *and* sustain a genuine product-based advantage. However, advertising has the power to shape, channel and enhance consumer's perceptions of a brand's delivery.
- Emotional affinity with the brand. This transformation of product perceptions is one of advertising's most powerful effects, empirically evident in blind versus branded product tests. Most markets will have a product with a taste or performance advantage in reality that evaporates when the brand identity is revealed – Skol used to have a 2:1 blind preference over Carlsberg, a score that reversed when the brands were revealed. Consumers were, literally, tasting the advertising.

■ Advertising is almost unique in its ability to establish personalities and positioning for brands. These may enhance the usage experience, but they also provide the hooks that enable consumers to feel that a brand is emotionally 'the one for them'. Are Levis really tougher than Lee Cooper or Wrangler? In a way it doesn't matter; the desirability bestowed on the brand by years of visible, innovative advertising is a driver of repeat purchase. Harley Davidson owners tattoo the brand name on their bodies – loyalty doesn't come much higher than that.

■ High regard and status. Advertising is also a powerful force for building and maintaining the standing and reputation of the brand in the broader marketplace. Importantly, in many cases this goes beyond the immediate target of the communication. One of the critical measures of a brand's status is its desirability outside the immediate user base.

Advertising is often criticized by advocates of narrower communication for its 'wastefulness'. However, it is the halo effect created by its ubiquity which can lead to enhanced valuation of a brand in the eyes even of those who could never afford it. When Audi was relaunched in the 1980s with the Quattro and 100, the decision to use television was derived from a marketing objective of making the cars desirable to those outside the potential purchaser circle, enhancing the self-image of owners.

Loyalty is transactional – it has to be earned. Unless the customer embarks on a long-term relationship in a motivated frame of mind, it is likely to turn into a shallow relationship, characterized by sporadic one-off encounters. A critical aspect of driving brand preference (ultimately the engine of loyalty and brand strength) is the complex pattern of beliefs that consumers will have. And just as no two individuals are ever alike, so the impressions of brands that live inside peoples' minds differ.

Innovatively expressed brand propositions through advertising media are a uniquely powerful way of generating these beliefs and impressions through a *shared experience* of a company or brand. It is this process of creating customer closeness, through involvement and a belief in the product's superiority, that creates real brand differentiation.

The suggestion is not that advertising is the only way to build a committed franchise, but by laying the foundations and interacting with other elements of the marketing plan, highly effective and cost-efficient results can be generated.

The mini-cases below provide evidence from the IPA databank, a collection of case histories spanning two decades, and show clear examples of some of these principles in practice:

Mini-case 1 – Colgate: Increasing loyalty in adverse circumstances

Issues:
- encroachment on branded toothpaste by own label
- vulnerability of leading brands in context of growing consumer belief that 'all toothpastes are the same'

Action:
- defence through attack
- drive competitive advantage via explicit dental professional endorsement
- strong brand identity through graphics
- focus on empirical differentiation

Loyalty measures:
- in area of heaviest weight, growth of penetration in two years from 47 per cent to 50 per cent
- solus usage among users up from 31 per cent to 40 per cent

Financial outcome:
- in UK Colgate outperformed other branded toothpastes by 25 per cent
- share up to highest level at 30 per cent
- Colgate UK value share up 12 per cent over two years. In rest of Europe, without corporate campaign, value share down 4 per cent
- profit generated three times cost of advertising investment, in addition to strategic importance of maintaining strength as other brands declined in face of own label gains

Mini-case 2 – Volkswagen: Increasing profit by attracting a less promiscuous customer

Issues:
- sales and share in decline
- Volkswagen perceived to be more expensive than it is
- margin being given away by increasingly demoralized dealers because of need to convert higher proportion of relatively small prospect base
- reduced overall profitability throughout business chain

Action:
- redeploy budgets from point of sale incentives to consumer communication
- aim of increasing desirability of VW, thereby driving demand
- 'Surprisingly low prices' theme to enhance perception of affordability and value for money, reducing need to do deals

Loyalty measures:

- decline in proportion of attitudinally bargain-oriented, promiscuous prospects from 20 per cent to 5 per cent of buyers (those least likely to stay with a marque, the least profitable long-term customers)
- VW dealers now showing highest level of satisfaction with own franchise of any in the industry

Financial outcome:

- fastest increase in sales of any brand of car in past 10 years
- percentage of buyers receiving no discount up from 10 per cent to 27 per cent
- average 10 per cent increase in actual price paid for each car relative to sector average
- increase of dealer margin by 50 per cent
- 10 per cent growth in residual values and boost to second-hand market (historically the higher the retained value, the greater the intention to repurchase same marque)

Mini-case 3 – Boots Advantage Card: Using advertising to differentiate a loyalty tool

Issues:

- at time of launch, over 55 million loyalty cards in circulation
- 74 per cent of adults had one or more, with a quarter of holders owning 3+
- AGB data showing that the difference between owning and not owning a store card tended to be expressed in share of trips made, rather than higher spend
- little apparent active use by companies of the captured databases, contrary to expectations

Action:

- focus of advertising strategy on positioning card as 'route to guilt-free indulgence', rather than as money-saving tool
- link to Boots brand strategy of shifting positioning from medicinal to 'looking good, feeling good'

Loyalty measures:

- rate of card uptake double that of test area, where no advertising took place and the card was promoted in store via point of sale and prompting by assistant at time of purchase

- 33 per cent of holders claimed that card ownership encouraged more frequent store visits
- 35 per cent buying things they would normally have bought elsewhere (against 24 per cent for their main supermarket card)

Financial outcome:
- only 29 per cent claimed to use the card to get money off, against 68 per cent for supermarket cards
- spend increase of 9 per cent on personal care items and 20 per cent on cosmetics (focus of advertising, strategic drive areas for Boots and higher margin categories)
- success of card highlighted in annual report as driver of business revival

Summary and conclusions

The benefits of customer loyalty can be traced straight through to the balance sheet.

Loyalty levels are a measure of both the current and long-term health of the brand. This is vital for more than just marketers. Arguably it is the responsibility of every chief executive or financial director to look to these indicators, not just the duty of marketing to evaluate them.

Loyalty is a complex subject. People are not disposed to be loyal in any aspect of their lives and their brand usage is no different. In fact, market forces positively reward and promote loose and uncommitted brand ties. The result is that the marketer spends their time trying to encourage loyalty in their own customers and promiscuity in that of others. In many markets, it is normal practice to lose half your customers from year to year. These changes do not happen overnight. They are the result of gradual shifts in beliefs and behaviour, which can go unnoticed until it is too late.

However, measuring loyalty goes beyond the simple analysis of buyer behaviour, which unless based on continuous panels, with their own attendant problems, can mask as much as it reveals.

Just as brands only exist in the minds of consumers, so true loyalty is an outcome of feelings as well as behaviour. The text contains three examples of research processes, which all recognize that loyalty and bonding need to be part of a holistic research process. Although the examples cited are all quantitatively based, they depend upon a close understanding of customer motivations, both at a category and brand level.

The role of advertising in generating loyalty tends to be diminished in much writing and the balance has shifted to communication areas which operate at a greater degree of customer closeness, typically loyalty cards.

However, if the principle is accepted that true loyalty is generated by building an emotional, rather than a mechanical, relationship with a brand, then well-targeted advertising that is built upon a brand and consumer truth is the medium best placed to deliver this.

References

Butterfield, L. and Haigh, D. (1998), *Understanding the Financial Value of Brands*, IPA Publications.

Heath, R. (1997), *Admap* (April), NTC Publications.

Hedges, A. (1982), *Testing to Destruction*, IPA Publications.

Millward Brown.

NPD Group.

Reichheld, F. (1996), *The Loyalty Effect*, Harvard Business School Press.

Richards, T. (1997), *Admap* (March), NTC Publications.

TGI (Target Group Index), BMRB International.

Overview: Chapter 14

After eight years as Chairman of the Training & Development Committee of the IPA, I stood down in 1997 and accepted an invitation to join the Value of Advertising Committee.

My role within this group over the last two years has been to examine, develop and publicize *general* proofs of the value of advertising. These, it was intended, should sit alongside the *specific* proofs encompassed within the IPA's Effectiveness Awards scheme.

In fact, this role has taken me much further afield than I ever envisaged. Initially it led to getting very involved in the area of brand valuation, culminating in the publishing of another IPA book, called *Understanding the Financial Value of Brands*. More recently, it has taken me into the whole area of how advertising can impact, both directly and indirectly, on shareholder value.

In this chapter, I have tried to distil the key learning from both of these avenues – since both are very much at the leading edge of current advertising and business thinking. I quote extensively from some of the most recent papers and research in the field, but I have tried to keep the chapter as jargon-free as possible.

My personal view is that this whole subject will be one of growing interest and relevance to advertisers and their agencies over the next few years.

As the last chapter in the book, it therefore represents both a springboard and a challenge to agencies as they move into the new millennium.

If agencies are prepared to grasp the nettle of accountability at this most commercial of all levels, then the rewards can be enormous.

Chapter 14

Advertising and shareholder value

Leslie Butterfield

Introduction

It was Oscar Wilde who said that a cynic is someone who knows the price of everything but the value of nothing. He was not talking about finance directors of marketing companies – and indeed this would be an uncharitable observation! But he might have been talking about some people's attitude towards brands, and expenditure on them. Because whilst in business one generally talks about the value of assets (rather than their price), it is only relatively recently that we have started to talk about brands as assets.

But we should, and until we do, many people elsewhere in those organizations will continue to view marketing and advertising expenditure in support of those assets as itself a cost rather than an investment. Yet an investment is what advertising expenditure is, and what it should be seen as.

This is true today more than ever before, for two reasons. Firstly, because brands represent trust, and trust is the precondition to loyalty. Ultimately it is loyalty that delivers sustainable income to brand owners. Readers may think 'trust' is a strange word. Unless, that is, they have read reviews of the 1998 Henley Centre research that places brands like Kellogg's, Heinz and Sainsbury's ahead of the police, the church and parliament in people's 'trust' league. It's not an accident that those brands also have a consistent history of quality advertising support. They've earned their trust – and it will stand them in good stead for years to come.

The second reason for this conviction is that brands are valuable. No surprises there, but if any convincing is needed, Figure 14.1 shows a chart

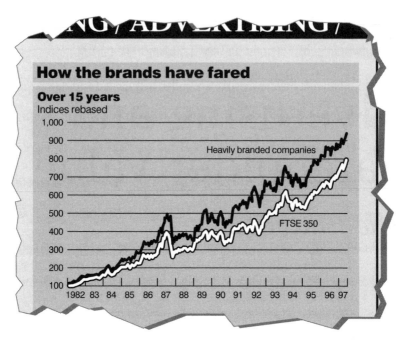

Figure 14.1 How the brands have fared. *Source: Financial Times, 1997*

reproduced from the *Financial Times* of an analysis that Interbrand and Citibank conducted on the stock market performance of heavily brand-dependent companies – and how they outperformed the rest of the FTSE 350 by between 15 and 20 per cent over a 15-year period. Patrick Hearne of Citibank, a co-author of the report that featured this analysis, concluded: *'I think we will see more companies refocusing their brand portfolios, and concentrating on the brands that create value for their business.'*

If anyone is in any doubt about the value of brands they need only do two things. Firstly, look at the extent to which the market capitalization of branded goods companies exceeds their tangible asset value. For the whole US stock market this figure has grown from around +50 per cent in 1993 to around +130 per cent in 1998. In the case of a company like Coca Cola, for example, the figure is as high as +4,000 per cent! In the UK, three examples will suffice: for Cadbury Schweppes the excess of market capitalization over tangibles totals some £1.5 bn (+33 per cent), for Sainsbury's it's £2.0 bn (+55 per cent) and for Scottish and Newcastle Breweries a whopping £3.5 bn (+158 per cent)!

Secondly, look at what acquisitive companies are prepared to pay for brands. In the States, Philip Morris paid £8 bn for Kraft, four times its book value as a business. Here, Nestlé paid £2.8 bn for Rowntree, five times its book value, for brands that included Kit Kat and Polo, both of which have subsequently been exploited and exported to their fuller potential.

Brands therefore are increasingly being recognized as critically important to many major corporations. Former Unilever chairman Sir Michael Perry summed this up almost perfectly when he said:

The major assets of a consumer business, overwhelmingly, are its brands. They are of incalculable value, representing both its heritage and its future. To succeed as a consumer products business there is no alternative but to invent, nurture and invest in brands.

That last point about investment is particularly interesting to those, like myself, who work in advertising. Because, seen in this way, brands are assets in which one invests – rather than, as at present, marketing 'items' against which costs are allocated, and accounted for only in the year in which they arise.

In parallel with the upsurge of interest in brands, there has also been a growing interest in the whole issue of brand valuation.

That subject has been elevated from a rather arcane discussion about balance sheet accounting, to a much more fundamental position of importance. Brand valuation allows marketing companies to quantify the actual financial value of their most prized assets. No longer need that value be, as Sir Michael says, incalculable.

From December 1998, the Accounting Standards Board's Financial Reporting Standards 10 and 11 came into effect, requiring for the first time that the value of acquired brands is included in a company's accounts. Finally, analysts and shareholders will be able to judge for themselves the real value of a company's brand assets.

The die for this change of approach was actually cast some ten years ago, when Rank Hovis McDougall included the value of its brands in its balance sheet as part of its successful defence against a hostile takeover bid from Goodman Fielder Wattie. RHM's actions, though controversial, changed the face of accounting for brands permanently, and since that time many major corporations have used brand valuations for a variety of reasons.

Diageo, Burmah Castrol, Cadbury Schweppes, ICI, Disney, SmithKline Beecham and Dalgety are just some of the 'blue-chip' companies who have employed the technique in pursuit of a range of corporate strategies from investor relations through internal marketing management to securitized borrowing and acquisitions.

The marketing contribution

Advertising comes and goes, but brands live on. And that's because it is brands rather than just their advertising that deliver sustainable long-term value to clients' businesses. 'Sustainable' because they can command loyalty. 'Long-term' because one is talking often about decades of contribution. And 'value' because, as we have seen, brands are valuable – to marketing companies, and therefore to agencies.

None of that will be any great revelation to the reader. Most will not need convincing of the part that brands can play in delivering sustainable long-term value. The real questions are: 'Do others appreciate this?' and, 'Is the marketing contribution to this value recognized?' At the moment, I suspect the answers here would be 'partially' and 'sometimes'.

Taking the first question, Figure 14.2 shows a copy of a memo. It's genuine, and genuinely frightening. It was sent to me by a former client of mine (the names have been disguised to protect the innocent!) with a note that just said 'Help'. I suspect like me you'd wonder where to start, so great is the gulf in understanding between the two disciplines. And, sadly, whilst extreme – this kind of gulf may not be so atypical.

In 1997 the IPA in conjunction with KPMG commissioned a survey of finance directors' attitudes to marketing and advertising. Figure 14.3–14.5 highlight three of the key findings from that survey.

In answer to the question, 'To what degree do you see the following as a necessary investment to long-term growth?', marketing came fifth out of five (Figure 14.3). But when it comes to cutting budgets when costs are under pressure, marketing and advertising are first (Figure 14.4). This is hardly surprising though when one realizes that the criteria that most FDs use to measure marketing and advertising effectiveness are pretty blunt (Figure 14.5). Sales volume is rated more than four times as important as brand image, for example, in making those judgements.

And as to the other question, about recognition of the marketing contribution, Dominic Cadbury, Chairman of Cadbury Schweppes, was quoted in *Marketing Week*, in June 1997, as saying:

> A fixation with advertising makes it unsurprising that marketing has a struggle to be taken seriously in the boardroom and that the notion of marketing as a source of competitive advantage is regarded with suspicion.

What a pity that such an eminent commentator should take such a dim view of the marketing and advertising contribution. In response to a letter from myself though, he substantiated his view as follows:

> I am committed to the importance of marketing in all its aspects as I am to improving the effectiveness of what we do. [However, he continues] I do think there is a growing issue around our accountability to our shareholders because I see them becoming more active in analysing and questioning marketing expenditures.

MEMO

To:	Advertising Manager
From:	Finance Director
Date:	14th December 199X

Dear Jeff,

Many thanks for demonstrating that you have a budget for this expense. However, I still have some concerns about the proposed advertising.

With car sales below plan, together with the adverse exchange rate expected below budget (£= 190-195 yen which is 25-30 yen below the budget rate, which means for Car Division's profit at planned volumes will be down by £2½-3 million!!) we must ensure that all expenditure adds value to the business.

To make gross profit of £0.5 million, we must sell 520 Corona's (13,000 for a net profit of £0.5m). I know that we have been asking agencies to measure the effect of our advertising. With this information and your department's analysis, will you please demonstrate that your proposed expenditure will earn net profit of £0.5m in addition to what we would earn without the cost. That is, will the advertising you propose generate 13,000 extra unit sales of Corona?

By the way, does your advertising analysis show that national or local advertising is the most effective in generating showroom traffic?

Thanks,

John

PS Assumptions of above are:

Gross profit per Car	£962.33	
Costs per car sold	£926.48	(budget)
Net Profit per car	**£35.85**	

Figure 14.2 Memo to AM from FD

Q. To what degree do you see the following as
a necessary investment for long-term growth?

	%
Training	94
Information technology	91
Human resources	79
Research and development	73
Marketing	**58**

Source: IPA/KPMG

Figure 14.3

Q. If business costs were under pressure,
which of these budgets would be cut *first*?

	%
Marketing and advertising	**23**
Human resources	18
Training	13
Research and development	9
Information technology	8

Source: IPA/KPMG

Figure 14.4

Q. Which criteria do you use to measure
marketing and advertising expenditure?

	%
Sales volume	**54**
Market share	**31**
Awareness levels	26
Brand image	12

Source: IPA/KPMG

Figure 14.5

Effectiveness and accountability

It is these twin issues of effectiveness and accountability that sit at the heart of the debate about brand valuation. The position today is that brand valuation points a way forward for marketing companies and their agencies in attempting seriously to monitor the value of their brands. In so doing it becomes a means to an end, not just an end in itself, by providing a common language at board level between the key functions of a branded business.

As preparation for writing this chapter and to gauge the current 'state of play', I consulted the finance directors of some of my own clients. Among these there are some pretty powerful brands – in many cases strong corporate brands, like Mercedes Benz, The Co-operative Bank, Emirates Airlines and Harley Davidson, who have the most to gain from directly enhancing their brand and its value. The overriding impression to come out of this was not, as Dominic Cadbury suggested, one of suspicion, but rather one of lack of understanding of the role that the brand could play – and above all the lack of a common language with which to construct that understanding.

It is in addressing issues such as this that brand valuation has a key role to play. Because it spans both disciplines, it can be the bridge between them, can unite the purpose of both, and can contribute to the greater understanding that is at the heart of some of the issues discussed above, whether it leads to putting a brand value on the balance sheet or not.

Within my own experience, I've seen the principle and, on occasion, the specific approach applied successfully in at least three areas:

- Defining the value of a retail subsidiary as a precursor to decisions about whether to merge, sell or invest in promoting that subsidiary
- Prioritizing brands within a portfolio as part of a review of where to make advertising investment decisions
- Evaluating the status of a single corporate brand as a guide to setting absolute levels of marketing expenditures.

Whilst the approach is not without its methodological drawbacks, these have, in all the cases I've just outlined, been more than outweighed by the strategic benefits that have been derived from the exercise. Of these benefits, by far the most important is the recognition by senior people *outside* the marketing area of just how valuable their intangible brand asset is.

Mini-case: The steps in a brand valuation

Brand valuations typically comprise four elements:

■ A market analysis (to understand the marketing environment)
■ A branded business analysis (to understand the brand's performance within the market)
■ A brand analysis (to determine what proportion of business earnings are attributable to the brand – Brand Value Added BVA^{TM})
■ A brand risk analysis (to assess the security of the brand franchise both with customers and with end-consumers – the BrandBeta^{TM})

The process can be flow-charted as follows:

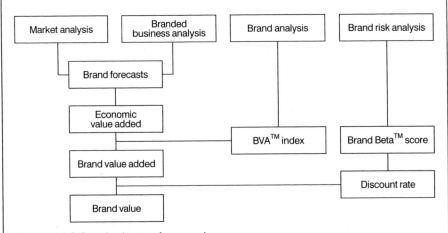

Figure 14.6 Brand valuation framework

A wide range of information is gathered about the brand, its performance and its history from a number of different sources. Data is collected by a mixture of desk research, questionnaires and face-to-face interviews. It is then analysed to assess the brand in various terms beginning with the financial data.

Calculating economic value added – Once a brand's background and its revenues, costs and capital employed have been established it is possible to produce a 5–10-year cash-flow forecast that can be assessed for reasonableness. Clear definition of the economic value added in the branded business is essential for valuation purposes. The earnings used to arrive at economic value added must be the fully absorbed earnings of the brand after the allocation of central overhead costs.

Elimination of private label production – The earnings used in the discounted cash-flow calculation must relate only to the brand being valued and not to other, unbranded goods which may be produced in parallel with the brand, but which are not sold under the brand name.

Remuneration of capital employed – To avoid overvaluation of the brand it is necessary to make a fair charge for the value of the tangible assets employed in the business; for example, the distribution system, the manufacturing plant and the stock. Until a fair return has been made on the fixed assets and working capital tied up in the business, it cannot be said that the brand is adding value to the business.

Taxation – The discount rate is always applied to post-tax earnings. The result of this analysis is a thorough assessment of the historic and prospective economic value added attributable to all the intangible assets employed in the branded business. The next step is to establish what proportion of the total economic value added relates to the brand as opposed to other intangible assets.

Calculating Brand Value Added BVA^{TM} – Different businesses rely in varying degrees on branding to stimulate demand and support price. By identifying what it is that drives demand in the specific market it is possible to estimate the contribution made to the business by the brand. This is typically achieved using a form of trade-off analysis.

This is known as the Brand Value Added BVA^{TM} Analysis. Although it is a judgmental exercise, it provides a systematized way in which to approach the question and produces reliable conclusions, particularly where it is supported by large sample trade-off or conjoint analysis. By applying the Brand Value Added BVA^{TM} Index to economic value added in the branded business, brand value added can be estimated.

Assessing brand risk – A brand value reflects not only the potential of a brand to generate income, but also the likelihood that the brand will do so. It is therefore necessary to determine an appropriate discount rate which takes into account economic, market and brand risks.

© BRAND FINANCE

Bridging the gap between marketing and finance

Rather than tolerate the 'parallel universes' of finance and marketing, companies can start to use brand valuation as a way of bridging between the two disciplines. And at this stage we can add a third 'universe': that of the

CEO. He or she also has an interest in the value of brands and hence the value of the marketing and advertising contribution to brands.

Within this triangular relationship between CEO, finance and marketing, all three of the 'linkages' can in part be better informed by a greater understanding of the value of brands to the business. The implications of this would be threefold:

- A more 'open' relationship between disciplines, because of the common goal
- Greater dialogue between all three because of the existence of a common language

and finally,

- Greater disclosure, both within *and outside* the company, of the marketing effort and investment going behind those brands.

The issue of disclosure is critically important if the role of brands and the professional marketing of them is to be taken seriously by the wider financial community.

In 1998, the IPA commissioned through Brand Finance Ltd a survey of City analysts' attitudes towards the nature and extent of disclosure in the published accounts of publicly quoted companies. The survey found there to be a strong and growing demand in the City for more comprehensive disclosure of marketing expenditure and brand value information by publicly quoted companies. This in turn reflects a growing recognition among investors that strong brands underpin growth in corporate value. Figure 14.7 highlights some of the key findings.

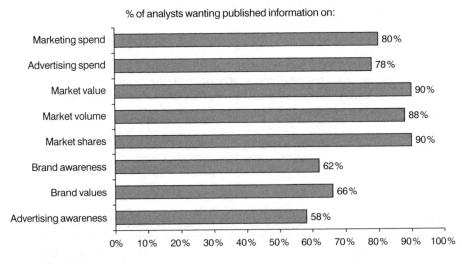

% of analysts wanting published information on:

Source: IPA/Brand Finance

Figure 14.7 Key findings

Some 80 per cent of analysts believed that stock exchange listed companies should publish more information on total marketing spend, while 78 per cent believed that more should be published on advertising spend levels. A substantial majority of these analysts claimed they would find a range of marketing information useful when making investment recommendations. For example, 88 per cent would like to see current market volume and 90 per cent value estimates; 90 per cent would like more information on market shares; 62 per cent would like to know the current level of brand awareness; and 66 per cent believe the publication of current brand values would be useful.

A way forward

The IPA is at the forefront of trying to promote a greater understanding of the financial value attributable to brands as a key measure of advertising effectiveness. For too long the focus in the advertising industry has been on the bottom half of the hierarchy shown in Figure 14.8. The IPA's Effectiveness

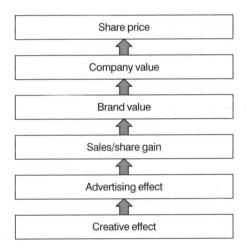

Figure 14.8 A hierarchy of effect

Awards scheme has concentrated, historically, on short-term advertising effects on sales and share and not enough on the harder-to-quantify effects on brand or even company value.

The IPA has already sought to broaden the criteria by which the Advertising Effectiveness Awards are judged, to take account of this expanded definition of advertising's role. Its mission now is to try and elevate the debate up the hierarchy shown here by demonstrating that brand valuation can also be a key measure of advertising effectiveness and that therefore it brings a whole new slant to marketing and advertising budget decisions. Even if it were only used as an internal tool, to get all disciplines within a branded business to focus on the asset value of their brands, this in turn might lead to those other disciplines viewing advertising expenditures as investments rather than just costs.

Mini-case: The Co-operative Bank

If a more general recognition of marketing's value is the aim, what contribution, and specifically what value, can advertising agencies add to the process and to the brand?

The conventional agency response – that advertising 'adds value' to products – is not good enough. What consumers increasingly want is to be shown the real, *intrinsic* value that the product or service possesses. They require product truths that match their personal needs.

Research that Partners BDDH did more than five years ago for The Co-operative Bank, taught us that using advertising to add a gloss to an imperfect offer (in the way that many banks have done) was an impoverished strategy when compared with the substantial claim that springs from a genuine truth that is intrinsic to that brand.

In the case of The Co-operative Bank, the truth was that it was an ethical bank, and Partners BDDH's mission became not so much about adding value, as about *extracting value* from this fact. In so doing it implied putting to work for the brand the most powerful weapon in the communications armoury – the truth – and then branding it.

The achievements of the campaign we developed were directly quantifiable. Over the initial period that we worked with them:

- Account closures were reduced by over 30 per cent.
- Account openings increased by 6 per cent per annum and average balances by nearly 20 per cent.
- 44 per cent of new account openings were claimed as due to the Bank's ethical positioning.
- The customer profile shifted significantly upmarket and to higher net worth individuals.
- And The Co-operative Bank became the biggest issuer of Gold Visa cards in Europe!

But the campaign went on to achieve much more than this. For the first time it gave the Bank a positioning and an identity on which to hang almost every aspect of its operation. At the very least this included branch materials, literature and direct marketing communications.

Figure 14.9

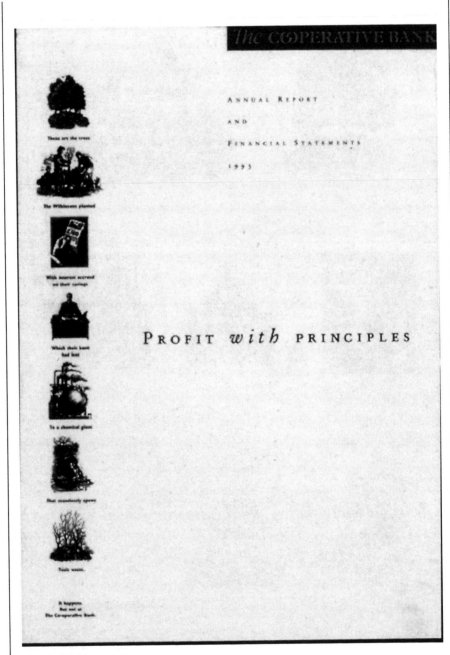

Figure 14.10

It carried through even to the Bank's Report and Accounts. As can be seen here, the press ad shown in Figure 14.9 above made it onto the front cover: frame for frame, word for word (Figure 14.10).

And that's significant *symbolically* too, because what it indicates is the *real* achievement of a campaign such as this.

By identifying and amplifying a core truth of the company, what we actually did was give meaning to the Bank's internal culture and value system. We gave customers a reason to choose them, but we also gave staff a reason to be proud of working for them and be ambassadors for them. We gave coherence to the Bank's identity, but we also gave the Bank's management an anchor point in terms of the internal focus of the company. We added value to the business, in other words, by extracting value from the brand.

	1991	1993	1995	1997	1998
Customer deposits					
Personal customers (£m)	609	728	1052	1785	1889
Business customers (£m)	414	572	855	1098	1280
Operating income (£m)	190	228	250	316	354
Profit before tax (£m)	(6)	18	37	55	74
Ad spend (£m)	0.6	2.5	4.2	1.9	1.9

Figure 14.11 Financial results

In this case, advertising quite literally helped transform the *fortunes* of the brand (see Figure 14.11). From 1991 to 1998:

- Deposits from both personal and business customers have trebled.
- Operating income is up by over 80 per cent. Profits have gone from minus £6 m to plus £74 m.
- And yet across the whole period, advertising spend has never exceeded £5 m.

In future it will only be by having evidence like this that agencies will be able to make a sustainable case for the economic benefit they deliver to their clients. And if agencies really want to be taken seriously they will need to raise their sights as well as their standards even beyond this. They will need to engage in the economic arguments at FD and CEO level, be prepared to demonstrate and be held accountable for the brand's financial value that they deliver, and even be remunerated accordingly.

In 1999, The Co-operative Bank undertook a brand valuation exercise. This revealed that a substantial proportion of total business value across all product sectors was coming from the contribution of The Co-operative Bank brand – a far cry from the position in 1991.

Advertising and shareholder value

I believe it is right that agencies should take responsibility for the effectiveness of their work for a client; effectiveness in all senses, including financial accountability. The ultimate contribution an agency can make is enhancing the shareholder value of its clients' business.

This brings me to the central purpose of this chapter – which is to examine the issue of how advertising can enhance shareholder value.

Because whilst brand valuation is a useful and important method for measuring the contribution of brands to the total value of a business, it doesn't of itself explain:

(a) *how* advertising contributes to brand value (and hence shareholder value) or
(b) *how* advertising can affect shareholder value via its impact on profitability, or indeed
(c) *how* advertising might even affect share prices *directly.*

A lot of the interest in the whole issue of advertising and shareholder value is coming out of the States. But amongst the various papers on the subject, one for me stood out above the rest: 'Market Based Assets and Shareholder Value' by Srivastava, Shervani and Fahey, delivered at the US Marketing Science Institute, in 1998.

The paper talks about a 'quiet revolution' in the way that marketing activities are being viewed by some marketing professionals, by CEOs and by enlightened finance directors.

In a nutshell, what the paper argues is that marketers will increasingly be called upon to view their ultimate purpose as contributing to the enhancement of financial returns.

This in turn will mean that customers (and indeed distribution channels) will be viewed as 'market-based assets' that need to be captured, cultivated and leveraged.

In tandem, marketers will need to move beyond traditional measures such as sales, share and margin to measures based on maximizing the net present value of future cash flows . . . and hence shareholder value.

Two things are worth clarifying at this point.

Firstly, by the 'net present value of future cash flows', we mean the value *today* of the income streams likely to accrue to the company over, say, a five-year period. That income being discounted at a rate which takes account of the degree of uncertainty that attaches to it.

Secondly, of the 'market-based assets' that the authors refer to, the most significant for us are what they call 'relational assets' – which are principally the relationships between a firm and its customers. To quote: 'Brand equity reflects the bonds between the firm and its customers and may be the result of extensive advertising and superior product functionality.'

So how do market-based assets specifically affect the shareholder value of the business?

At its simplest, the market value of a firm is the net present value of all future cash flows expected to accrue to the firm. The importance of this perspective is underlined by the fact that a large proportion of the value of firms is based on perceived growth potential and associated risks. That value is based on *expectations* of future performance.

Because shareholder value is largely composed of the present value of cash flows during a defined period, the value of any strategy is inherently driven by:

1 Accelerating the *speed* with which cash flows are generated (earlier cash flows are preferred because risk and time adjustments reduce the value of later cash flows).
2 An increase in the *level* of cash flows generated through its various components (e.g. higher revenues and lower costs, working capital, and fixed investments).
3 A reduction in *risk* associated with future cash flows (e.g. via reduction in both volatility and vulnerability of future cash flows), hence, indirectly, the firm's cost of capital.

Now, if we take each of these three shareholder value drivers, let's examine how marketing and advertising activity can affect and enhance each one in turn.

1 *Accelerating cash flows:* The authors cite evidence from numerous published studies that demonstrates that market-based assets can accelerate cash flows by increasing the responsiveness of the market place to marketing activity, e.g. speeding up trial, adoption and referral rates for new or next generation products or brand extensions from the same company.
2 *Increasing or enhancing cash flows:* The authors here cite examples of enhanced cash flows as a result of
   (a) established brands being able to command a price premium
   (b) higher customer retention and therefore lower customer 'recruitment' costs
   (c) greater responsiveness of loyal customers to advertising and promotions (therefore lower marginal costs of sales and marketing)
   (d) greater uptake of brand extensions.
3 *Influencing the volatility of cash flows:* Volatility (and vulnerability) of cash flows is reduced when customer satisfaction, loyalty and retention are increased. Importantly the net present value of a less volatile cash flow is greater than that of a more erratic one – again contributing directly to shareholder value.

The bottom line (literally) is that advertising affects the quality of a brand's relationship with its customers, which in turn can be demonstrated to affect cash flow, which directly impacts shareholder value.

The impact on profitability

If you don't want to get into that level of debate, what about something a little more straightforward – like 'does advertising affect profitability?' (Which of course itself affects shareholder value.)

Well, here too the answer is 'yes' – and this time the evidence comes from closer to home (the UK and Europe) and is a bit simpler to explain.

The data source is PIMS (which stands for Profit Impact of Market Strategy), and the focus for this study were the 200+ companies operating principally in branded consumer products in Europe.

The analysis described here conducted by myself, PIMS and the IPA focuses specifically on the relationship between advertising and profitability – both directly and, perhaps more importantly, indirectly, via the medium of perceived quality.

Figure 14.12 illustrates the well-established causal relationships that PIMS know to exist within the main database. PIMS are unequivocal that, on the basis of the *whole* sample of 3000+ businesses, providing a superior value offering to customers is a prime driver of growth and profitability.

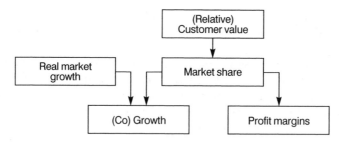

Figure 14.12 Links from customer value to profitability and growth

Customer value in turn is defined from the customer's perspective as a combination of quality of total offering, and price, both of these being measured *relative* to competitors. Of these two, it is relative perceived quality that is of most interest to us. Finally, we also know that one of the principal *components* of relative quality is 'product image and company reputation'.

Armed with these numerous linkages and relationships, we now went on to examine the extent to which we could demonstrate the role that advertising spend can play in shaping and influencing the above factors.

Our first special analysis was designed to examine the relationship between absolute levels of advertising spend (expressed as a percentage of sales) and relative quality of offering. The results were disappointing: there was little correlation between absolute levels of advertising spend and relative quality of offering.

Spirits rose considerably, though, when we repeated the analysis, but this time relative to competitors . . . effectively a measure of 'share of voice' relative to share of market. Figure 14.13 shows the findings from this analysis and the result is clear: advertising spend *relative to competitors* is strongly correlated with relative perceived quality of offering.

Advertising spend relative to competitors is strongly correlated with relative quality of offering

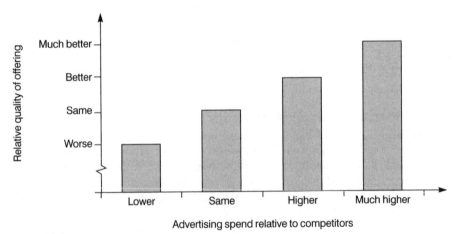

Advertising spend relative to competitors

Figure 14.13

The conclusion here is clear and important. Namely that in influencing customer perceptions of the quality of your product (and hence its value) it is not a question of how *much* you spend, but of how much you *out*spend your competitors.

(The point about outspending competitors should not be taken as a 'counsel of despair' by No. 2 brands and below! What we are saying here is that those brands need to outspend (in share of voice terms) *relative to their share of market* – not absolutely more than, for example, the brand leader.)

This same logic held true when we went on to examine the key component of perceived quality: product image and company reputation. Again the analysis showed little evidence of correlation between *absolute* spends and this component. But when we examined our *relative* spend measure (i.e. share of voice, relative to share of market) the correlation was very powerful

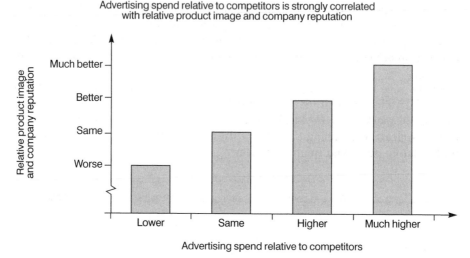

Figure 14.14

(Figure 14.14). It is this analysis that leads to the second key conclusion from this study.

Because 'product image and company reputation' is both a component of quality and a *driver of it*, we would suggest that it is not just 'any old advertising' that matters, but rather advertising that seeks and succeeds in building quality perceptions of the product, either directly or through the intermediary of product image and company reputation.

The combination of these two special analyses, and the conclusions that stem from them, mean that we can now extend the model that we examined earlier. Figure 14.15 shows that extended model – with the top three levels having been added as a result of the analyses reported here.

Whilst it would have been delightful to show a simple causal relationship between advertising and profitability, the real world influence of other factors means that we have had to demonstrate causality through a set of intervening variables. Of these, by far the most important is relative customer value – and we are able to demonstrate the impact of advertising on this variable through its effect on relative perceived quality.

Advertising and share prices

If that's still too convoluted, what about if we really got down to brass tacks?

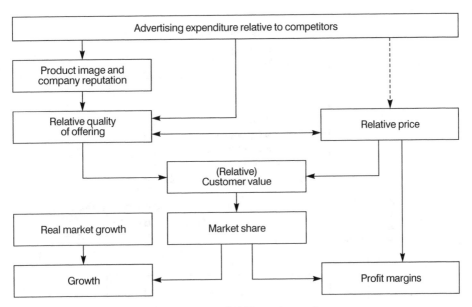

Figure 14.15 Links from advertising to profitability and growth

What if we were able to demonstrate not just that advertising affects cash flows and profitability, and that these impact on shareholder value – but that advertising can directly affect share price itself!

Well we can. But we've got to go back to the States again for the evidence here.

To Connecticut to be precise, to a company called Corporate Branding Partnership, who have developed a model to disentangle the various linkages and drivers that affect the stock prices of listed companies.

Of these linkages, the ones that they focus on, and that are of most interest to us, are those between communications, corporate image and shareholder value. Figure 14.16 demonstrates the chain of events that link corporate brand communications, corporate image, and share price.

The factors that impact stock price, based on this research, are illustrated in Figure 14.17. CBP's analysis explains 87 per cent of the variance in stock price by a number of factors, most of which are business related.

Cash flow, earnings, and dividends explain 30 per cent of the stock price. Another 20 per cent piece of the pie is expected cash flow growth. Company size accounts for 6 per cent of the pie. (Companies that are either very small or very big carry a real disadvantage in terms of stock-market valuation.)

But the really interesting bit is this!

CBP's research has shown that *image* alone explains 5 per cent of the variation in stock price. Image is not a huge percentage when you compare it

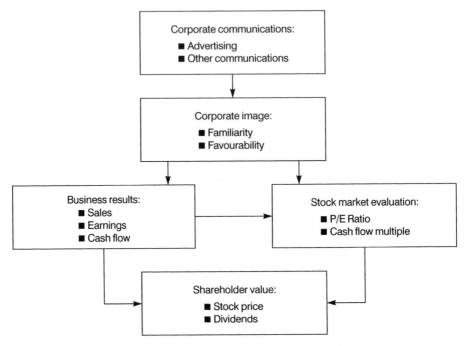

Figure 14.16 Linkages between corporate communication and stock prices

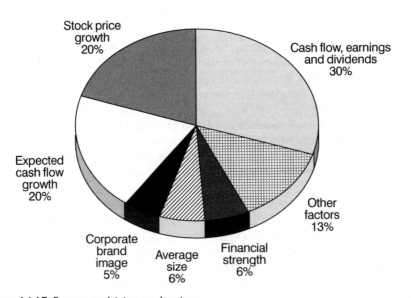

Figure 14.17 Factors explaining stock prices

to cash flow, earnings, and dividends, but it is definitely significant, and an important contributor.

CBP suggest that amongst other business-related factors that a company has little control over, image is a real leverage factor, a tool that can be used to affect a company's stock price. The fact that it is nearly as important a factor as the 6 per cent explained by financial strength (a company's soundness based on stable earnings and amount of debt) in determining stock price is, they say, worth noting.

In addition to having a direct impact on stock price, CBP argue that image also indirectly influences perceptions of cash flow, earnings and dividends, stock price growth, and expected cash flow growth (Figure 14.18).

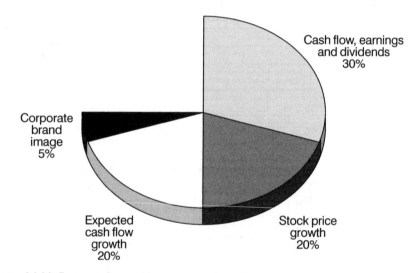

Figure 14.18 Factors influenced by corporate brand image

So, when you add up both direct and indirect influences on stock price, image has an effect on 75 per cent of the factors explaining stock price.

Finally, CBP were able also to quantify the most significant factors explaining corporate brand image. Not surprisingly, the biggest single influencer of image was (you guessed it) advertising.

Now . . . back to the UK. Tim Ambler, Research Fellow at London Business School, has picked up on the work that Corporate Branding Partnership have been doing, and has incorporated it into a model that he has developed of how marketing impacts on shareholder value.

He sees a movement having taken place from the traditional view of marketing's effect on profits (Figure 14.19) to a new view of marketing's effect on shareholder value (Figure 14.20).

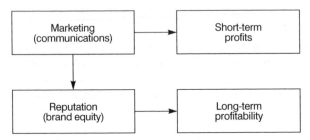

Figure 14.19 Traditional view of marketing's effect on profits

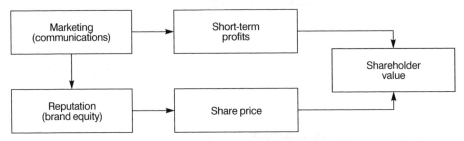

Figure 14.20 A new view of marketing's effect on shareholder value

A number of the factors that we have discussed here would support this observation, although I personally feel that the learning on cash flow adds an extra stage of effect that perhaps his model understates.

Mini-case: Orange

Whilst price-cuts might have seemed the obvious strategy for Orange, this would have been fundamentally opposed to Orange plc's business strategy of value growth. Instead Orange has pursued a three-pronged strategy, with advertising contributing across every element.

1. Earnings growth

By creating a positive predisposition towards Orange prior to the purchase decision, econometric modelling has shown that advertising was responsible for at least 15.27 per cent of additional subscribers since flotation, equivalent to a lifetime value of £144.34 million.

In addition, advertising has contributed to a higher subscriber revenue by:

■ **Attracting high-usage customers.** Analysis of the customer database demonstrated that customers who responded to the advertising were more valuable. This has contributed to Orange having the highest average revenue per customer.

■ **Increasing usage.** By showing a correlation between advertising support and network traffic, Orange demonstrated how advertising has exploited the tendency of customers to be more aware of their own brand's advertising. Orange users have been educated to use their network.

Via these effects, advertising's quantifiable contribution to maximizing subscriber revenue can be calculated as £22 million.

2. Earnings security

For Orange plc to be confident of maximizing shareholder value it must not only attract and cultivate *quality* customers, but maintain them and deliver *earnings security*.

Orange has the highest customer lifetime in the marketplace, and advertising has contributed to this enviable level. Research identified that *coverage* and *cost* were the two main reasons why customers chose to leave the Orange network. By educating customers about Orange's improved coverage and value added features, advertising has improved customer loyalty by 3.43 months, equivalent to an additional earnings security of £102.6 million.

3. Risk diversification

Orange has an obligation to create further shareholder value through the diversification of its interests. Advertising's role in *risk diversification* can be highlighted in two areas:

1 *Foreign licence bids.* Given the slow rate of growth of the UK marketplace, Orange has sought to obtain mobile licences abroad. The strength of the brand has given Orange plc a huge headstart in these foreign bids, playing a fundamental role in Orange plc's success in Switzerland and Belgium.
2 *Brand transferability.* Through exploratory research amongst consumers, Orange has confirmed the potential of the brand to enter new markets (e.g. banking). Whilst this strength remains latent, it will undoubtedly play an important role in Orange plc's future business plans.

Valuing advertising's contribution

There can be little doubt about the high regard in which the City holds Orange advertising. Research amongst City analysts consistently rates Orange marketing and advertising as the company's single most powerful inherent strength. However, in order to obtain a quantitative valuation of Orange advertising's

Table 14.1 Lehman Brothers current equity
market valuation

Discount rate	9%
NPV cash flows	1,035
PV terminal value (£m)	6,396
Enterprise value Orange PCS	7,432
Other businesses	459
Asset/enterprise value	7,891
Net debt (projected end 98)	(1,571)
Equity value	6,320
Implied value per share (pence)	528
Current share price (pence)	443
Current discount/premium	+16%

impact on shareholder value, in 1998 Orange and their advertising agency, WCRS, enlisted the help of Lehman Brothers.

Their spreadsheet methodology put the implied value per share of Orange at 528p (compared to the then current market value of 443p), implying that Orange was a *buy* stock.

Lehman Brothers then reworked their valuation on the assumption that advertising's effects on net subscriber growth, customer revenue and churn had not applied. The implied value per share dropped to 279p.

Table 14.2 Lehman Brothers equity market
valuation removing advertising's contribution

Discount rate	9%
NPV cash flows	328
PV terminal value (£m)	4,172
Enterprise value Orange PCS	4,500
Other businesses	459
Asset/enterprise value	4,959
Net debt (projected end 98)	(1,616)
Equity value	3,343
Implied value per share (pence)	279
Current share price (pence)	443
Current discount/premium	−59%

Conclusion

The success of Orange plc over the last three years is due in no small part to the company's belief in the manifold power of advertising; a power which has created a conventional earnings payback in excess of six times the advertising investment.

With the help of Lehman Brothers, Orange and WCRS have been able to calculate advertising's capacity to increase Orange plc's implied value per share by £2.49. This is equivalent to an increased market capitalization of £3.0 billion. There can be few more powerful demonstrations of the impact of advertising on shareholder value than this.

The opportunity for agencies

Advertising agencies are increasingly trying to reposition themselves as business partners to their clients – often in an attempt to cement their upstream, top-table position with clients. Here, of course, they face the encroachment of management consultants, in what is increasingly becoming an advice market.

But whilst management consultants have numerous skills, branding and the understanding of consumers' relationships with brands are not their strong suit. For this reason, and also because it is in agencies' own interests to promote the value of brands for investment purposes, agencies should take more interest in the whole area of brand valuation and shareholder value. And if they are interested, they are well placed to make a real and valuable contribution. There are both skill and structure reasons for this unique position.

In terms of their skill base, the contrast with management consultants in respect of brand knowledge has already been mentioned. Beyond this, it is often the case that high-quality pure research skills (especially in the area of econometrics) still reside in agencies more than in many client companies.

In 1998, the discipline of account planning within advertising agencies celebrated its thirtieth anniversary. Planning (and hopefully planners) have come a long way since Stanley Pollitt's original vision of a 'new breed' of researcher. Nowadays, planners have to combine their traditional position of 'spokesperson for the consumer' in the creative process with a third dimension of skills in the area of business performance (see Figure 14.21).

As such (and often in combination with enlightened account directors and agency managers), they are increasingly called upon to assess the financial performance of brands for which they are the guardians. Likewise, the best planners are well equipped to prioritize the importance of the various research

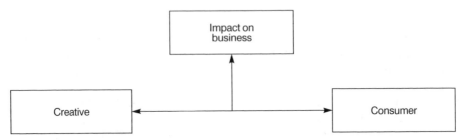

Figure 14.21 The third dimension of planning

inputs outlined below. Their remit is broader, their expertise often more varied and their perspective more commercial than many client research personnel.

Structurally, agencies enjoy a privileged role vis-à-vis their clients as being, at the same time, both impartial observers and intimate confidants of their clients. This should allow them to see the brand in all its guises (and from a consumer perspective), and yet be objective about the strength of relationship that that brand enjoys with its user base. Furthermore this 'expert' standpoint is often fuelled by the length and continuity of relationship that the agency has had with the client and its brands. This often far outlasts the equivalent timescale of the client's own marketing personnel.

Finally, agencies have access to normative data from other categories, or direct experience of valuations for other brands, that can give them a rare expertise relevant to the brand in question. Trend data, syndicated studies and competitive information may all be more readily available to agencies than to the client company. All of these can be powerful and influential data sources for the valuer.

Implications for research

Some parts of the process of brand valuation in particular rely heavily on high-quality research inputs, whether they be quantitative inputs such as awareness and loyalty measure, or 'softer' measure such as brand personality. As an example of how broad this research input can be, Table 14.3 shows David Aaker's 'Brand Equity Ten' – the measures he says should be embraced by marketers concerned to understand, evaluate and measure over time the strength of their brand.

Some of these form direct or indirect inputs into the principal brand valuation methodologies. All of them imply the use, usually on an ongoing basis, of a considerable portfolio of research measures and techniques.

This sort of research process is good news for the marketing community – and for advertising agencies too. The rigour that it implies will force a positive

Table 14.3 Brand Equity Ten

1 Price Premium
2 Satisfaction/Loyalty
3 Perceived Quality
4 Leadership/Popularity
5 Perceived Value
6 Brand Personality
7 Organizational Associations
8 Brand Awareness
9 Market Share
10 Market Price and Distribution Coverage

Source: David Aaker, *Building Strong Brands*

re-evaluation by the board and by the financial community of the role and value of brands, and of the marketing and advertising support for those brands. As a result, the better clients (and their agencies) will prosper and may, one day, even see their remuneration and fees linked to changes in brand value.

Conclusion

Beyond the rhetoric about 'brands on the balance sheet', beyond even the laudable goal of bridging the gap between marketing and finance, there lies an even bigger prize: the elevation of brands to being recognized as centrally important and enormously valuable corporate assets. Agencies have much to gain from contributing to this elevation.

Within branded business a new paradigm of appreciation is emerging that does increasingly recognize the role and value of brands. Brand valuation and the demonstrable contribution of advertising to shareholder value are powerful ways to cement this recognition.

And in the consumer marketplace, something else is happening. Partly because of the demise of faith in traditional institutions, partly because of the speed of change (especially technological change) in many markets, a new and greater 'appetite for trust' is developing in many sectors.

As a result of this, the whole issue of brand extension into disparate categories has become a really hot topic in the marketing world. Mars' entry into the ice-cream market is an example of this strategy working to best effect. The ambition is synergy, as a result of transferring a favourable reputation from one sector into others. But there is also a risk.

The risk is that rather than achieving synergy (classically the formula of 2 + 2 = 5), the extended brand actually produces what I have labelled 'antergy'. Antergy would be defined as the whole being *less* than the sum of the parts (or 2 + 2 = 3). And it stems from the careless or ill-judged extension of a brand into an area that then diminishes the value of the whole.

Virgin's controversial foray into the rail network might, at least in the short term, be an example of this. Only time will tell whether the consistent underperformance of the Virgin product in this area will override the benefit of the doubt that this brand might have earned for itself through excellence in other areas. One thing is for sure though: Virgin's recent entry into other new markets will now be scrutinized even more closely to see what value it can add, or whether these areas represent a brand-extension too far.

It is in managing situations such as these that brand valuation in particular has a part to play – hopefully as a way of gauging risk in advance rather than assessing damage in hindsight. It is also in areas such as this that agencies, once again, have a key role. As brand guardians, or just as business partners to their clients, they can help steer brand strategies from a perspective of expert consumer advice, to temper more opportunistic financial arguments in areas such as brand extension.

Brand valuation might well become a powerful weapon in the armoury in debates such as these. The advertising agency might, in parallel, become the initiator of such analyses – or at least the 'matchmaker' between client and brand valuer.

As regards shareholder value, I can do no better by way of conclusion than draw together a 'crib sheet' of ten ways in which advertising can have an impact! The list may not be exhaustive, but at least it provides the ammunition for anyone who cares to, to point at specific, empirical, financial effects of advertising.

Ten ways in which advertising can impact on shareholder value

1 By directly impacting sales and/or brand share and hence the value of the brand.
2 By speeding up trial, adoption and referral rates for new products and hence accelerating cash flows.
3 By contributing to a brand's ability to command a price premium and hence increasing cash flow.
4 By creating greater customer loyalty and hence enhancing cash flows through lower recruitment costs or more effective promotional programmes.
5 By contributing to the greater uptake of brand extensions and hence increasing cash flow.
6 By generating greater customer satisfaction and retention and hence reducing the volatility of future cash flows.

7 By impacting perceived quality of product, which in turn affects the profitability of that product's corporate owner (*Source*: PIMS).

8 By impacting product image and/or reputation of a company which again affects profitability (*Source*: PIMS).

9 By directly affecting share price. (Up to 5 per cent of variation explained this way. (*Source*: CBP.)

10 By indirectly affecting share price via its effect on *perceptions* of cash flow, earnings and dividends, stock price growth and expected cash flow growth (*Source*: CBP).

More than ever in the future, marketers, agency people and senior managers will need to understand and be able to demonstrate these kinds of effects if they are to secure and grow the advertising investment in brands. My guess is that they will.

References

Aaker, D. (1996), *Building Strong Brands*, Free Press.

Ambler, T. (1998), *Marketing and Shareholder Value*, London Business School (Marketing Metrics Partnership Presentation).

Butterfield, L. (1998), 'Economic Benefits of Branding', *Admap*, April, pp. 14–16.

Butterfield, L. and Haigh, D. (1998), *Understanding the Financial Value of Brands*, IPA.

Butterfield, L., PIMS and IPA (1998), 'How Advertising Impacts on Profitability', *IPA Advalue Series*, Issue One.

The Co-operative Bank (1995), IPA Advertising Effectiveness Award paper, reproduced in *Adworks 8*, IPA.

Financial Times (1997).

Financial Times/Interbrand/Citibank/Patrick Hearne report

Gregory, J. (1997), *The Impact of Advertising on Stock Performance*, Corporate Branding Partnership/AAAA.

Orange (1998), IPA Advertising Effectiveness Award paper, reproduced in *Adworks 10*, IPA.

Srivastava, R.K., Shervani, T.A. and Fahey, L. (1998), *Market Based Assets and Shareholder Value*, Marketing Science Institute.

Index

A&I (Analysis and interpretation) *see*
  Qualitative research
Aaker, David, 292
ABCD checklist (Appreciation, Branding,
  Communication and Desired effect),
  220
Account direction, 178
Account directors, 177–8, 187–90
Account planners, 153, 154, 193, 197, 222,
  291
Accountability, at TSB Bank plc, 54
Accounting Standards Board's Financial
  Reporting Standards, 267
Acquisition, of brands, 16–19
Adopted proposition vs perceived
  intention, 126
Advertising:
  and attitudinal loyalty creation, 257–8
  for bond building with public, 73
  and brand building, 26, 73
  and brands, 16
  and business performance, 26
  contribution of, 25–6, 34–6
  and creativity, 40
  direct/indirect response to, 65
  evaluation of, 215–27
  from product to band, 26–9
  how it contributes to profit, 222–6
  how it works, 63–5
  Joyce's model, 64

as a loyalty driver, 247–62
not synonymous with marketing, 57–8
role in strategy development, 72–5
and share prices, 284–91
and shareholder value, 280–2, 294
short term judgement of, 223
for transformation to differentiation,
  40
TV advertising, 162–3
value of *see* Brands as assets
Advertising agencies:
  adapting to client pressures, 56–7
  agency models, need for new, 58–9
  agency–client relationships, 58–9
    all for one and one for all, 240–1
    discipline total, 241
    à la carte, 240
    product total, 241
    virtual, 241–2
  as business partners, 291–2
  client structures
    central marketing department, 239
    classical brand management, 239
    strategic business unit (SBU), 239
  delegation of responsibility to, 238
  knowing your, 180
  'lead agency' concept, 59
  need to adapt to changing market, 60
  strategies required, 60
  understanding the clients of, 181–2

AGB's Superpanel, 257
Agencies *see* Advertising agencies
AIDA, 64
Aiwa, 167
Alliance and Leicester, 101–3
Ambler, Tim, 287–8
Analysis and interpretation (A&I)
    see Qualitative research
Antergy, 294
Apple PC, 35, 74
Archimedes and the lever, 136
ARS Persuasion testing, 217
ASDA, 189
'Audience Media Network', 210
Average Issue Readership (AIR), 206
Award Databank, 215–16
Awareness index, 219

Badge brands, 77
Banking:
    bank's customer loyalty, 251
    changes to, 53
    see also Financial services
Bartle Bogle Hegarty agency, 30
BAV™, 224
Bernbach, Bill, 41
Black and Decker, 4, 235
BMRB's Target Group Index, 95,
    98–100
BMW, 12, 168
    'Ultimate Driving Machine', 223
Boddington's beer, 37–9
Body language, 121
Boots Advantage Card, 260–1
Boston Matrix, 47
Brand acquaintanceships, 248
Brand Asset Valuator™, 223–5
Brand communication strategy, 235–7
    clarity, 236
    coherence, 236
    commitment, 236–7
    consistency, 236
    contact, 237
    control, 236
    customer driven, 237
BrandDynamic Pyramid, 251–2
Brand Finance Ltd survey, 274

Brand growth direction matrix, 10–11
Brand loyalty, 8–9, 12
    advertising, value of, 256–7, 257–8
    attitudinal loyalty, 257–61
    behavioural loyalty, 256–7
    benefits of, 247–8
    bonded consumers, 252
    brand shift and switch, 249–50
    Conversion Model, 254–6
    and emotional affinity to a brand,
        257
    erosion mapping, 250
    forces against, 248–9
    measurement of, 250–1
    true and behavioural loyalty, 251–6
Brand management structures, 239
Brand personalities, 6, 9–10, 166–70
Brand status, and strategy development,
    68, 69
Brand valuation *see* Brands as assets
Brand-building, 223
Brandbuilder model (NPD Group),
    253–4
Brandes, Burckhard, 218
Branding, 4, 56–7
    and competition, 9–10
Brands:
    acquisition of, 16–19
    advantages of, 234–5
    and advertising, 16, 26–9, 73
    audience for, 202–5
    building, 56–7, 73
    buy vs build, 16–19
    complexity of, 29–31
    depreciation of, 5
    differentiation between, 4–5, 10, 15–16,
        29, 32–3, 225
    durability, 33
    extension strategies, 19–20
    getting data on, 95
    and habit, 5
    image of, 5
    importance of, 33–4
    niche, 6–8
    pioneering, 15
    positioning, 30
    power and importance of, 232–3
    and products, 29, 31–2, 36

rational and emotional areas, 30
successful brands, 3–5
    creation of, 12–16
    value of, 6–12
support required, 5
types of, 235
value of *see* Brands as assets
what is a brand?, 234
why bother?, 232–3
working principles, 5–6
see also Brand loyalty; Brands as assets
Brands as assets, 265–95
    advertising and share
        prices/shareholder value, 284–91
    agencies, opportunities for, 291–2
    brand image vs sales volume, 268
    brand risk assessment, 273
    brand valuation, steps in, 272–3
    Brand Value Added (BVA™), 273
    economic value added calculation, 272
    effectiveness and accountability, 271–3
    IPA contribution to better
        understanding of, 275–6
    marketing contribution, 267–70
    marketing/finance relations, 273–5
    private label production elimination,
        273
    product image and company
        reputation, 284
    profitability, impact on, 282–4
    remuneration of capital employed, 273
    research implications, 292–3
    taxation, 273
    value of brands, 21, 31–2, 265–7
Briefing, 135–8, 151–6
    creative people as target group, 151
    creative perspectives, 161–74
        brand personality importance,
            166–70
        creative starters, 172–3
        defining the target market, 170–2
        doing something different, 162–6
        making the brief inspiring, 173–4
    critical nature of, 154–5
    making it interesting, 155–6
    reacting to the work, 156
Briefs:
    creative brief forms, 135–8

principles of good briefs, 139–46
    clear directions, 140–4
    directional properties, 139
    inspirational properties, 139
    language, 144–6
    in qualitative research, 111–12
    structure, 146–51
        complex brands, 150–1
        examples of bad, 148–50
        guidance vs rigidity, 151
        mandatories, 150
        proposition, 146–7
        requirement, 150
        support, 148
        tone, 148
British Airways, 75
British companies, preference for
    financial goals, 17–18
British gas, selling electricity, 233
British Telecom, 4, 75, 194, 204
Broadbent, Simon, 223
Brown & Polson, 47
BTR, 18
Bull, George, 32
Bullmore, Jeremy, 29, 58, 172
Business objectives, and marketing
    objectives, 68–72
Business performance, and advertising,
    26
Butterfield, Leslie, 256
    Butterfield's diamond shape
        framework analysis, 198, 199

Cadbury, Dominic, 268
Cadbury Schweppes, 27, 235, 266
Car advertising, 163
Cash Cows, Stars and Dogs, 48–9
Cash flow, 281–2
Causality and correlation, 218–19
Channel proliferation, 71, 72
Christian Aid advertisements, 124
Cinemas, change with television, 195
Citibank performance, 223
Clemmow, Simon, 200–1
Client pressures, how agencies can
    adapt, 56–7

Clients:
　'clients thing', interpreting, 124–30
　pressures on, 45–60
Cluster analysis, 203
Coca Cola, 5, 11, 266
Colgate, 259
Competition, and branding, 9–10
Competitive analysis, strategy
　development, 75–8
Competitive depositioning, 11
Competitor analysis, 87–9
Complaint handling, and brand strength,
　14–15
Constructive conflict, 184–5
Consumer–media relationship, 200–1,
　209–11
Consumer loyalty *see* Brand loyalty
Consumer perspective, 88, 195–7
Conversion Model, of brand loyalty,
　254–6
The Co-operative Bank, 276–80
Coopers & Lybrand, 181–2
Corporate Branding Partnership (CBD),
　285–7
Correlation and causality, 218–19
Correspondence analysis, 95, 203
CPC (UK) Ltd:
　company profile, 46–7
　portfolio appraisal, 47–9
　resource reallocation, 49–50
Creative briefing *see* Briefing
Creative development work, in
　qualitative research, 112
Creative people, 178
　as target people for brief, 151–4
Creativity, and advertising, 40
Credibility and relevance, 126
Criticism, 162

Daewoo cars, 152–3
'Dead Frog Syndrome', 197
Denotive versus Connotive, 126
Diageo's brand portfolio, 223
Differential advantage, 4–5
　brands, 4–5
Digital Audio Tape, 167
Discussion groups, for research, 204

Dogs, Cash Cows and Stars, 48–9
Doyle, Peter, 33
Drucker, Peter, 190

Egg, as a unique brand personality, 168
Ehrenberg, Professor Andrew, 88–9
Electricity companies, selling gas, 233
Emotion:
　and advertising, 35
　and branding, 31
Emotional selling proposition (ESP), 35

Fashion industry, 167
Fast moving consumer goods (FMCG),
　35, 40, 56–7
　panel data, 100
　range extensions in, 249
　vs service industries, 242
Federal Express, 9
Feldwick, Paul, 223
Financial services:
　at TSB Bank plc, 64
　and brands, 232–3
　and customer power, 233
　tactical alignments, 233
　transparent banking, 54
　see also Banking
First Direct, 168
　market share, 251
'Five Questions' planning cycle, 65–7
FMCG *see* Fast moving consumer goods
Food manufacturing vs food retailing,
　advertising/marketing, 57
Fothergill and Ehrenberg (1965), 217

Gallup, George, 216, 222
Geodemography, 203
Global branding, 11
Gordon, Wendy, 119

Hägen-Dazs, 36, 37
Haigh, David, 256
Halifax 'house', 127–30
Hall & Partners, 219

Hanson, 18
Harris research, 182
Hayward, Wendy, 119
Heath, Robert, 254
Heathrow Express advertisement, 67
Hedges, Alan, 68, 114, 249
Heineken, 138
Hellmann's, 46–7, 49–50
Henley Centre, 248
Henry, Steve, 204
Hillyer, Tony, 165
Hiring people in advertising, 178–9
Holiday advertising, 163
Hoover, 234
HPI Research Group, 219, 220
Hygiene factor, 169
Hypothesis notepad, for qualitative
    research, 117

IBM, 4, 6, 12, 74
Identity versus disposition, 126
In-house clients, 185
Informational coherence, 231
Interbrand performance, 223
Interpretation, in qualitative research,
    113
Involvement advertising, 220
IPA Advertising Effectiveness Awards,
    37, 215–16, 221, 222, 225–6
IPA databank, 258

Japanese companies, preference for
    market share, 17–18
Johnson & Johnson's Baby Shampoo, 11
Jones, Professor John Philip, 218
Joyce, Timothy, 64
    Joyce's model, advertising, 64
JWT's T-Plan, 217

Kellogg's, 20
Kenco, 97
King, Stephen:
    on consumer response, 216–17
    'Five Questions' planning cycle, 65
    scale of immediacy, 64, 65

Lannon, Judie, 104
Leadership, 190
Lehman Brothers, 290
    analysis, 226
Levi's jeans, 38–9, 137–8
Loyalty *see* Brand loyalty
Loyalty cards, 257

Macdonald, Colin, 218
Macleans toothpaste, 235
Market attractiveness grid, 47
Market economics, 87–9
Market leaders, penetration of, 248–9
Market share:
    'right-handed' companies, 17–18
    successful brands, 6–7
Market study reports, 90–1
Market-based assets, 281
Marketing, not synonymous with
    advertising, 57–8
Marketing departments, central
    structures, 239
Marketing movies, MGM cinemas, 55–6
Marketing objectives, and business
    objectives, 68
Marks & Spencer, 12
Martini, 169–70
Mazda, 163–4
Mazola, 46–7
Meat and livestock Commission, 121–2
Media, 193–211
    changing role of, 193–5
    cinema advertising, 195
    consumer–media relationship, 200–1
    consumption patterns, 204, 205–7
    objectives and strategy, 207–9
    radio advertising, 195
    research studies on, 206
    TV advertising, 194–7
Media planners, 197, 198, 200, 205, 208
Media Usage and Attitudes study
    (U&A), 206
Mercedes-Benz, 20
MGM cinemas:
    company profile, 55
    marketing movies, 55–6
'Middle England', advertising to, 171

Millward Brown, 217, 223, 251–3
Monty Python's *Life of Brian*, 193–4
Moving Annual Totals (MATs), 91–2

National Lottery, 75
Nestlé, 266
Net present value of future cash flows,
    280–1
New technology, 11
Niche brands, value of, 6–8
'Nine box' portfolio appraisal, 47
NPD investment, 47

Objectives, media, 207–9
Objectives setting, personal, 179–80
Omnibus survey, 103
Orange mobile telecoms network, 226,
    289–91
  brand improvement, 103
Outdoor advertising, 195

Partners BDDM agency, 276
People in advertising, getting best out of,
    177–90
  accepting responsibility, 188
  account directors, 187
  arch manipulators, 185–6
  e-mailers, 186–7
  in-house clients, 185
  reluctant go-betweens, 184
  rewarding performance, 183–4
  tyrants, 183
Pepsi, 5
Perry, Michael, 33
'Personal Media Network', 196
Persuasion advertising, 220
Persuasion testing, 217
PG Tips chimps campaign, 223
Pharmaton, 149
Phileas Fogg snacks, 38–9
Philip Morris, 266
PIMS (Profit Impact of Market Strategy)
    study, 6, 282
Pioneering brands, 15
Planners/planning, 197–8, *see also*
    Account planners; Media planners

Planning cycle, Stephen King, 65–7
Portfolio appraisal, CPC (UK) Ltd, 47–9
Postman Pat, 210
Procter & Gamble, 20, 194
Product interrogation, strategy
    development, 78
Product life cycle, 10
Product values-centred advertising, 126
Products:
  and brands, 29, 31–2, 36
  definition of, 3–4
  value of, 4
Profit(s):
  how advertising contributes, 222–6
  with successful brands, 6
  ways to increase, 94
  see also Brands as assets
Project design, in qualitative research,
    112–13
Prudential, 168
Psychometric testing, 178
Purchase loyalty levels, 253–4
  Prospects and Vulnerables, 254

QMR (qualitative market research)
    see Qualitative research
Qualitative research (analysis and
    interpretation), 109–32
  functional issues, 113–19
    'dump' notes and/or dicta-tapes, 119
    notes by observer, 118
    tape recordings, 114–19
    transcripts, 116–18
  interpretation for, 120–7, 131
    'clients thing', 124–30
    what people say/think/mean, 120–4
  orientation and inputs, 110–13
    the brief, 111–12
    project design elements, 112–13
Quality, for brand strength, 13
Quantitative research, 83–106
  competitor analysis, 87–9
  consumers' relationship with
    advertising, 89–90
  consumers' relationship with brands, 89
  consumers' relationship with products,
    89

detective type use of, 85–6
FMCG panel data, 100
market economics, 87–9
market study reports, 90–1
omnibus survey, 103
questions
  design of, 104–5
  use of, 84, 87
retail audits, 91
  distribution, 93
  Moving Annual Totals (MATs), 91–2
  price, 93
  rate of sale (ROS), 93–4
  value versus volume, 91–3
Target Group Index (TGI), 95–100
tracking studies, 101–3
usage and attitude surveys, 100
volumetric analysis, 98–100
when consumed, data on, 94–103
Question design, 104–5
'Question Marks', 48

Radio, growth of commercial stations,
  195
Range extensions, in FMCG markets, 249
Rank Hovis McDougall, 267
Rate of sale (ROS), 93–4
Relationship marketing, at TSB Bank plc,
  54
Relative market share calculation, 47–8
Relevance and credibility, 126
Repeat users/consumers, 248
Research:
  on brand messages received per day,
    209
  how advertising researchers think
    advertising works, 216–21
  techniques for, 221–2
Research Business International, 221
Resource reallocation, CPC (UK) Ltd,
  49–50
Retail audits *see* Quantitative research
Return on investment, by 'left-handed'
  companies, 17–18
Revlon Cosmetics, 4
Revson, Charles, 29
Richards, Trevor, 254

Roddick, Anita, 164
Rolling hypotheses, 111
Rowntree, 266
Rule breaking, 164

Safeway, 75
Sainsbury's, 266
Sales, ways to increase, 95
Sales response advertising, 219–20
Salience advertising, 220
Scale of immediacy, 64
Schwerin, Horace, 217, 222
Scottish and Newcastle Breweries, 266
Service, for brand strength, 13–14
Services, as products, 3
Sex, for good advertisement recall,
  216–17
Share prices/shareholder value of
  brands *see* Brands as assets
Short Term Advertising Strength (STAS),
  218
Singapore Airlines, 12
Society of Motor Manufacturers and
  Traders, 90
Soft drinks, 165–6
Sony, 35, 70
Stakeholders, motivation of, 12
Stars, Cash Cows and Dogs, 48–9
Strategic business units (SBUs), 239
Strategy development:
  brand status, 68, 69
  and brand's total marketing situation,
    200
  business and marketing objectives, 68–72
  Butterfield's diamond shape
    framework analysis, 198, 199
  competitive analysis, 75–8
  how does advertising work?, 63–5
  implementation, 78–9
  media, 207–9
  the planning cycle, 65–7
  product interrogation, 78
  role for advertising, 72–5
  target audience understanding, 78
  see also Brand communication strategy;
    Quantitative research; Total
    communications strategy

Subconscious interpretative thoughts, 119
Sustainable differential advantage, 4–5
SWOT strategy audit:
  TSB Bank plc, 53–4
  Woolworths, 51–3
Synergy, and brand acquisition, 18
Synesis, study by, 182

'Tablecloth' transcript analysis, 117
Tape recordings, for qualitative research, 114–19
  'dump' notes and or dicta-tapes, 119
  skilled observer notes, 118
  transcripts, 116–18
Target audience understanding, strategy development, 78
Target Group Index (TGI), 95–100
Target market, 170–2
Team member assessment, 179
Television:
  changes affecting advertising, 196
  increasing importance of, 194–5
Testing products in market, blind and named, 27–9
TGI *see* Target Group Index
Total communications strategy, 231–43
  agency structures, 240
  agency–client relationships, 240–2
  blockers to, 238–9
  client structures, 239
  issues and challenges, 242
  levers to pull, 238
  rules for, 243
  see also Brand communication strategy
Tracking studies, quantitative research, 101–3

Transcripts, for qualitative research, 116–18
Transcripts of interviews, 116–18
Transparent banking, 54
Treats, 166
TSB Bank plc:
  accountability at, 54
  marketing function reorganization, 53–4
  relationship marketing, 54
  SWOT analysis, 53–4
TV advertising, 162–3
Tylenol, 9

Unilever, 194
Unique Selling Personality, 168
Unique Selling Proposition (USP), 63, 166–7

Value, of products, 4
Venn Diagram, 129–30
Virgin, 232, 294
  one account advertisement, 67
Vodka, 99–100
Volkswagen, 259–60
Volumetric analysis, 98–100

Webb Young, J., 63–4
Wells, Stephen, 111
'Wild Cards', 48
Wonderbra, 75
Woolworths:
  company profile, 50–1
  SWOT strategy audit, 51–3